Archaeology at Home

Archaeology at Home

Notes on Things, Life and Time

Hein Bjartmann Bjerck

eQuinox

SHEFFIELD UK   BRISTOL CT

Published by Equinox Publishing Ltd.

UK: Office 415, The Workstation, 15 Paternoster Row, Sheffield, South Yorkshire S1 2BX
USA: ISD, 70 Enterprise Drive, Bristol, CT 06010

www.equinoxpub.com

First published 2022

British Library Cataloguing-in-Publication Data

A catalogue record for this book is available from the British Library.

ISBN-13   978 1 80050072 3 (hardback)
          978 1 80050073 0 (paperback)
          978 1 80050074 7 (ePDF)
          978 1 80050243 7 (ePub)

Library of Congress Cataloging-in-Publication Data
Names: Bjerck, Hein Bjartmann, author.
Title: Archaeology at home : notes on things, life and time / Hein B. Bjerck.
Description: Sheffield, South Yorkshire ; Bristol, CT : Equinox Publishing Ltd., 2022. | Includes bibliographical references. | Summary: "Archaeology at Home takes a deep dive into the entanglements between humans and their things, exploring the notion that things themselves "remember" when left by "their" people and illustrating how the integration of humans and things involves connections running all the way from the present into deep time. The author presents three case studies of homes all intimately known to him - the home of his father after his abrupt passing, the home of his uncle that was lost in a fire, and a Stone Age home he excavated many years ago. This evocative approach to archaeologies of memory will be appreciated by professional archaeologists as well as members of the general public who are drawn to the study of the past and things that connect us with it"-- Provided by publisher.
Identifiers: LCCN 2022001178 (print) | LCCN 2022001179 (ebook) | ISBN 9781800500723 (hardback) | ISBN 9781800500730 (paperback) | ISBN 9781800500747 (pdf) | ISBN 9781800502437 (epub)
Subjects: LCSH: Bjerck, Hein Bjartmann--Homes and haunts. | Household archaeology. | Personal belongings--Social aspects. | Dwellings. | Memory. | Material culture--Norway.
Classification: LCC CC77.H68 B54 2022 (print) | LCC CC77.H68 (ebook) | DDC 930.1--dc23/eng/20220513
LC record available at https://lccn.loc.gov/2022001178
LC ebook record available at https://lccn.loc.gov/2022001179

Typeset by S.J.I. Services, New Delhi, India

Contents

List of Figures

numerous boat trips. However, fjords may be large or small, wide or narrow, but they all have ends, defining how far you can travel. I was in my teens before I saw the unbroken horizon of the ocean for the first time – this limitless body that had had no end, and the eerie freedom in sensing that it was up to you how far you would go. Would I have become a different archaeologist if my father had dared to show me this earlier – the prospects of the unsafe and limitless?   195

Acknowledgements

In memory of Pappa, my father, mentor and good friend, and also my exotic uncle Faste, grandmother Mommo, grandfather Nils in Nordland, and the unnamed Stoneager seafarers in the Åsgarden encampment on Vega. I will also include the late Asle Bruen Olsen, who introduced me to Stone Age craftsmanship. I like to think that you are all in the same peaceful void – safe in the confidence that you all made a difference to your futures – your heart-beats still resonate in the world.

Thanks to Elin Andreassen, my companion in life as well as in profession, artist, co-author, and guide towards the fruitful peripheries of scholarly disciplines – that perhaps are actually the centres for understanding life. I am also grateful to my mother Siv, my two brothers Børge and Snorre, and my nephew Erlend for their support, information and photos. And to Kyrre, Trygve, Helge and Lola – a sincere thankfulness for handling my thingly realm when the day comes. It may not be as straightforward as you may think.

In writing this book, I cannot overvalue the insights, inspirations and support from Bjørnar J. Olsen and members of his research projects *After Discourse* at the Centre of Advanced Studies (CAS), the Norwegian Academy of Science and Letters in Oslo (2016–2017), *Ruin Memories: Materialities, Aesthetics and the Archaeology of the Recent Past* (2009–2013) and *Objects Matters: Archaeology and Heritage in the 21st Century* (2015–2019), financed by the Norwegian Research Council. I am indebted to the long row of scholars included in these projects as members and guests, in particular Bjørnar, Elin, Saphinaz Amal-Naguib, Doug Bailey, Torgeir Rinke Bangstad, Levi Bryant, Mats Burström, Denis Byrne, Caitlin DeSilvey, Stein Farstadvoll, Alfredo González-Ruibal, Graham Harman, Gavin Lucas, Tim LeCain, Robert Macfarlane, Laurent Olivier, Þóra Pétursdóttir, Kerstin Smeds and Christopher Witmore. I am grateful to each and every one for their sharing and mind-opening perspectives, and for their support and encouragement to present the intimate accounts in *Archaeology at Home*.

The chapter 'My Father's Things' is an edited and expanded version of the similarly-named chapter in the volume *Ruin Memories: Materialities, Aesthetics and the Archaeology of the Recent Past*, edited by Bjørnar Olsen and Þóra Pétursdóttir (Routledge, 2014).

The Vega Project was financed and organized by the Norwegian Ministry of Environment, and the institution that now is the NTNU University Museum. The initial field crew (1985) was Berit Gjerland, Lisa Bostwick and Martinus Hauglid. Later crew members were Evy Berg, Snorre Bjerck, Lisa Bostwick, Dagrunn Brattset, Martinus Hauglid and Kristine Johansen (1986), and Lisa Bostwick, Dagrunn Brattset, Martinus Hauglid and Kjersti Schanche (1987). The Vega municipality administration added to the field staff with summer jobs for a number of local students, who also came with treasured local knowledge – Trond Steinbru, Lillian Nielsen, Trond Tøgersen, Monika Mortensen and Margrethe Wika. Many thanks for their encouraging support go to Vega major Osvald Floa and his staff, Per Morten Gullsvåg and Jens Einar Johansen in particular. Thanks to Hårek Fredriksen and Aud Halmøy for bringing their baby daughter Isa to the field, and to Isa for being so loud and clear that she managed to revive the Åsgarden soundscape for me. Had she been a more modest whiner, things may have turned out differently.

I am also greatly indebted to close friends and companions in the business of things, time, life and memories, old and new – luckily they have few limits on what is worthy of debate: Knut Andreas Bergsvik, Terje Brattli, Heidi M. Breivik, Martin Callanan, Axel Christophersen, Jo Sindre Eidshaug, Ellen Grav Ellingsen, Oddmunn Farbregd, Linda Fluge, the artist duo Hertling & Andreassen (Elin Andreassen and Ann-Cathrin Hertling), Åge Hojem, Henning Holmelid, Tora Hultgreen, Arne B. Johansen, Trond Lødøen, Ernesto Piana, Morten Ramstad, Heidrun Stebergløkken, Birgitte Skar, Atilio J. Francisco Zangrando and Leif Inge Åstveit.

Thanks to Equinox Publishing and Janet Joyce for taking on the volume in their production, Valerie Hall, Sarah Lee and Daniel Gronow (constructive proof-reading and Copy Editor).

Last but not least, I am indebted to Elin Andreassen (Photo Editor) for assisting in the selecting, adjusting and arranging of the figures – her combination of professional skills and in-depth knowledge of things and people 'at home' are highly appreciated.

...

Admittedly, I had to reach the third revision of these acknowledgements to realise that I had become like the 'lone and unsupported' adventurer to the South Pole mentioned by Bjørnar Olsen – in forgetting to see, value and thank all non-humans that are intermingled and were decisive for this book. There is a 'deep irony' in this, that for a book on exactly this subject, frequently flogging other thing-neglecters, even in these circumstances things managed to escape my expressed gratitude.

In an interview with philosopher and ecologist Timothy Morton that was published in *The New Yorker* this week[1], Morton puzzles the journalist by insisting on referring to him by the pronouns 'them' and 'they'– to underscore that Morton considers his own being as an inseparable aggregation of human and non-human entities – hyper-objects like the bacteria and viruses that 'they' cannot live without, 'their' T-shirt, the car they arrived in, their home, where there is also a cat named Oliver that they obviously care much for.

For my own sake, the interview was a timely reminder to pay respect to all non-human things that were a part of making this book, that despite sudden death, fire and ages of weathering managed to slip away from their normal withdrawal and attract my attention – as I have tried to show in the long list in the next pages.

Thank you for the brief companionship, you sleeping giants, I wish you all luck in the times beyond me.

Trondheim, October 2021
Hein B. Bjerck

Humans and Non-Humans that Found Their Way into this Book

1 kilometre, the approx. distance from our home in Firdavegen to the family tailoring shop.

11,421 years AD, the year when the Åsgarden camp will be as far from the present as today it is from the past.

¹⁴C, radioactive carbon isotope with a half-life of 5730 years, used to date organic substances.

24, the number of years that the same dried straws were in the black vase in the home of uncle Faste.

24-hour clock, a clock with which uncle Faste wanted to separate day from night.

30, the number of almonds included in my father's breakfast routine.

4/-, the price of steel wool that I erroneously mistook for 41-.

557, the number of kilometres Elin and I drove to reach Florø when my father died.

8 mm, the format of my father's movies.

9400 years BP, the approx. heyday of the Åsgarden encampment.

Aaslaug, my former boss, who had lost a keyring that I miraculously found in the grass.

AD, *Anno Domini* (or years After Christ), a dating reference that may not exist 11,421 years from now.

Alma Charlotte Liseth (1906–1997), the wife of Nils, my maternal grandfather.

Alpinist, not asked much about what he really saw along the track.

Among Wizards and Cannibals, the title of a book Siv gave her finance Rolf for Christmas in 1952.

Animal Planet, a TV channel that my father cherished watching.

Animate vs. inanimate, living vs. non-living entities.

Anna and Abraham Terdal, former owners of the farm with our family cabin.

ANT, Actor-Network Theory, demonstrating the active intermingling of humans and non-humans.

Anthropocene, the current geological age, when human activity has been a dominant influence on climate and the environment.

Artefact, any human-made thing.

Åsgarden, a Stoneager encampment that we found and excavated on Vega.

Auto-archaeology, the things and events to be studied in your own, lived yesterdays.

Awl, a lithic instrument we found that has listened to Stoneager conversations.

Baby of local policeman on Vega, who turned out to be Isa Halmøy Fredriksen.

Ball of chewing gum, that my father left on a plate by the TV-chair on his last evening.

Ball-shaped lamp, that Karl Ove Knausgård suddenly noticed on his desk as he returned from Denmark.

Bananas, the seven spotless bananas that my father left when he passed.

Bathtub, pink, torn out as uncle Faste's home was demolished.

Ben-Hur, the protagonist in a feature movie, whose story my father told more vividly than the original movie.

Birgitte Skar, archaeologist, expert in refitting flaked lithic artefacts.

Bjartmann Spektronikk A/S, uncle Faste's firm, which produced automatized technical inventions.

Bjartmann, the surname Mommo invented for her children after divorcing their father.

Bjercks Konfeksjon, our family tailoring business.

Bjørn Faste Bjartmann (1927–2019), my maternal uncle.

Bjørnar Julius Olsen, archaeologist, friend and mentor, who brought spicy things for dinner and debates from the UK.

Blade, elongated, sharp lithic implement used as part of a variety of Stone Age instruments.

Blanket, that retained the shape of my father, and waited in vain for his return.

Blown kisses, a thing uncle Faste was accused of, to another girl.

Bob Bartman, the name uncle Faste took in Australia.

Bomberos in Ushuaia, Tierra del Fuego, they keep my father's jeans in reserve for a person in need.

Boomerang, aborigine throwing instrument that was stolen from uncle Faste's burnt house.

Børge Bjartmann Bjerck (1958), my brother, who suddenly appeared as my father filmed Stone Age rock art, accidentally bringing the moment back to our own time.

BP, Before Present, reference for archaeological dates in calendric years.

Bridge, a card game my grandfather Oluf played with friends, unaware of the fact that his sons cut open and later stitched together their overcoats to learn details of how pockets were made.

Broken leg, in the winter, that made a man wonder about the Stone Age.

Carpet, that could be made into a landscape within the living room.

Charcoal, that could remember the approx. time since they were warming embers.

Chlorine, the smell of embarrassment.

City-Hotel Ansbach, Berlin, from where my PC with photos was stolen.

Clocks, running in separate paces in a jeweller's shop in a Tunström novel.

Contemporary archaeology, studies of material remains from the recent past.

Cow, that uncovered rock art that was repainted by an unknown man.

Cyborg, a mix of human and non-human parts, as Donna Haraway sees it, like a woman riding a bike.

Denis Byrne, Australian archaeologist who smiled to the wind and waves in a Sydney harbour.

Donkey, with melted eyes.

Doubling the dishwashing, what my father said if dirty plates were stacked on top of each other.

Dreaming the Stone Age, dreams that seem to never happen.

Earthling, a world member, independent of time.

Electrical wall heater, supporting coffee cups, and keeping them warm.

Elin Andreassen (1965), my wife, artist, who led me beyond the archaeological horizon.

Elsa Eikaas Bjerck (1937–2016), my aunt, wife of uncle Oluf jnr.

Embers, that hid in the wall and tricked uncle Faste in believing they had died.

Enough rope, that my father always made sure was in the boat.

Equinox Publishing, a 'human-thing-machine' in the UK that produced this book.

Erlend Book Bjerck (1988), my nephew, son of Børge, who now owns the house of my father.

Erling Kagge, adventurer claiming to have gone 'unassisted and alone' to the South Pole, whom Bjørnar writes about.

Ernesto Piana, archaeologist and Argentinean compañero, who advised what to do with the jeans.

European tour diary 1952, that my father wrote during my parent's pre-wedding trip.

Firdaposten, the local newspaper in Florø, that Pappa used to save to update me when I had been away.

Firdavegen, the road by our house, where Snorre obediently waited for a car to pass before he crossed.

Fire alarm typhoon, that I mistook for the sound of fire.

Fish gratin, a favourite dish that I made with bacon slices that were too thick for Bjørnar's liking.

Fish puddings, home-made, the ones that Solfrid made.

Flamenco dancer figurine, from Torremolinos, scorched, now gone.

Flat-topped boulder, that Stoneagers discovered when they excavated a pit for their home.

Flint, the rock type that Stoneagers cherished for their instruments.

Fløibanen, a funicular in Bergen controlled by a device that uncle Faste made.

Ford Taunus, a light blue company van, with 'Bjerck's Garments Everywhere' on the back door.

Fossil Devonian wave-ripples, that we found and brought home to show.

Fram, the former communal house in Florø, where my parents watched *Ben-Hur*.

Frank Aarebrot, the scholar who narrated *The War in 200 Minutes* on TV.

Furniture covers, leftovers from the shop, usable for a number of other things.

Gabbro, or black granite, a coarse-grained black/dark green igneous rock my father took an interest in.

Gabriela Paterito Tonko, Kaweskar woman whom Elin and I met in Puerto Edén, Chile.

Gaute Solheim Olsen, Jostein's son, who rescued uncle Faste from running back into the burning house.

Gelatine mould, party snacks that were cherished leftovers from our parents' parties.

Göran Tunström, Swedish novelist.

Gunnar Ekeland (1945), my mother's husband, we both needed cigarettes after visiting the National Archives.

Hair dryer, that looked like an alien attacker, emitting a smell reminding me of past pre-party anticipation.

Heart-shaped fish burgers, that my father kept in the freezer downstairs.

Helge Bostwick Bjerck (1992), my son, who visited the grave of Nils.

Hilmar Reksten, the renowned ship owner in Bergen who employed my grandfather.

Hioduwä, Yanomamö Indian who went to see the Pope and Roman ruins.

Home, difficult to define precisely in few words.

Honey-coloured soap, that had teeth marks in my fantasy of a Stoneager friend.

Hyper-objects, real things that we live among that are too big to see, which Tim Morton writes about.

Jack Frost, DI in the TV series *A Touch of Frost*, whom uncle Faste cherished.

Ingerd, a girl who claimed that Faste loved *her*, and not Oddrun.

Jimi Hendrix, famous guitarist/singer who probably would have liked the red trousers my father made me.

Jimmy Button, Yamana Indian who went to England with Darwin on-board the HMS Beagle.

Jiu-Jitsu, traditional Chinese self-defence that uncle Oluf and my father practised.

Jostein Solheim Olsen, my father's friend, he frequently came by to visit.

Karl Ove Knausgård, Norwegian novelist.

Kaweskar, the indigenous group in Southern Chile that Gabriela belongs to.

Kingdome, a demolished sports arena in Seattle.

Kennedy, President of USA, Mommo learned that he was shot from irregular news on the radio, and made a note.

Koala bear, a kangaroo-skin toy that uncle Faste brought to me from Australia.

Kofes, an impossible thing to make that Tunström talks about.

Kyrre Bostwick Bjerck (1979), my son, who saw the 'Pearly Gates' when he was a baby.

Lesbian, the two women's bikes combined by uncle Faste.

Letter, that was lost in the loft, and never answered.

Levi Bryant, American philosopher who authored a book on Machine-Oriented Ontology.

Lighter, a thing my imagined Stoneager friend came to call 'Father of Fire'.

Lithic artefact with lateral retouch, as we were educated to say in the University.

Lithic instruments, Stone Age tools that came back to human hands with other skills.

Machines, as noted by Levi Bryant, they work the world.

Magne Salomon Bjerck (1934–2021), my paternal uncle.

Magnus Holen, archaeologist who studies lithic blade technology.

Male egg-laying bird, that I once thought I had heard of.

Map of Australia, that uncle Faste believed a woman was reading.

Mart., Martinus Hauglid, who found the first flints at the Åsgarden site.

Mary, woman in an imagined psychological experiment.

Mathilde Nilsen Bjerck (1896–1980), my paternal grandmother.

Merlin Sheldrake, botanist who talks about the dark twins of scientific papers.

Meshwork, describing the intermingling flow of the myriad entities in the world, by Tim Ingold.

Mesolithic, a time period within the Stone Age, 11,500 – 6000 years BP.

Microliths, minute worked lithic blades inserted into composite Stone Age tools, normally projectiles.

Middagsskarheia, Stoneager hunting station on Vega.

Mommo, my maternal grandmother, Ruth Liset.

MOO, Machine-Oriented Ontology, formulated by the American philosopher Levi Bryant.

My father, Rolf Bjerck.

My mother, Siv Liset, who told stories so vividly that I now believe I was there when they happened.

Nail, a thing my father believed should not be hammered in all the way, in case it needed to be removed.

Nils Liseth (1901–1969), my maternal grandfather in Nordland.

Non-human, all other animate or inanimate things in the world.

NS, Nazified political party in which my grandfather Nils enlisted.

Nuts, the ones my father bought, and his fatherless sons ate after he passed.

Oddrun xxxxxxxxx, the young girl who wrote a letter to Bjørn Faste that was never responded to.

Oluf Martin Bjerck jnr. (1921–2012), my paternal uncle.

Oluf Livius Bjerck snr. (1892–1970), my paternal grandfather.

OOO, Object-Oriented Ontology, formulated by Graham Harman, American philosopher.

Pearly Gates, an artistic metal chain curtain that Mommo made.

Pencil, a miniscule remnant I found in one of my father's pockets.

Percussion bulb, a percussion mark in flaked lithic artefacts.

Phenomenology, how the world is perceived by those who live in it.

Piezo-resistivity, a thing uncle Faste mentioned, I do not know what it means.

Pirlo (2014), our cat, whom I imagined a Stoneager friend would chase.

Plane crash site, in Svalbard, a disturbing thing to see.

Pocket knife, a thing my father is buried with – he could not understand how his sons could manage without one.

Pork chop, warm, that Pappa had to leave on his plate as the fire alarm sounded.

Presentism, a perspective that holds that things from past times are here and now.

Pyramiden, an abandoned Soviet mining town in Svalbard that Elin, Bjørnar and I wrote a book about.

Red marker I, marking the 60-meter shoreline, making Vega remember past seascapes, and helping us to find the Åsgarden site.

Red marker II, that I regretted giving to my imagined Stoneager friend.

Rerebawä, Yanomamö Indian whom Napoleon Chagnon brought to Caracas, Venezuela.

Rimski-Korsakoff, Russian composer whom Mommo cherished.

Robert Macfarlane, who endures hardships to reach the many things he writes about.

Rock art, paintings or engravings on rock surfaces.

Rolf Bjerck (1923–2009), my father, Pappa.

Ruth's Bok I–III, the extensive memoirs Mommo wrote after she retired from her teaching position. She gave the books to me before she passed in 1991.

Ruth Liset (1902–1991), my Mommo, maternal grandmother, who loved her own telephone number.

Sawdust, in uncle Faste's bed, from firemen hunting down embers.

SCN, the suprachiasmic nucleus, that measures time in nerve cells.

Seascape, a landscape with more sea than land.

Shelf in the toilet of 'Huset' in Longyearbyen, that Elin photographed when I met her.

Shiny trousers, of red lining, a thing Jimi Hendrix probably would have liked.

Shore lines, elevated by land rise after the Ice Age.

Shorts, mended in a comical way to my embarrassment.

Sila, Inuit phrase that Pelle Tejsner writes about.

Siv Liset (1933), my mother, Mamma, she was tense as we opened the container and saw the letters in her father's pen.

Smoke alarm, that saved uncle Faste, but could not save his home.

Snakeskin, that uncle Faste brought from Africa.

Snorre Bjartmann Bjerck (1963), my brother, who thought it was much worse when the cat had died.

Soft-boiled eggs, timed by singing a psalm.

Solfrid Andreassen (1944), Elin's mother, my mother-in-law.

Sølve Bjartmann (1925–1990), my maternal uncle, he chased Faste, held him down and tickled to see a letter from a girl.

Sound wall, a phrase Mommo wrote, that uncle Faste corrected to 'sound barrier (typical mother)'.

Spanish dress w/grey complet w/orcidé, garment Mommo wore to Børge's confirmation.

Stone Age, in Norway, the time period 11,500 – 32,000 years BP (also referred to as 'the Mesolitic').

Stoneager friend, whom I imagined, I am sorry that my fantasy made him into a villain.

Sun helmet, mysterious protection needed in hard sun, like in Australia.

Tarzan, the lone human in 'The Valley Time Forgot', in the carpet-landscape we made in our living room.

Test pit, a peephole in the ground to locate the remains of prehistoric sites.

Theory of Snoring, a theory I invented to charm Elin, a verisimilitude.

Things, all planetary realities that are often taken for granted and under-communicated.

Tom Cruise, the famous actor who appeared in a dream I had.

Toyota Corolla 1.6Xli, uncle Faste's car when he lost his way.

Travel Channel, that my father liked to watch on TV.

Trygve Bostwick Bjerck (1983), my son, who appeared as a young boy in a recent dream.

Tupolev Tu-154M, a Russian plane that crashed in Svalbard (Vnukovo Airlines Flight 2801).

Uncle Faste, Bjørn Faste Bjartmann.

Unnamed man from Vega, who assessed seascapes from below for the first time.

Unnamed Romanian, a neighbour and friend to uncle Faste.

Unnamed woman in cemetery, who remembered grandfather Nils.

Vase I, black, painful heritage, a 'celebration' of my grandparent's divorce.

Vase II, of copper, a wedding gift that turned to a fallen heirloom.

Vega, island that remembered how it was in the Stone Age.

Verisimilitude, something not proven to be true, but that may very well be so.

Villa Farris, a soda-pop uncle Faste wanted to buy.

Wedding portrait, that was lowered on the wall to bewilder my parents.

Withdrawal, a thing things do to avoid human attention.

WoodWideWeb, the communication between plants, by roots underground.

Yámana (or Yagan), an indigenous group in the archipelagos of Southern Patagonia.

'Later, Elin would complain about teeth marks in the honey-coloured soap.'

When Does the Past Begin?

As a trained archaeologist, I know where to look, and I know what to look for. One eye is on the ground, always, when I sense that there is a chance to find something, remnants from people of the past. Surprisingly often, there are things to be found – arrangements of stones or ditches, forgotten paths and fences, boat runs, lumps of iron slag, Stone Age lithic waste, house foundations, fireplaces, cairns, a pitfall for moose, cleared fields overgrown by trees, in rare cases also inscriptions and rock art.

One Monday morning at work, in the 1990s, Aaslaug (my boss at the time) complained that she had lost her keyring during her Sunday stroll, and was totally handicapped. She and Jostein had been walking along the beach at Straumøya across the fjord from Bodø in Northern Norway. On their return, the keys were gone. Now, she elaborated on the drama of the situation. How the keys might have fallen out of her pocket. How stupid she was to bring them along. The luck that they had happened to use Jostein's car. The trouble to get into her home. Who they had had to call. Locks that might have to be changed. To organise a search seemed futile: their walk was many kilometres long, they had followed no path, and the heather was high. The keys were gone. Period. Along with the rest of the staff, even her archaeologists could do nothing more than sympathise for her loss and her struggle to replace the keys, one by one – to reopen her life as it used to be.

Weeks later, I launched my kayak at the town side of the fjord. The sea was calm, the sun was low, but nights were many weeks distant, as in all summers in the north. I intended to paddle across the four-kilometre-wide fjord to Straumøya. There, on a ridge at some distance from the beach, were Iron Age grave cairns I wanted to explore. They were magnificent overlooking the fjord, and, vice versa, the cairns on the ridge were prominent for all seafarers. Time had deprived the buried persons of their names, their deeds, friends and foes, probably even their bodies and bones. But their souls were still clinging to the cairns, the view persisted, and they still ruled the fjord mouth. They emitted an eerie kind of silent power, an ambition to own a sliver of eternity, to beat time, somehow. For more than one thousand years now, their venture has been successful.

I stayed there for a long time, enjoying the scenery, the out-of-time-feeling, coffee from a flask, sandwiches and a couple of cigarettes – taking care to remove the cigarette stumps and all other evidence of my visit, as if my visit was some kind of break-in. My only worry was what the tide could have done to the kayak landing. On returning to the shore, I stepped on a bundle of keys in the grass. As I picked them up, I recalled Aaslaug's loss – could the keys be hers? It was plainly unbelievable. I had happened to cross her track twice, perhaps merely two meters of her many-kilometre-long walk. I scrutinized the individual keys. One of them, the 0005, resembled my own key to the office. I had to reach home to compare – the 0005 matched my own key to the office – they were in fact Aaslaug's keys. As I returned them to her the next day, and told of the circumstances of my finding them, she looked at me with suspicion, as if I had stolen them from her in some miraculous way (that actually seemed more plausible). The recovery was 'stranger than fiction', it was something you could anticipate in a confused dream, but not in real life.

I worried that I had spent my whole share of luck all at once – how could I be a professional archaeologist without luck? In hindsight, I had been thinking that the unbelievable episode contained pivotal elements of what is archaeology. Initially, you depend on a certain portion of plain luck to discover. Admittedly, the finding of the keys demanded unseen amounts of good fortune, but even disproportionate luck would have been wasted without the possession of certain expectations and knowledge: a reference to understand and contextualise what was found: a key, so to speak. In the case of the finding at Straumøya, I possessed a (theoretical) framework that enabled a recognition of what keys look like, and the pre-conception of the lost keys. In opposition to most finders, I also possessed a key to compare against, a reference collection in my own bundle of keys – a method of proving (or falsifying). The success of my discovery (or publication) depended on all this – Aaslaug's lost keys as much as any other archaeological objects that have found their way to recognition.

It is one of the perks of being trained in archaeology, this capability to spot and identify things that bear marks the past. You may think that the vestiges of bygone times are somewhere else, distant and out of reach. On the contrary, they are here and now; the ground we tread on is a giant scratch card, with frequent winnings. The things that have survived the ravages of time are still here in our midst, Aaslaug's keyring and Iron Age grave cairns alike, the rest are in museum showcases and storages, on display in collectors' dens, bagged and marked in researchers' desk drawers – although the majority are buried, unfound and unknown. The things in and of themselves are not old, they are as present here and now as your bike or yesterday's garbage. Yet they carry memories of events that happened in the past. To study and understand the memories inherent in objects is the real challenge for archaeologists, to study how things were made and used, their role and importance in events that are old, what they did in the past.[1]

Very often, the surface is already scratched to expose things buried: newly-ploughed farmland, a fresh ditch in the city, tree falls or trails that have tattered and penetrated the veil of time that covers most abandoned things. They are perhaps hidden, but are ever ready for new attention.

Independently of being discovered or not, the vestiges of the past have already made a difference in the world. They made up a large part of the human world as it is today – their subtle touch educed the functions and stability needed to form societies, or perhaps made adjustments, changes. In their newly exposed state, things demonstrate their ability to come back, sharing their memories in new settings, inducing new actions.

Anyway. Archaeology prompts us to find, to discover, to be in places that once were significant and well known to many, now forgotten. Large base camps, stone quarries, rock art sites, hillforts, a chief's grave, farmsteads, court sites, fences, paths and road markings, houses that once were homes. It prompts us to connect findings, to try to understand patterns. To walk the faint outline of the remains of a house, to observe its surroundings, to ask why here, when? To move along abandoned roads, to study what they connect, to wonder about what fences kept apart. To listen to locals, to researchers, to read, to discuss, to travel and to see new places, different things.

As an archaeologist, I have the good fortune to have frequent up close and personal interactions with abandoned things from bygone people. I get to hold objects that acted in ancient times in my hands, such as a stone adze – turning it around, slowly, feeling its weight and smooth surface, holding it up against the light to study striations that reveal how it was made, scrutinising the chips and the polish along the edge that show how it was used back then, in the forgotten depths of the Stone Age. Quite often, when excavating at a settlement, I am the lucky one to lift out a flint arrowhead, to free it from the damp darkness of the soil where it lay dormant for thousands of years. This implement, it was here for all those years, entirely forgotten by humans – and now, back in the light of the day, it is exposed to different times, included in another context, in a world that has since changed.

In the confined silence of the square I am carefully scraping, I wait for a moment before I announce my finding to others in the crew, enjoying the instant in which I am the only one who knows about its recovery from its long sleep. If I were to drop dead in this instant, this projectile point would perhaps have to wait another eight thousand years to get back into the hands of a human. I cherish the feeling of being the first to touch this thing since it parted from the faceless someone who had depended on it functioning well for success in hunting 10,000 years ago. Sometimes, if needed, I may lick away the last of the soil to study the details of how the point was made – and experience the thrill of this close and eerie relation to an individual who was here, at this very spot, all that time ago. The arrowhead between my fingers, still as sharp as when it was meant to kill, it has proved its capacity to keep something in reserve, to be something else other than what it was in the grip of its maker. Once, when it was shaped and used, it 'collected' memories of function, tradition, competence and intention. It became one of the hunter's helpers; brought around as part of the gear in the search for game, it was a decisive instrument in bringing that game down, in succeeding.

Now, it has proved its ability to come back, to slip out of its long dormancy. Patience pays, here is yet another chance to be handled by a human (as if it cares), to be lifted to the light, to be seen, admired, to receive attention and esteem, to be talked about, to make a heart skip a beat.

The implement is an able player in the hands of humans, able to remember fragments of events before its long sleep. However, it wakes up to something different than what was. Never more to be pointed at an animal it was meant to maim and kill, never more the vibrant flight from a bowstring, the brutal impact, to be embedded in an animal soon to lose its life, never more to be praised for its efficiency during the subsequent feasting, feeding everybody. Now, after this brief flash of light in my palm, a new semi-oblivion awaits – it is bagged, marked and put to sleep again in a specially-adapted Styrofoam bed, in the deep darkness of the museum storage. Indifferent to it all, it is not even waiting for new action from a future student, researcher, curator, a person with a particular interest in the past in this specific local community where it was rediscovered. Archaeology is not only about finding things. It is also about examining the memories things bring along, how things once worked, were held or hafted, technological traditions, the materials chosen for instruments – there is always more to be found and studied.

... he never returned the red marker

In the silence of the square I am digging, touching things, I am wondering about things and humans, time and happenings, how things from the past are still here among us. The very soil I am scraping is saturated with unseen components of whatever was left here. Sometimes, I try to imagine how I would manage if I could in some miraculous way go back through time and be among the people here, to see their Stone Age world, their homes and garments, the construction details in their boats and how they communicated, to learn about their complete material world that comes to us as mere fragments – how it all was alive. Would I be killed on sight? ...or perhaps survive some hours tied to a pole? Would I be saved by the wonders of my Swiss-army-tool and cherish happy times as an infamous Mesolithic[2] celebrity? Would I like the food they prepared? Usually, I end up thinking that I soon would miss the perks of my present life, the sofa and the binge-watching of TV series, my wok and Asian spices.

After this, I may try to see it from the opposite direction, switching the direction of time, imagining a man (in my prejudiced mind it is always a male) from the past appearing from the bushes on the north side of our excavation field. The wonderful things that this Beforeigner[3] could reveal, what he could tell me, from mundane details to stories of life, where he travels, the location of other camps. His reactions to the most normal things of our time, a glass bottle or a rain-proof garment, a passing ship, a plane in the sky. The evasiveness and indifferent gazes among individuals in a crowd of people, he would perhaps think they were 'the living dead'. The myriads of city lights at midnight, he would think they were individual campfires, a feast of astronomical proportions. He would wonder why there was no smoke. Or maybe things are so utterly different, beyond all his references, that the man would be indifferent to it all.

My mind drifts to something I once read about Rerebawä, a Yanomamö Indian from the untamed parts of Amazonas, who accompanied the anthropologist Napoleon Chagnon to an airport on the way to Caracas.[4] An endless array of wonders passed the man, a myriad of queries to be asked – perhaps he was too estranged even to formulate questions. On seeing the airstrip, he sat down, touched it carefully and asked where they 'had found so many flat stones to make such a big trail'. Flat stones, although of unseen proportions, he could relate to that. Later, in Caracas, he was shown a soda pop machine in the hotel corridor. What impressed him was not the orange soda pop, the chilled container, the sweet fluid, or the intricate mechanism of the machine – but the speed of the operation. He could relate to giving a gift (the coin) and have a gift (the orange soda pop) returned at some later point, but never ever had he experienced a gift exchange that was this rapid, in the very same instant as his gift was given. He envisioned presenting the gift-giving wonder during a feast in his encampment in the depths of Amazonas.

Or the story about Jemmy Button, Fuegia Basket, York Minister and Boat Memory, the four Fuegian teenagers, nicknamed by the Europeans, whom Capt. Fitzroy brought to England from Tierra del Fuego on-board the HMS Beagle in the mid-1800s.[5] Along the way, they anchored in the harbour of Buenos Aires, which was already a blooming city at the time. The crew, among them Charles Darwin, were curious as to the teenagers' reactions to this vision of wonder, but, disappointingly, the wild bunch seemed indifferent to it all – until they spotted a long-horned bull: they stared at it for hours, the size of it, the horns, that they could get near, that the bull obeyed orders and could pull a wagon – they could relate to this in a way, it was the same as home, but remarkably different.

I would start with something simpler for my imaginary Stone Age friend, a softer adaption to modernity, something he could relate to. Like a red permanent marker, the eternal red line in the wake of its tip would surely fascinate him. He would draw shapes that I perhaps would recognize from ancient incisions in bone implements, or rock art. I would be thrilled to see these motifs shaped 'live', a dream come true (in a dream). Repeatedly, he would examine the marker thoroughly. More than the bright colour, he would be enthralled by stingy scent from the tip, and the remarkable fact that it never stopped producing colour. Likewise, he would be deeply fascinated by the instant, ever-ready flame of my lighter, how it may be regulated, that fire could be stored safely in your pocket without any harm. After learning this, he would touch the flame to his finger, to test if it was fake, as

Figure 1. A Stoneager man I envisioned as a schoolboy. His simple and basic life enticed me. At the time, I would easily have agreed with a similarly-aged schoolboy who concluded his report on his class's re-enactment of Stoneager life (sleeping in tents, using stone-tools, and cooking by open fire) with this well-reflected statement: 'The Stone Age must have been a good time to be in. This is probably the reason why it lasted for so long.'

he would so many other things in this strange world he had arrived in. Like the marker, he would comment that the fire was stored within this instrument for eternity (or for 'all-times', as he would say). Just as much as the actual flame, he would be amused that he could 'kill it' by a simple blow, or just by 'ungripping' the instrument – nevertheless, it was always ready to produce a new flame. The fire that could never die. I would not reveal that the lighter *would* be emptied, eventually.

I could stream a catchy tune (lots of drums) via Spotify on my mobile phone, take a selfie of the two of us, perhaps. I could probably show him things that would scare him, a passing car close by, challenging him to touch an electrical fence, but would I be able to say or do something that would charm him, make him laugh? A funny face? I could find out if 'falling in water' is an eternal amusement among human onlookers. Could he make me smile? Maybe a funny ring to a word he would utter – would he notice my reaction, and repeat his action to provoke another smile?

At some point during my enticing fantasy, my working hours are over, and I am facing a dilemma: what to do with my newfound Stoneager[6] pal? I could not leave him among his now plastic-bagged belongings in the storeroom – I would have to bring him along, to my home. Very soon, I would realize that he was a problem. I would have to open the car door for him, and close it too. He would not like to be buckled in the seatbelt, and panic as I started the engine. He would perhaps try to escape as the car started moving, climb to the back seat, as he could not manage to open the door. And perhaps he would lose all composure when we met another car on the road. He would know right from left, but the yellow line that divides traffic would mean nothing to him.

The situation would worsen as we arrived at my home. At first, I would be charmed that he labels the refrigerator in the kitchen the 'home of the winter', and his fascination for colourful plastic objects. However, the fantasy would soon be redirected by my inclination to catastrophe-thinking.

Eventually, he would use the red marker that he never returned to make 'rock art' on the white walls in our guest room. I would have to always watch him, or he would harass Elin. He would surely chase our cat around the house, and I would be deeply disturbed by his hinting at the need for a winter hat. He would look behind my wide screen TV upon the appearance of an edible animal. I would show him the bathroom, how to flush the toilet. He would be fascinated. All afternoon he would sneak back to flush it again. I would hear him splashing the running water. Later, Elin would complain about teeth marks in the honey-coloured soap.

I would fail to take back the lighter (or 'Father of Fire', as he comes to call it) after he ignites our decoration of straws in the living room – he would overpower me, his muscles as tough as car tires, it would be scary. He would steal my best shirt and kitchen utensils. There would be a mess in his wake as he rumbles around in our cosy home. He would sneak out at dusk, I would have to search the neighbourhood for him, he would already be in the next garden chasing their leashed-up dog.

As he invades my imagination, my Stoneager friend turns to a villain in every sense – I have to remind myself to blame my fantasy going wild, rather than him.

The things he would communicate would never touch upon what I am interested in; archaeological enquiries into how to make up and fuel a fire, the basic lay-out of his social structure, mobility patterns and the carrying capacity of boats, site catchment areas, social identity, or cosmology. I suddenly realize that he would not understand any of my words, as I would not understand his. He would keep repeating one peculiar sound, some kind of throat clicking, I would not even know whether it was a word, a warning or a sign of confidence. I would fail to explain my profession, he would not understand deep time – like *Hioduwä*, the Yanomamö man who was granted an audience with the Pope in 1971. More than the 'awesomeness and pomp' of the meeting with the Pope, he was impressed by the Roman ruins, '...the old, abandoned villages of their ancestors'. As Chagnon comments, it was perhaps a testimony to the fact that the 'past is connected to the present in an intimate, concrete way – as it is in the Yanomamö myth where present, past, and future are unchanging and indistinguishable'.[7]

After a while, I am usually happy that I chose the silenced archaeology over noisy anthropology, and slip back to the routines of the excavation, scraping the soil, picking up the silent things and putting them in marked plastic bags, thinking of my upcoming vacation in Sicily or a new annoying administrative routine from my University, awaiting the lunch hour and all the rest of the familiar things of modern times, and happy that time-machines are not yet invented.

Dreaming the past

Some years back, I was dreaming of my son Trygve. It was the kind of dream that lingers for days, a dream that brings on a distinct feeling, it stays on unconsciously, colouring events and actions without you actually knowing, and evokes a rush of joy each time you remember it. In the dream, Trygve was a boy of perhaps six years, open-minded and attentive, with his blonde unruly hair and colourful training suit; we were outside the house we lived in in Bodø. I was looking down at my cherished boy – he was telling me something about a new gadget given to a friend, intense and meticulous in his elaboration of what the thing could do. There was nothing particular in the event – just the fact that he was exactly how he was at the time, and how I was too. The dream evoked an intense longing for this charming boy, it was a feeling of something precious that had fallen into oblivion – although

I loved Trygve in the moment of dreaming this as I did *in* the dream. It was one of those many things that you think are lost in the depths of the forgotten, but which you catch sharp glimpses of, not only remembering the facts of a situation, but the emotional ballast of past moments. I think the mind has the capacity to store complex vivid emotions; perhaps they are more accurate than what happens, where and when, the persons and non-humans that a dream may include.

I am becoming increasingly aware of a fact about myself: in spite of a deep and long-lived engagement with the past, facts and fantasies, I have never ever *dreamt* that I was in the Stone Age, or, for that matter, in any other parts of the past beyond myself. Of course, 'archaeology' is a frequent occurrence in my dreams. In the night, deep in my sleep, my mind roams freely in my personal universe of experiences, mixing dreams from a vast repertoire of delights, fears, friends and foes, places and happenings, private and professional. The most absurd combinations and entanglements may occur, and quite often they relate to archaeology. I may dream that I discover something worthy of attention, like an object from that past that is especially large or well shaped, a flint blade that is close to a metre long, or a bulb of percussion the size of half an apple. Or that I suddenly discover that the ground in front of the now long-gone newspaper kiosk in my home town of Florø is packed with Stone Age lithic artefacts. I wake up and wish that the dream would stay with me longer – and recall that this exact spot was a place of frequent findings of lost coins when I was a kid.

Just as frequently, my unconscious realm relates to archaeological humiliation and failure. Valuable and well-preserved artefacts disintegrate before my eyes, in my clumsy clasp. A beautiful polished slate dagger with astonishing incisions slips out of my hands as my colleague proudly hands it to me to admire. The impressive implement breaks, or is lost, and I cannot find it back in the grass. The stratigraphy I thought was straightforward changes to something impossible. I have messed up the information on the plastic bags, and lack the courage to confess, as the threatening truth slowly closes in on me – if I am lucky, I wake up before my secret mess is revealed to others in my team. I may dream that I arrive at a conference, and suddenly discover that I am still in my pyjamas (or worse), and that there is no time to change before I am on. Occasionally, I wake up remembering a dream of distinct clarity: after a conference dinner, I went to the bar in the next room; Tom Cruise was there. I talked to him, he was a bit drunk-happy and friendly, although I was suddenly unable to remember any of the movies he was in. He was impressed by the fact that I was a real archaeologist. When my colleagues came to the scene, Tom had vanished, and nobody would believe what had happened. I fell out of the dream, and realized that my colleagues were right, unfortunately.

Figure 2. An expedition into the jungle, as I imagined it in school – inspired by the canvas tents my grandfather Oluf had made. The mysterious 'sun helmet' from uncle Faste's Australia-things is also included.

In my dreams, even the most absurd, I am always myself, the *archaeologist*; I experience the victories and humiliating defeats of being an archaeologist. I am never a human *in* the past, and never ever a human among humans of past times. I may dream my own past, but the moment I came into this world seem to be the outer limits of my unconscious reach into the past.

I have been wondering about this, and perhaps I would like it to happen – to be dragged into my imaginary Mesolithic, immersed in an entanglement of my being-in-the-world and my profound engagement with the deep past. I have been wondering about the absence of the past in my dreams to the point that I have asked fellow archaeologists and students. It seems like I am not the only one. Never have any of my colleagues retold dreams about happy times spent in sunny Bronze Age days, or the perils of being sold as a slave in Viking times. Once an undergraduate student said that she had dreamt about herself in the medieval period. Perhaps it was because her archaeological training had yet not reached the level where it would block her imagination, she had not yet experienced an archaeological 'taming' of her mind. I believe that this is what it is all about. Our archaeological knowledge, explorations, studies and findings of objects are always fragmentary compared to lived lives. Archaeological vestiges that are memories of past events and interactions are part of, but never close to, the entangled lived lives of past peoples. And just as often, the archaeological foci are generalisations and trajectories that were never seen or experienced by the people who were part of them, changes that were too slow to be sensed and acknowledged by the actors that *lived* them.

Dreams relate to the holistic, lived completeness of experiences of being alive in the world – in opposition to the wealth of single strands, trajectories and fragments from life that is archaeology. The apparent reluctance of dreams to cross this line is a reminder of exactly this. We may speak of and fantasise about past realities, but we cannot force the unconscious mind to translate the archaeological fragments into actually being alive in and members of bygone times. I think this illustrates the impassable gap between the archaeological and the lived past – perhaps this division is a necessary thing to acknowledge in archaeology. It is a gap that perfectly preserved and complete archaeological contexts may narrow, but cannot close. Not Pompeii-like ash-buried instances, armies of detailed terracotta warriors, mummified Pharaohs in the unscathed, murky chambers in the heart of Egyptian pyramids, not even a frozen parade of Ötzis rediscovered in the blue ice of the Alps.[8]

Broken leg ...in the winter

I recall another encounter with past realities; it taught me a lesson. Some years ago now, as part of a student field course, we arranged a meeting with the local community in the area where we were working. Judging by the many that came, there was a great interest in our doings and discoveries. The students presented our findings; we had discovered several Stone Age encampments in their community: maps with markings were on display in the community hall, things to be shown, including things that had been found in our different test pits – 11,000-year-old stone tools, projectile points, a knife just as sharp on this day as it was when it lay in a Stone Age hand all that time ago. It was a perfect and all-encompassing presentation that ended in an invitation for questions and comments from the local audience. Both students and teachers were proud of our major contribution to the knowledge of the past in their local surroundings, their ancestors – and we were eager to elaborate on details that the locals might want to know more about.

After a brief moment of hesitating silence, an older man in the third row raised his hand and was invited to speak. There was something he had been thinking of, he told us: if he had been living in the Stone Age, and if he had broken a leg in the autumn, would he have survived the winter, and would he still be alive in the spring (as it was spring at the time). I still remember my reaction: that this was an utterly stupid question that was not at all related to our detailed account of scientific details. I rolled my eyeballs upwards and drew in air slowly and very deeply through my nose, as I let the students answer the 'we-don't-know-exactly-s' and the usual 'unfortunate lack of organic preservation'. As suspected, the man had in fact broken his leg the previous fall and had had ample time to reflect on his own situation, with his foot in its cast on a stool in front of the wood stove during the snowfall and heavy winds of a long winter. Obviously, he had taken comfort in this, that he in this situation was very lucky to be a member of modern society – and not a Stone Age man.

On second thought, as I was listening to the students' struggle to redirect the ex-crippled man to the patchy world of 'real archaeology', I felt a creeping shame about my reaction. Exactly how stupid was this question? After all, it touched upon basic human issues, on individual care within the Stone Age society, their medical competence, their settlement pattern and housing, their mobility pattern, to name but a few. The problem was that his curiosity was directed towards what was outside the frame of our predefined archaeological record, beyond the fragments we collect. Thus, the man had put the finger on our largely neglected, but still sore point: that most of what relates to *being* a human in the past is not included in the problems we explore. The people who are unaware of the limits of archaeology, lines that we, as professionals, have learned not to cross, are free to wonder about how the world was. Perhaps the man with the healed leg injury, unfettered by scholarly limitations, had even managed to dream the past.

The man's question was far from unwise, not at all. It was a question that we should have asked more often, to remind ourselves of the fragmentary basis of our discipline, to see beyond the horizon of traditional archaeology.

I am not saying that the things we explore and reflect upon are unimportant or futile – but our efforts will never bring us even close to a comprehensive understanding of the *lives* of past peoples. And now, before my eyes, I was in the process of 'taming' a new generation of archaeologists to stay safe within the disciplinary fences...

In many ways, our scientific training as archaeologists has distracted us from holistic past realities. We are led to believe that archaeology is about 'everything', all-encompassing. In one way, that is true, in the sense that there are perhaps no limits to what that may explored. Nevertheless, we cannot escape the fact that we can never track more than fragments, aspects, trajectories of humankind. The search for facts has taken us to increasingly smaller objective details that tell us increasingly precise truths about smaller and smaller fragments about lived lives in the past. Or to the higher, more general levels, overviews and trajectories that were never seen in the past, that perhaps were beyond the planetary awareness of Beforeigners. We learn about climate changes – but the only thing the past individuals could ever see was the weather.[9]

We have been educated to be very aware of the fact that little from the present can illuminate the past – that 'the past is a foreign country'.[10] An archaeologist proper must consider her/himself as contaminated, a danger to his/her ability to explore the past. To top it off, we are taught that we can never escape ourselves as members of our time. As archaeologists, so to speak, we are our own worst enemies; our best option is to withdraw from our own beings, and communicate anonymously, to refrain from coming out as speculative and non-scientific 'I's. Through the years as a professional, truth-seeking archaeologist, I have experienced a growing feeling that this is not sufficient. Our traditional style of writing up archaeology is too confined. It is not the intention – but certainly a result; the strict and objective way of researching and writing excludes many important aspects of human life – like the broken leg. In fact, the combination of not being able to experience lived lives of the past and the self-inflicted restrictions on consulting the only living human (yourself) that we may fully access is problematic. Strict academic work in IMRAD-style (Introduction-Methods-Research-And-Discussion) is important, but there must be room for other styles of writing.[11]

The young plant scientist Merlin Sheldrake hints at the same in his conversation with Robert Macfarlane, albeit about a different scientific discipline: 'It's so weird to me how science always presents its knowledge as *clean*'. He announces his plan of publishing the dark twin of every scientific paper, its underground mirror-piece – '...the true story of how data for that cool, tidy hypothesis-evidence-proof paper *actually* got acquired... this frothy, mad network that underlies and interconnects all scientific knowledge – but about which we so rarely say anything.'[12]

I recall my dubious 'Theory of Snoring', initially invented in despair to charm Elin after an unfortunate noisy night; '...it is because I love you – a man who doesn't snore is without care for his dearests'. I claimed that snoring was actually 'a remnant of the Stone Age man that still lingers in the depths of me', that it materialises in a tiny flap of skin that lowers itself into my respiration system to make abrupt sounds intended to scare predators and enemies when in deep, defenceless sleep. A wishful fact (perhaps), hard to prove (of course), although I checked and found that most primates snore in their sleep, to strengthen my case.

Later, during a dinner get-together, partly as a joke and partly to support other male snorers, I retold the 'theory', and we ended up in a debate as to the limits of archaeological science. My 'theory' was ridiculed and dismissed as impossible to test, and hence uninteresting. Admittedly, the theory of snoring is scientifically weak, but is it unfeasible, uninteresting? There is a logic to it, abrupt snoring *would* scare away threatening beings that once lurked too close to sleeping humans, and human bodies carry other unnecessary things, like extra molars, a tail bone and an appendix, all of which are remnants of things that were, the physical body is too slow to keep up with evolution – to root out benign vestiges. The point is, should all things that are difficult or impossible to prove be left out of the scientific discourse?

'Nothing floats into the world from nowhere', is a famous quote from the philosopher Alfred North Whitehead. The world consists of things that came about from somewhere, that have roots and origins. There is not a single place name that emerged from an arbitrary sequence of sounds, they are all rooted in meanings. Routines have deep roots, as do our clothes, what we eat, how we speak, our tools and means of transport, our forks and spoons and the mugs we sip from. Some of these roots are easy to track, others may be hard to follow – but should scientific discourse be restricted to the thin lines that may be proved as facts? Should the dark twins of factual knowledge be shown? Wild ideas are the cradle of what it may eventually be possible to explore scientifically, in the ever-expanding archaeological workshop. When does the uncertainty of 'past' begin; where does the 'now' start to dwindle?

Contemporary archaeology

'Archaeology of the recent past' or 'contemporary archaeology' is about studying ourselves and our 'amongstness' with the planet – humans, and all their seamless engagements with nonhuman entities, animate as well as inanimate – humankind within what Timothy Morton labels 'the symbiotic real'.[13] Materiality – things in their widest sense, their basic nature and what they do in the world – is at centre. The *now* allows us to study things that are near to us and hence more recognisable, albeit unseen in their conspicuous familiarity, taken for granted to a degree that they are overlooked.[14] This neglect of things is luminously exemplified in Bjørnar Olsen's comment on Erling Kagge's book *Alone to the South Pole* (1993), advertised as relating 'the first solo and unsupported expedition to the South Pole':

And you start to wonder – alone? Solo? Unsupported? Didn't he have the help of a pair of skis, the company of a sledge, the protection of some clothes, the comfort of a tent and a sleeping bag, nutrition from some freeze-dried food, the 'eyes' of a navigator, communication links to some satellites crossing the sky above his head, etc, etc? Of course, he had – but all the honour and fame is once again claimed by a single actor, the human subject, when in reality a whole company of actors actually crossed the Antarctic.[15]

Contemporary archaeology strives towards a deeper understanding of timeless human-thing entanglements – what things do to humans and vice versa. Archaeological things are more than a steady drizzle of material remains through the times. These things were also active players in how the world worked, intended and unpremeditated effects alike. Engagement with the materiality humans are born into entails discovering a next to unlimited array of possibilities and limitations to be acted upon – challenges that call for reorientations. This notion of *symmetry* between humans and non-humans is essential in most of the theoretical perspectives that modern archaeological research leans upon, e.g., Actor-Network-Theory (ANT), Symmetrical Archaeology, and the dynamic lines of Meshwork, Object-Oriented-Ontology (OOO) and Machine-Oriented-Ontology (MOO) that will be elaborated on in the following.

As a fairly new branch of the discipline, contemporary archaeology brings about an openness to experimental research and alternative ways of communicating.[16] I have had the lucky opportunity of being a member in research groups focusing on the various aspects of contemporary archaeology.[17] I do not hesitate to admit that fellow group members reinvigorated my archaeological thinking and perspectives, as did the many invited scholars who visited our meetings – joined in search of a deeper understanding of *things*, *time* and *heritage*, how humans co-reside with non-humans, the entanglements of materiality in its widest sense. Not everything was new to me, but all things were seen from new angles, elaborated on and put together in different manners. One recurring theme was styles of communicating, styles of writing. Another was the nature of working with fragments, as archaeologists always do. We explored the hallmarks of our time, the Anthropocene; how things remember, things and memories; the 'affect of things', how things may constantly surprise, strike or annoy their living co-residents; the 'ethics of things', how things have values of their own, outside of what they do for humanity.

It is claimed that contemporary archaeology has its roots in ethno-archaeology.[18] Ethno-archaeology aimed at better insights into human behaviour and material remains, such as Lewis Binford's classic study of the Mask site in Arctic North America. Binford studied the minute details of how the actions of an Inuit hunting band were mirrored in the vestiges of their camp. I also vividly recall Robson Bonnichsen's fascinating study of

Millie's camp, and how her quarters reflected her lifestyle.[19] In parallel with a widening critical approach to the archaeological discipline, questions were asked about the search for extant 'primitive' societies to expand the knowledge of things and human behaviour. It certainly did not accord with growing anti-colonial norms. Perhaps the study of our own postmodern material engagement could be likewise instructive? Since then, from the late 1990s onwards, we have seen an ever-expanding array of new types of research and study objects, academic writings narrowing in on the world of materiality, of non-humans and humans.[20] They have all contributed to a deeper and wider understanding of things, time and the human dependency on their surrounding materiality, and have even challenged the human–nature division itself.[21] It is claimed that humans bodies include about 1.5 kg of bacteria that is genetically different from us, organisms that we cannot survive without, and that a large part of a mother's milk is evidently not food for her baby, but for bacteria that protect the baby's inner organs.[22] Human lives are intermingled with animal pets as well as livestock, plants, metals, corrosion, smoke, fire, weather and climate. Where does the 'human' end; where does 'nature' begin?

These issues have provoked a growing interest in research history, epistemology, theory building, ontology, and the phenomena of time. The latter entails 'Presentism', i.e., that all surviving materiality from past events are here and now, and that the present is ridden with 'stuff' from all times; all past things that have not since disintegrated are among us in the contemporaneous – in exhibitions, in museum collections, in drawers in researcher's offices, and above all in the dark depths of the soils beneath us. This is not exclusive of our own time – people of the past surely stumbled across masses of things from their own pasts. Bronze Age people did not inhabit a clean 'Bronze Age' world, but a Bronze Age that included all stuff from earlier times. Thus, 'there is no archaeology of the twenty-first century but only an archaeology of the twenty-first and all its pasts, mixed and entangled', to quote Alfredo González-Ruibal.[23]

However, things *remember* past events, they bear the marks of what happened to them through the times, how they were shaped and used, and their changing roles in all their moments through time, as sharp instruments, in abandonment and oblivion, as archaeological objects with added catalogue numbers in museums, on display, or in the protected darkness of collections. Archaeologists study how things remember past happenings, how to understand and interpret their marks – it is a special skill in our discipline. Archaeological objects prove things' ability to 'come back', always to a changed world, always to something else than what was. Our collections are full of tools meant to cut, maim and kill, to shine, to impress, to signify social status. Now they are seemingly passive and innocent, dormant in their new and comfortable beds in climate-controlled museum stores. But beware – they are still ever ready to engage the hands of humans with different skills and intentions. Now, they may be objects to study the bygone times they were part of, but also enter future trajectories, whether intended or unintended, good, evil, wise or unwitting alike. Most of them will survive us, their future roles and connections even more in the unknown than their past. 'Objects are sleeping giants holding their forces in reserve, and do not unleash all their energies at once', as phrased by Graham Harman.[24]

Rodney Harrison and John Schofield have attempted to sum up different rationales for studying the archaeologies of the contemporary past.[25] The ever-accelerating development of our time entails that recent things and technologies fade away and are forgotten. Recent things may enlighten what is omitted or obscured in written sources, and also normally excluded in traditional cultural heritage – the subaltern, the painstakingly ordinary and normal, the abject, the painful, the unimportant. Harrison and Schofield point out that archaeologies of the recent past are more 'democratic' than archaeologies of antique periods. Educated scholars of the discipline have a deeper knowledge of past vestiges than laypeople – hence, archaeologists have authoritative views and claims regarding past periods. The present and recent past belong to the majority and are lived by everyone alike – and are hence more multivocal and democratic.[26] It is certain that 'archaeologies of the recent' embrace more experimental types of research and are considerably more tolerant of non-traditional styles of scholarly writing than traditional academic texts – supported, perhaps, by precisely its multivocal character. Although there are pronounced ambitions to be scientific, academic and objective, the scope of what 'archaeology' *is* is considerably widened, including questions of what is proper empirical data, methods, theory building, what neighbouring disciplines are relevant, and how to write it up studies – how to communicate.

In the more 'democratic' realm of the recent past, traditional limits between different academic disciplines are blurred, as demonstrated in several publications of our time. A great many authors have crossed the scholarly borderlines, and have ended up somewhere that is multidisciplinary, albeit hardly without a sound scholarly footing. It seems archaeology is one of many fields of interest, among many other sciences. Very few will dispute the thorough scholarly foundations of the celebrated works of Robert Macfarlane, touching upon archaeology, history and geology, language and literature, place names, landscapes and mobility, Anthropocene and deep time alike.[27] His books do not belong in any specific discipline, much like Yuval Harari's best-selling books.[28] Maybe the lack of disciplinary confinement is exactly what elevates these writings.

In the early spring of 2017, I happened to meet Macfarlane – as a member of Bjørnar Olsen's year-long research project *After Discourse* at the Centre of Advanced Studies (CAS) in Oslo. Macfarlane presented a seminar on scholarly writing and had forwarded a reading list of thought-provoking examples. Without revealing details, he talked about a new book that was underway

– *Underland* – it was about the wealth of obscured realities underground, mines and grave chambers, how plants communicate by root systems in the WoodWideWeb, the blue depths of glaciers, catacombs ...and caves.[29] In fact, he was combining the Oslo visit with a journey to the Lofoten islands to study the coastal cave 'Kollhellaren', with its ancient paintings, positioned on the remote and harsh western shores. It happened that I had studied Kollhellaren as part of my published research on the subject. My own visit to the cave had included hiring a boat for transport – to avoid crossing the risky mountains to reach to the cave.

Macfarlane was eager to seek my advice on this and that in his preparation for the visit. To my surprise, I realised that the man actually planned to cross the jagged and scree-faced mountains by foot, spend the night in a tent, and study the cave the next day. This sympathetic and slender British man – well proportioned, but he did not meet the worn-leather-look I anticipated from a mountaineer roughneck. To my even greater astonishment, I learned that his trip was going to take place the next week – it was still March and winter up there. At first, I thought that he needed much more than a healthy advice from me – he needed help to save himself from his maniacal plans. As I was gradually convinced that the man was actually an able mountain climber and that his trip was well-planned, including an awareness of hazards – I could do nothing but wish him good luck, although I was keen to learn how it all went.

What he told in an email some weeks later (he was alive!) was even worse than I could have foreseen. The weather had not been the best, a fresh heavy snowfall meant that he had had to wade in snow up to his knees most of the way. After struggling to reach the steep and rugged pass he had been advised to cross, there had been a gale that had brought heavy sleet. His tent had threatened to collapse during the night; he had needed to relocate it in the dark. As he finally entered the cold silence of the cave and could see the ancient stick-men figures, he could not help crying. The mix of emotions, evoked by his experience of the gigantic dimensions of the cave, the flogging sleet and frothy sea, and all other hardships in reaching the place, was overwhelming. As a result, his attentiveness included things I never saw during my smooth visit. What he later wrote about this endeavour in *Underland* reflects this close encounter with something bigger than himself.

Of course, as I eventually understood – from reading *Underland* and other writings of his – his hardships were pivotal parts of how he encountered things. The perils were more than unintended accidents. To be outspokenly immersed in the context of what he writes about, that intimate bodily presence is a vital part of his successful writings. Most of them could be dismissed as personal experiences that he had no way of knowing were relevant to what he observed or not. But as so many times before, this observant presence added things to what he wrote that objective information never could. His very presence in his text was imperative, and the book on all that is 'underland' became another addition to the reading list that he had presented in our seminar in Oslo.

Macfarlane's venture helped me to realise why I was drawn to similar presences in many other writings. They were more than readable texts with attentive observations. They also included a sensation of being brought along, a familiar recognition that facilitated shared understandings.

There is also Bjørnar Olsen's remarkable account of 'Halldor's truck' – a thing that was a part of his tiny village in Finnmark in Northern Norway. At the time when Halldor's truck was launched onto land from a boat in the harbour, the car-less village had merely a few kilometres of road. The truck was dragged through the snow to a place less than a kilometre from the harbour, where it was left. Decades of still-stand followed; Halldor refused even to rent out the truck to the road-construction company when the village was finally coupled to the general road system. These circumstances, in parallel with the unused truck's familiar presence, the bizarre affect of a thing that never got the chance to demonstrate is functional capabilities – nevertheless, the truck was still a thing that did something in the world.[30] Then there is Chris Witmore and his texts about walking the old roads in Greece, attuning himself to the landscapes, ancient monuments and mythical accounts, how all this mingled into observations of real life today.[31] And the elegant elaborations on the reclamation in Elizabeth Bay at the shores of Sydney by Denis Byrne – how he could manage to see a reclamation as an object to elaborate on, and how he could involve seemingly endless connections to geological times as well as the most minute and sensual details of the Anthropocene:[32]

> Meanwhile, the same warm breeze that was creating waves on the harbour's surface was blowing on my surface, my skin, as if to underline the impossibility that I could ever be a disembodied observer here. Would the wind on my face create ripples that would alter the pattern of native creases that would materialize, for instance, if I smiled? Naturally, this thought, triggered by the wind and waves, made me smile.[33]

There are the ways in which Þóra Pétursdóttir contemplates and writes about the accumulations of drift-matter along ocean beaches – seen by many, but rarely acknowledged as anything more than unruly matter that needs to be cleared away – Pétursdóttir demonstrates that drift matter is telling heritage of the Anthropocene, however unruly.[34] Alfredo González-Ruibal has written intimate accounts for excavations of heart-breaking contexts from the Spanish civil war and the shadows it casts onto human fates – back then and also very much today.[35] There is Mats Burström's engagement with recollections of valuables hidden away around the fluctuating fronts during the turmoil of WW2 in Estonia, involving memories in things, treasure maps and stories told, field surveys and excavations, and finds to be rejoiced in;[36] the mingling presence of times observed by Laurent Oliver as he examines the black box of valuables inherited after the passing of his mother;[37] Rachel Kiddey's involving of homeless persons in her study of the archaeology of the homeless and the much debated cartoon publication that followed.[38] Then there are Stein Farstadvoll's observations of the maze of plant descendants in the abandoned Retiro Park near Molde, the metal bolt Lucas Introna stepped on by accident on the road, initially a thing of annoyance that he eventually kept as a memory, even the destructive experiments and texts by Doug Bailey, crushing ceramic vessels or using chlorine baths to remove layers of emulsion from discarded slides.[39]

These are merely a tiny fragment of scholarly writings with an outspoken positioning of the author on the inside of observations, of what is being studied – in opposition to objective positivism, to what Donna Haraway has labelled 'the god-trick of seeing everything from nowhere',[40] in advocating the need to expose, not obscure, the position of writers. Things need to be seen from somewhere.

Auto-ethnography – and auto-archaeology?

An important hallmark of 'archaeology' is the concept of 'past' and 'old', as embedded in the very name of the discipline. Thus, archaeologists are quite familiar with *not* being alive among the things they study – everything is normally abandoned, brought down and not moving, decayed and dead long before us; the past is referred to as 'another country'. It is deeply acknowledged that past peoples lived different lives, that lifestyles and social systems were different, as were world views, cultural references, and what was near and what was far. Also acknowledged is the fact that we, as researchers and authors, cannot rid ourselves of our own presence, that our embedded experience of being-in-the-world is more of a problem than an asset to our understanding of the past. We are infested by our own time, so to speak. This is clearly demonstrated by the ways in which phenomenological studies in archaeology are criticised and dismissed as futile endeavours.[41]

This seems different to neighbouring humanistic disciplines like anthropology and ethnography – where studies are often integrated among the living. As in archaeology, anthropology and ethnography are very aware of the pitfalls of studying 'the other'. Nevertheless, there is perhaps a longer scholarly tradition of studying the very role of the researcher/author as part of what is studied. Apart from seeing the challenges, there is a will to turn this problem to advantage. Already in papers from the 1980s, the phenomena of 'auto-anthropology' and 'anthropology at home' are highlighted.[42] Ethnographers have elaborated on this perspective under the label of 'auto-ethnography'. Auto-ethnography is more or less a different field of study, on its own terms – different to classical ethnography.[43] I am surprised to discover that there are a great many studies and writings about the essence of auto-ethnography. In their review, Ellis, Adams and Bochner define auto-ethnography as

...an approach to research and writing that seeks to describe and systematically analyze (*graphy*) personal experience (*auto*) in order to understand cultural experience (*ethno*). ... A researcher uses tenets of *autobiography* and *ethnography* to do and write *autoethnograpy*. Thus, as a method, autoethnography is both a process and a product.[44]

'Auto-ethnography' thus labels a research method whereby researchers/ authors are an integral and constituting part of what is studied, 'a critical response to the alienating effects on both researchers and audiences of impersonal, passionless, abstract claims on truth generated by such research practices and clothed in exclusionary scientific discourse'.[45] Auto-ethnography rejects the deep-rooted and theory-ridden hypothesis of testing research methods based on positivist epistemology, and the binary opposition between 'researcher and the researched, objectivity-subjectivity, process and product, self and others, art and science, and the personal and the political'.[46] As opposed to concealing, trying to hide the 'I' – auto-ethnography foregrounds the researcher's subjectivity, making the 'self' active and visible to the reader.[47]

Laurel Richardson suggests the following five criteria to define auto-ethnography. First, the contribution has to be substantive. Does the piece contribute to our understanding of social life? Second, there has to be aesthetic merit. Does this piece succeed aesthetically? Is the text artistically shaped, satisfyingly complex, and not boring? Third, there has to be an element of reflexivity. How did the author come to write this text? How has the author's subjectivity been both a producer and a product of this text? Fourth, there must be impactfulness. Does the text affect me emotionally and/or intellectually? Does it generate new questions or move me to action? Five, the text has to expresses a reality. Does this text embody a fleshed-out sense of lived experience?[48] More recently, goals for assessing auto-ethnography stress the importance of making contributions to knowledge, of valuing the personal and experiential, of demonstrating the power, craft and responsibilities of stories and storytelling, and of taking a relationally-responsible approach to research practice and representation.[49] However, it is impossible to present an accurate definition; the limits of auto-ethnography are by nature blurred and entangled.

Ethnography is a discipline with a different focus to archaeology, oriented more towards observed human behaviour, praxis and social mechanisms. Archaeology has a basic empirical base in things and materiality, perhaps a realm of things freed from its people, albeit not without a deep interest in human societies. In line with the increasing interest in the recent past and a contemporary world, it is perhaps worthwhile to advocate for an 'auto-archaeology' oriented towards things and humans in a wider sense. Actually, there is no need to subtract or add much from the referred, quite neutral definition by Ellis, Adams and Bochner. However, auto-archaeology does not need to be reserved for the recent past. As mentioned, the notion of 'Presentism' implies that the materiality of the past is here and now, with all survived things, places and structures that were entangled in human lives in deep time. In principle, then, there is little difference between encountering an abandoned gas station from the 1950s and the remains of a settlement that was inhabited in the Mesolithic. Perhaps 'the abandoned' are more important than 'the ancient' in circumscribing the scholarly sphere of what 'archaeology' is. Auto-archaeology is more about how you encounter this material world, using the gravity of your personal experience as a reference and an asset, as a way of peeping behind the horizon of traditional archaeology. Obviously, there are limits to what may be seen here. 'Truths' are perhaps hard to achieve. Perhaps this does not matter. Perhaps instead we should aim at what auto-ethnography labels 'verisimilitudes', i.e. what *resemble truths and realities.*

I think auto-archaeology is a proper nave for the intentions of *Archaeology at Home.* A study of things and thing-regimes that you have been part of in some way, things you have lived among; not trying to escape what cannot be escaped, being openly present in your study, but also trying to explore the limits of the scholarly. The point is not a circumscribing definition of auto-archaeology – but rather to allow for another approach to what things are and how they remember – personal perspectives that welcome human experience, seeking substantial verisimilitudes rather than factual fragments.

Machine-Oriented-Ontology (MOO) – making the invisible appear

Perhaps we need to acknowledge that what was most important to past people is not necessarily what appears as dominant in the archaeological record. As an example, climate fluctuations through the times, including precipitation, temperature and the configurations of animals and plants – most archaeologists know them by heart, and include them as premises in research strategies. However, these changes were never really observed by the individuals in the past, as they are too slow to be perceived by human senses. It was the weather that was observed and that called for action, as obscured to us as climate was to them.[50] However, we may trust that the past included night and day, and the sequence of the seasons. To acknowledge the differences between what is most obvious in scientific records and what humans saw and acted upon is imperative. To advance, I believe it fruitful to include the more elusive and less visible in this discussion. Recent archaeological advancements entail increasingly detailed insights into smaller and smaller facts. Each and every one are scholarly victories, but are in vain without the verisimilitudes of the setting – speculations on the dynamics of the unseen.

Figure 3. A sunny morning, probably a Sunday around 1957, when my parents decided to set the breakfast table in the rough, newly blasted-out foundation for their house. My father is in a white shirt with a fresh newspaper and a close shave, coffee and a soft-boiled egg on the side, a kitchen towel to shield the bread slices from the sun, and my mother's magazine *NÅ* (*NOW*) – the wheelbarrow is resting in the background. It is a celebration of the prospects of their home to be, a statement of independence and adherence to a patch of the world that you 'own'. Today, this green and white tablecloth is one of my dear keepsakes from my father's home.

Recent 'thing-theory' explores the existential nature of things (in the widest sense), and what they do in the world. It aims at insights into how things relate and co-work to make up the worlds that humans are part of, and is just as relevant for deep-time studies as for the present-day.

Subsistence systems and ecologies may be viewed as 'machines', in line with Levi Bryant's theory of machines and media, elaborated on in his 'Machine-Oriented-Ontology'.[51] Bryant stresses that the world is made up of stuff, and that all stuff are 'things':

> Even ideas and concepts have their materiality. ...I only mean to say that the world is composed of physical things such as trees, rocks, stars, wombats, and automobiles, that thought and concepts only exists in brains, on paper, and in computer data banks, and that ideas can only be transmitted through physical media such as fiber optic cables, smoke signals, oxygen-rich atmospheres, and so on.[52]

He labels things as 'machines' to underline the notion that all things consist of and combine smaller parts, and also that things are integrated in more extensive co-working wholes. The label 'machine' highlights this meshwork of integrated, co-working parts. In Bryant's words, 'a machine is a system of operations that perform transformations on inputs, thereby producing outputs'.[53]

Bryant stands on the shoulders of those who formulated 'Actor-Network Theory' and theories of 'entanglements', 'meshwork' and 'speculative realism'. But Bryant's machines are freed from any anthropocentric bias – machines may include both human and non-human parts, animate as well as inanimate. A bird in your garden is a machine – as is your bicycle. A man riding a bicycle on the road is also a machine, a machine that has abilities other than those of the naked bicycle, or, for that matter, of a human without a bicycle. An insurance company with its people and material infrastructure is yet another, but far more complex machine, as is a Bronze Age ship with its crew and cargo, or a camp of Mesolithic hunters. Even a simple lithic flake combines a multitude of parts and is a machine in itself, but it is also a part of bigger machines. Flakes take part in the shaping of an implement, in the blows inflicted by a human, and involve the skills, experience and intentions of that human being, as well as relating to the wider world, the surrounding social system and ecology. A Mesolithic machine involves a wide array of non-human actors; there is a 'gravity' between tools and equipment, garments, transport facilities and topography, animals and ambient factors, fireplaces and fuel, dwelling structures for sure, probably also dogs, perhaps boats, remedies for production and maintenance, seasonal movements, relations to neighbouring groups. Each of these are machines that have certain capabilities, and their combination in bigger integrations expand those capabilities.

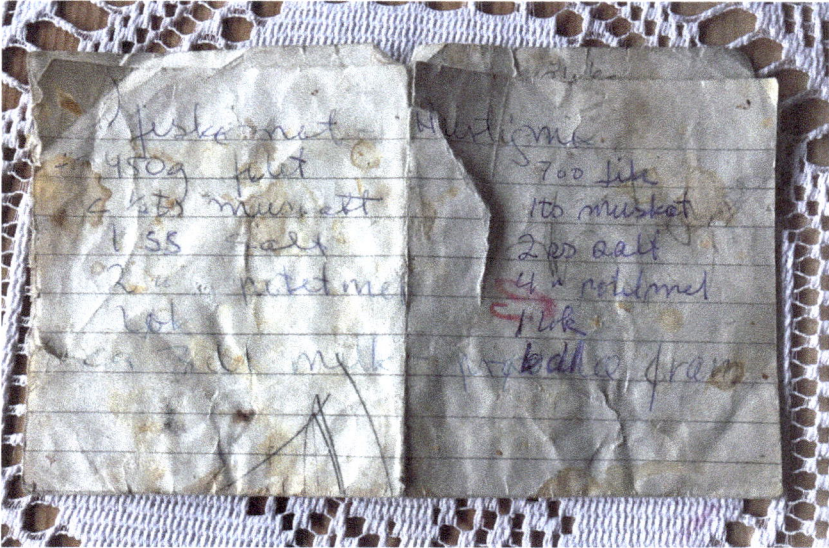

Figure 4. Solfrid's fish-pudding recipe, a 'machine part' as good as any, co-working with other parts – containers, the fish, onion, milk, knife, blender, electricity, Solfrid's skills, the table, stove, and so on. It is adjusted for a doubled output: 700 g fish fillet, 1 teaspoon nutmeg, 2 tablespoons salt, 4 tablespoons cornflour, 1 onion, 6 dl milk. Not only is the recipe regulating the ingredients involved, it has also accidentally been stained by material remains from them – thus, the recipe note is more than its textual content.

Bryant's machines are also beyond time. Mesolithic camps and the home of your father are alike, as is the kitchen of my mother-in-law Solfrid as she prepares the traditional fish pudding, involving things that are machines on their own, fish fillets and onions, cornflour, spices, the blender, the stove to bake the puddings, the supplier of electrical power, her own skills and the tattered handwritten note that is the recipe, which ensures that the ingredients (or machine parts) are combined in the right proportions. However, the output, the tasty fish pudding, is not a dead-end product, it continues to act as a part of new machines, to nourish human bodies, tighten bonds between friends and families in meals, or to be presented as a gift to lubricate social relations. Whatever more these machines may do in the world, it is difficult to foresee.

Thus, machines are a series of meaningful and definable entities that are linked and joined in more complex machines. Their outer limits are difficult to imagine, and even harder to delimit. But what lies within is a series of entangled entities that rule how the world works. As machines are always material, I believe that there is hope for archaeology – the discipline of

things.[54] As material fragments, many of the parts of past machines are recognisable to the archaeological eye. In fact, all things in the archaeological
record are remnants of delicate machineries that were once active in past
livelihoods. The machine parts are still active today, but produce something
different to what they once did.

Once a machine gets going, the integration of its many parts is a self-
stabilising factor. It is held together by its function, so to speak, and may
account for the stability of traditions that we observe in the archaeological
record. However, entropy is always near.[55] A machine may need new parts to
cope with new challenges. A vital input that the machine depends on may
no longer be available. New parts may be difficult to adapt to old parts. Small
changes may cause substantial rearrangements and allow for new things.
This could be a changed subsistence system – machinery that produces new
outputs from different inputs. However, no machine is totally new in the
world, there are always parts that relates to the old. In short, viewing subsistence systems as machines may account for repetition and stability. But
it is likewise clear that machines (like traditions) change, sometimes slowly,
other times quickly – here are the ever-going debates of stability and change
that are so well-known to archaeology.

One of the many consequences of Bryant's Machine-Oriented-Ontology
is that it highlights fragments in the archaeological record that were once
parts of well-greased machines that once co-worked. The parts that are no
longer present are brought to light. The attention may shift from sorting
artefacts in size-groups and typological listings to studying their integration in past machineries. The imperative question is not what things are
(as in most archaeological studies) – but *what things do*. Machine-Oriented-
Ontology does not discriminate between humans and non-human parts,
it brings attention to the invisible entities that are rarely considered as
archaeological facts, but at the same time were indispensable in how the
world worked for past people. It stresses 'amongstness' and blurs the
nature-culture dichotomy as well as the distinction between animate and
non-animate parts. It bridges Timothy Morton's non-observable 'hyper-
objects'[56] (e.g., the solar system, ecological biotopes, ocean currents, climate, atmospheric pressure), to reach what were tangible for past people
and called for action – like weather-worlds and animal life within the range
of their mobility.

Homes – two recent and one ancient

In this book, I will elaborate on three case studies. They are all related
to homes that have been near and dear to me, homes that at present
are disrupted and abandoned; they are silenced thing-regimes left by

their people. 'Homes' are thing-regimes that rule over and are ruled by humans, a special and very common human-thing collective – 'homes' are 'machines'.

The first case is the home of my father, where I grew up, in the small town of Florø on the outermost west coast of Norway. Then, the home next to it, my late uncle's home, that was also the former home of his mother, my grandma, Mommo. Two homes that I have been in and out of countless times, in many ways the backbone of my own being-in-the-world. They are both gone now – both examples of homes that were terminated, at the same time similar as well as opposites. My father left his things exactly how they were when he suddenly left life one spring day morning in 2009. Shortly after, his thingly regime was dismantled by his closest descendants, among them me. My father's things were suddenly 'homeless'; overnight, the home changed into a 'house with things'. The 'home-machine' had lost a vital part.

In the second home, everything was the opposite. In 2013, my uncle's home was attacked by fire. Luckily, uncle Faste survived the fire, but he lost all his material belongings – including the blackened and smelly clothes in which he had fought the flames. The fire brigade managed to put out the fire in time for many things to survive, but in a maimed state. They were melted and twisted, wet, blackened and stinking, but were stubbornly clinging to their memory value.

Things retain memories of events, are fossils from realities that time left behind. The abandoned homes of my father and uncle are thing-realms that also illustrate the ephemeral character of things in a home: the speedy turnover of valued and important things, illustrating, perhaps, that very few, surprisingly few, possess old things, things that are older than a couple of generations as part of their homes. Nevertheless, the things are not gone, they are merely pushed over the borderline to the world of 'wild' things in the ground... the archaeological record. The two derelict homes both mark the very moment when vibrant machines were changed into what are archaeological remains.

The third and final case is an encounter with a home in the Stone Age encampment of 'Åsgarden', situated on the island of Vega off the coast of Northern Norway. The settlement was abandoned some 9400 years ago. The discovery of the site, going back to my early days as an archaeologist in the mid-1980s, had a profound impact on my professional life. Now, close to 40 years later, I will return to the ancient settlement with a different gaze. The long-abandoned settlement is still there among the cliffs, but my perspectives have changed. Perhaps the ancient home in Åsgarden is not as distant as I initially thought?

Figure 5. Our home in Firdavegen, Florø – a drawing I made at school. It includes the gravel path, the sandbox with two cars and a dinosaur, the reindeer antlers between the windows upstairs, the lamps in the main window of the living room, even the little lamp on the corner of the house and the cropped trees in our garden.

Figure 6. The home of my grandmother Mommo (and eventually uncle Faste), our nearest neighbour. This drawing, from 'Summer 1952' from 'Ruth's Bok', illustrates uncle Faste's vision of their extended home, 'Bjartheim', which never materialised.

Figure 7. A slide frame containing a photo from the 1990 excavations at the new-found Åsgarden Stone Age encampment.

'The stripped chair sounded like 'Herb Albert and the Tijuana Brass' and muffled voices intermingled with waves of laughter – the calming and confident soundscape of a party downstairs when you were snug in bed upstairs, with a treat on the side.'

2 My Father's Things

In 2009, at almost 86 years old, my father died. He lived alone and was in good health. His death came suddenly – I suspect that he never knew what happened, and that he left life with less pain than when he was born. My brother found him one Sunday afternoon; he was lying in the bathroom, in his nightclothes. All lights were switched off, indicating that he had died that morning, as it would have been dark when he settled for the night the evening before. We believe that it happened immediately after his routine morning gymnastics. It was a ritual not observed by anyone, as he systematically skipped exercises when anyone visited. But he enjoyed talking about his exercise routines and other efforts to keep fit – like his equally-structured meals: 30 almonds, two teaspoons of ground cinnamon, fruits and cereals for breakfast – three kinds of vegetables included in every dinner – butter was banned, but he enjoyed some rather unhealthy biscuits as an evening snack in front of the TV.

The day after this shocking news, Elin and I drove down the 557 kilometres to my home town of Florø on the Norwegian west coast. It was a whole day's drive, with ample time to think and talk. I was surprised to find that I was able to speak of what had happened without getting all choked up; I could even make jokes about how he was, his numerous idiosyncrasies – and was starting to think that it was not as hard to cope with the loss as I had feared. However, as we approached his home, I could sense the uncanny feeling that it was there – in his house, among all the familiar things, in his silenced home – that I would be confronted by the fact that he was gone.

It was perhaps the worst moment of all – to arrive at his dark and quiet house – and to see for myself that he was no longer there.

As if this was not plenty bad enough, I was soon to realise that I had lost more than my father. Overnight, his home, the place in which I had been born and bred – and which I still recognised as pivotal in my own being-in-the-world, was no longer a home. What had happened included the fact that my father's home had changed to a constellation of things and material structures – an early phase of an archaeological site. I came to realise that a 'home' is this complex integration of human–thing-relations, and that the human component represents some kind of coherent force that keeps this material realm in place as a functional whole. Without my father, my former home was like a huge orchestra without the conductor. All of the musicians, their instruments and notes, microphones, speakers and wires, the hall with all facilities, were there. All parts worked; everything was ready at hand.

They could play many a song from their time, but no longer could they perform the songs of my father's home.

His absence accentuated the presence of his material world – and enhanced an awareness of how his being emerged as an imprint on his things. And also the other way around, how his material realm reflected the entanglement of times and changing worlds of his life. This evoked a professional interest – amid of all of this, I was also an archaeologist with a particular interest in the recent past. Thus, I photographed rooms, overviews and details, things on the walls, furniture, constellations and positions, the 'African corner' with souvenirs on display, his bookshelves. This semi-analytical component became a kind of comforting companion in the process of handling it all, perhaps a way of gaining a mental distance from the emotional hardships of the situation.

Figure 8. My ever-curious father, exploring the fjord from Brandsøyåsen near Florø in the early 1950s, looking through the 'monocular' he had recently purchased in London. As it turned out, the Ausevik rock art site is located approximately where he is, unknowingly, pointing the lens.

Over the next weeks and months, my two good brothers and I – like sons and daughters of all times and all places – had to cope with the material realm of our father and good friend. This included cleaning and tidying, the initial sorting of things and the subsequent decisions of what to do with it all, and, at the end of the line, the displacements, givings away, discardings, and the integration of selected fragments in our own homes. When the job was done, it was painfully clear to me how volatile the memories of a person are. We remember histories and events for some time, and transfer selected material fragments of what once was an integrated entity into new homes, where most of it is destined to a future out of place.

How much of this will survive the next transfer – beyond me? This last point was made painfully apparent when Elin and I were robbed in City-hotel Ansbach in Berlin the following summer – losing, among other things, the PC with most of the photos of my father's house. Elin said to me, 'You just have to see this as part of the fact that all things get lost, eventually'. However, this also illustrates the fact that lost things do not necessarily disappear; in most cases they are just out of reach of the person who suffers the loss. It is very likely that my digital photographs still exist somewhere deep in the digital darkness of my slaughtered computer, somewhere in the shady parts of Berlin.

Seven spotless bananas

I will start this journey into my father's material realm with the initial 'forensic' confrontation with his silenced home – the harsh but comforting evidence at the scene of his death, where my brother had found him, in the bathroom. In his fall, probably resulting from a deadly stroke or a heart attack, he had hit his head on the toilet-roll holder. In removing the blood-stained carpet, I could see no signs of movements or distress, no attempt to get help, meaning that he had entered the big silence without any pain or fear. In washing the stain on the floor, I felt only a calming, peaceful sadness.

To me, the confrontation with all his things was the worst. They revealed a heart-breaking normality that was miles and eons away from death. All and everything was waiting for him, ready for new action, as if they were unable to perceive that their normal world was over. In a sense, they had died too. All things were interlocked in a logical structure that related to the minutest details of my father's being, his last movements and actions. If he still was here, he could account for it all, even the strangest things and placements. Now, things had to speak for themselves. Now, on their own, they might also tell other stories, things too small, too big or too slow for him to see, or even things he would have avoided and ignored.

His chair in front of the TV – the blanket, still with strands of his thick grey hair, exactly as he had folded it to get out of the chair, like it was waiting for his return. Close by, the smallest of his set of nested tables, perfectly placed within an arm's reach of his chair. On the table, the square plastic plate with rounded corners, the unbreakable one that he had bought to be used in the boat. On the side of the plate, a ball of chewing gum, and tiny crumbs from his evening snack – a biscuit – the very reason for putting away the chewing gum for a while. The seven perfect bananas in the basket on the kitchen table, bright yellow, so normal, yet so unexpected in the house of a dead person. The frying pan still on the stove, tilted, so that the oil he had used to heat the fish burgers had gathered to one side. Plate and cutlery in the sink. On the kitchen counter, a bundle of receipts held together by a rubber band. He had been shopping the day before, for the bananas, two bags of his favourite coffee. Ordinary things, so absurd to be the last shopping of a man who had been shopping for more than 80 years.

It was a comfort to find a receipt from a somewhat later moment that same afternoon, probably after a visit to the café on the second floor of the shopping centre. Evidently, he had later returned to the store for a Saturday treat, chocolate, nuts and VG, his favourite newspaper. The chocolate bar was gone, its shiny paper in the waste bin, the newspaper on the nested table in front of the TV, already with pencil crossings in the TV section, marking things he had planned to watch during the weekend. How unthinkable in that evening that these programmes were for times past him. The nuts were still on the kitchen counter – and eventually, we ate them. How absurd, when he took them from the shelf in the store that Saturday afternoon, that his fatherless sons would eat them when he was no more among the living.

All this normality, all of the familiar things in place, present-at-hand, motionless, waiting for a mild touch from their master. But his caring hand, the hand they were ever ready to guide through daily routines, was no longer present. Now, all they did for us was make his absence even more conspicuous. It was disturbing. It went without saying that we could not stay overnight, we could no longer sleep in the beds that had kept us snug and safe all these years.

The urge to clean

In parallel with observing all this, we started to clean and wash. We did not discuss the necessity of this action (our father was a tidy man), nor did we make a plan – we just did it. In the kitchen, we washed the dishes, counter, stove, cupboards, floors, and shook the carpets outside. We threw away all opened food in the fridge, cheese, butter, jars with jam and pickles, vegetables. In the shelf of the fridge door was a note that we saved for a while, it was the list of his breakfast ingredients, the prescribed cinnamon, and the exact number of almonds. In the bathroom, soap, toothbrush and dental floss, containers of toothpaste and cream, combs, razor, scissors, mouthwash, vitamin pills and medicine, towels – along with the few unwashed clothes we could find – all thrown away.

Where did this urge to wash, clean out and tidy come from? It was as though the place that two days earlier had been completely normal had suddenly been infected – with what? Why was it imperative to remove the most intimate details, all of the things in which his bodily existence was most evident? Nobody had told us to do this. We just did it – without discussing it – and felt good about it afterwards – as if we had helped him in some way. On the surface, it was an act of removing all of the things that were not clean, that might show signs of decay or develop a ghoulish smell. What we really did was make his presence fainter, as if to make a more distinct border between our dead father and his things. Was this our unspoken intention? I still do not know. The absence of him had caused a disturbing aura to appear around these most intimate things. Even though they were perfectly situated and had not moved a millimetre, still in the exact same positions as they had been as inconspicuous members of the home 48 hours earlier – now, without him, they had turned to matter out of place, which could not be tolerated.

Perhaps our cleaning was some kind of initial phase of his funeral, which took place the week after. We had chosen one of his nice self-made suits for him for this last occasion, the coffee-brown wool suit with ivory-coloured stripes. In the left inner pocket, we put his well-used folding knife. He totally depended on this tool – 'You boys... I do not understand how you can manage without a pocketknife', he had told us in triumph so many times, on the many occasions when he had solved an acute problem with this instrument before our eyes, cutting a string, removing a sliver from a finger, opening something, tightening a loose screw, slicing a piece of dried herring during a lunch in the open, making a toothpick from a match. Of course, he also needed the knife now.

Seeing him for the last time, in his coffin the evening before we buried him, he was so still, his skin cold but smooth. A faint bloodstain from the wound still lingered, peaceful and disturbing at the same time. The moment called for soothing thoughts. I thought that the fact that he was not without his knife would be one of them. It was not. Remembering this insignificant thing – its dark brown Bakelite sides shiny from years of polish in his pocket, the smallest of the knife blades that he used most frequently turned concave by meticulous sharpening – only made it worse. The corkscrew, it could not be opened with bare fingers any longer... in memory of his modest intake of alcoholic drinks.

'Death, it seemed, gave a better overview'

In the days to come, I was startled to find that the fact that my father had left life changed how he appeared to me. It was a paradox, to find that he was closer in his very absence. Now, as his presence was formed increasingly by the memories emitted from his realm of things, the scope widened, and more and more he came to me as he had been throughout his lifetime. When he was still among us, I believe his very presence in the 'now' overshadowed how he had been through all the years we had spent together, as though his appearance as an ageing man deprived him of other parts of his lifetime, as a teenager, a father of small kids, a friend, a husband to my mother, a grand-father to my children – always ready with a witty comment, a supporting hand. The entanglement of memories evoked by the things he had left us expanded the scope of how and who he was. Each and every one of these memories brought others to life through an abundance of associations, which in turn awoke dormant sentiments, events and conversations, words of wisdom and annoyances alike. The playful father who once showed me a pointed rock protruding from the gravel road outside his workshop... per-haps, he told me, it was the very top of a huge pyramid from ancient times. It was a decisive moment for my interest in the mysteries of archaeology. 'Life seems to get in the way. Death, it seemed, gave a better overview'.[1]

He was not an authoritarian father with a capital 'F'. He was 'Dad', our 'Pappa'. Memories were mixed and marbleised: funny situations, mellow moments, disturbing bites from remembering failures to show attention and gratitude. The masses of happy times were as yet unbearable to think of. I took comfort in the fact that I had visited him several times during his last year. On every visit, he had exercised a next to unlimited hospitality. Arriving to him after a lengthy travel from wherever I was living, seeing him waiting for us in the window by the electric wall heater, we knew that the lavish evening meal had been ready for hours in advance: paprika fla-voured potato chips, chicken, cured leg of lamb, salami, 'Nøtte' (hazelnut) and 'Sjokade' (chocolate) bread spreads he knew his grandsons cherished, raspberry jam... bread.

Now, there was a sting attached to remembering the bread, a shame: I could be annoyed about the bread not being day fresh, I was ungrateful, a spoiled brat. The fact was that the care he had laid down in the meal spilled over into 'over-preparation', planning and shopping days ahead. In the kitchen, when cleaning the table afterwards:

> '...no, no, come on, Hein, sit down and relax after the long drive, you must be exhausted ... I will clear the table. I saved a bunch of Firdaposten[2] for you to read...'

Now, in his silenced kitchen, a thing came to mind. I remembered his rational assessment of what was necessary:

> 'Hein. Hein (he had the habit of saying names twice) – look here... now you just doubled the dish washing.'

I had stacked the used plates on top of each other, the clean backsides on top of the dirty faces. He recommended that I place them individually on the counter, to save us from having to wash both sides.

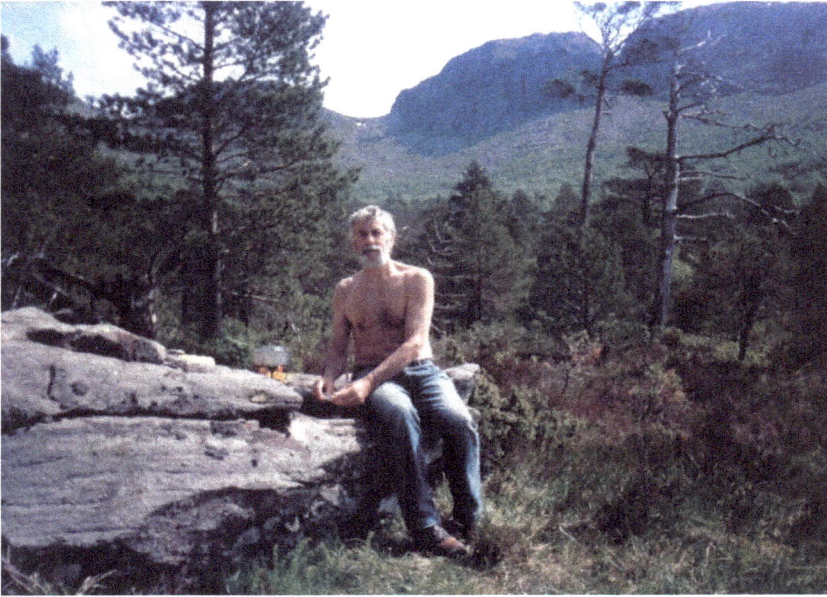

Figure 9. My father, preparing a simple lunch and fresh coffee in the open during one of his many trips to Terdalen, close to the family cabin near Florø.

On top of the fridge, I could find the paperwork from his meticulous preparations for bygone family meals, columns named for each visitor, and individual lines for what was needed for whom at the table: plates (all), coffee (grown-ups only) or a teacup (if Elin was along), glasses for juice, forks (not needed for kids) and knives, etc. At the bottom, the number of items of each kind was added up, to save him unnecessary returns to the kitchen cupboards for things forgotten. There were lists of what he needed to buy, what (and when) he needed to take out from the freezer (bread). Now, in hindsight, there was a sting in remembering that I had once commented on his irritating habit of eating and talking in parallel – keeping silent all the time he was stuffing his mouth with food, then starting to talk in a semi-understandable babble. Even in the moment it happened, as I saw him putting on a brave face to hide the humiliation from his grandsons and daughter-in-law, concentrating on mute eating... there was immediate remorse for losing my temper at this minor annoyance amid all his well-meaning efforts. Huff.

All things in the house, colour combinations and patterns, a ladle, the pancake batter bowl, the red beams above the dining table, the sound from the three bells we used to signal that we were ready to eat, the touch from the rippled surface of the grey wood stove, wallpaper designs, a knitted egg warmer, the kneeling clay figurine of Joseph on the window sill, the souvenirs from Tunis, the dishwasher brush, the Dutch salt and pepper kit, the black telephone in the hall, a sauce pan, a whiff of scent from a cupboard, the familiar faint squeak from closing the door to the toilet, the view from a window upstairs. Sensing all of this evoked recollections of things he used to say:

(When eating soup): 'They say that you are supposed to tilt the bowl *away* from you when you are eating the last part, not *towards*, as we normally do.'

(When I was doing something with a sharp or pointed instrument): 'Watch your eyes! You know, remember I told you about ... (referring to some accident in the past).'

(When sitting at the breakfast table with my kids): 'Hein... do you think they would like to eat (something)'... it annoyed me that he could not ask them directly.

(When hammering in a nail): '...don't hammer it all the way in!!! You may have to take it out.'

(When in the boat I): '...have you checked that the cooling water is running?'

(When in the boat II): '...are you sure we have enough rope?'

(When in the boat III, on a clear summer day): '...I have the fog horn right here, just to be sure.'

(Only said once, as he discovered that my brother had a girlfriend in his room, door locked): 'Are you engaged to be married, or just a complete idiot?'

(When lighting a candle): 'Have you checked that nothing can catch fire? Remember I told you about ... (some fatal fire).'

(After a couple of sunny days): '...I have to say that you have been really lucky with the weather this week'... I was irritated – after all, he had enjoyed the same good weather as me.

(When unsure of something): '...I must ask Oluf about this...'

(When dining I): '...are you sure you don't want some of the (something that was not on the table), ... I can warm it up for you. It takes only five minutes.'

(When dining II): 'What would you like to eat tomorrow?'

(Mornings after I had been to all-night parties): 'Who else was at the party yesterday?'... I was always reluctant to answer this simple and well-meaning question.

Why could I remember so many things I had been annoyed about, his over-care, all of the just-to-be-sure precautions? The price I paid was perhaps my inclination to carelessness, to sloppy preparations that were short-cuts to all-too-many failures. Where were the memories of all the kindnesses, favours, wit, funny comments, tender teasing, and the myriads of vivid images he imparted?

My parents had been to the cinema in 'Fram' – it must have been the six-thirty show, as I was still awake when they came home. Pappa came upstairs and sat down on the bed; the film must have impressed him, and he 'told it' to me. It was *Ben-Hur*, a film I was far too young to have been allowed to see at the time. The brutal Romans, gladiator fights, sea battles, galley ships with spiked battering rams in the prow, catapults slinging balls of fire. The galley slaves below, in separate floors, chained to the oars as they tried to escape the doomed ship. It was gruesome, but I am confident that Pappa withdraw violent details, and adjusted the drama to what he knew I could tolerate. *Ben-Hur*, with its highs and lows, brave rescues, duels and deeds of unseen proportions. Many years later, when I actually saw the movie, it was a bleak twin of the *Ben-Hur* my father had brought forward that night. Charlton Heston's character was simplistic and anaemic compared to the imaginary, multi-dimensional and colourful Ben-Hur in my father's version. It was not a bad movie, not at all. But my dad just knew better all that needed to be triggered in 'telling' the story.

Furniture covers

I was looking at the textile covers on the furniture of his muzzled living room. Pieces of fabric, all different in colour and pattern, as they all came from the ample supply of leftovers from the family tailoring business, 'Bjercks Konfeksjon'. Now, the covers reminded me how my father took care of things, and how things could always be used for something else when they were no longer suitable for their primary function. A length of good wool fabric too short for a woman's coat in the shop fitted perfectly as a chair cover at home. Furniture was for a lifetime; pieces of cloth were free, could be exchanged with little effort. The covers were a second chance, a freedom. They allowed kids to sit in the good chairs to enjoy an evening sandwich – sticky fingers and runny jelly – without too many worries. After a bath, or in cold mornings, still in your pyjamas, the covers might be turned into blankets, as you tucked yourself all in, curling up your legs. The cover was a part of the chair for us, we thought as little of the covers as we did of the chair's hind legs.

On occasion, if locked inside by bad weather or in the long days of fever convalescence, the covers were used to build play huts in the living room. Børge, Snorre and I were able blanket-house-constructors; the operation put an end to all kinds of quarrelling. We rearranged the furniture: the chairs made up the sturdy elements, while covers were turned into roofs and walls. The construction was kept together by an ample number of clothes pins, and furnished with pillows and blankets, and, on occasion, also a lamp, but then we had to be extremely careful. 'Remember what happened to the chair!' The alarming burn mark on the side of one of our good chairs was still visible as I studied the now silenced room. The electricity had been down, as frequently happened in stormy weather at the time. I had been playing motorcycle with the cooled electrical heater and had 'parked' it next to the chair. When electricity was restored, the plugged-in heather scorched the chair, threatening to start a fire:

> 'Luckily, thank God, I must say, I was in the kitchen making pancakes at the moment, I smelled something disturbing, and went to check. There was already smoke! What if we had been away, a visit to the store? We would have lost the whole house, ...and everything else we own', our mother frequently reminded us.

If the play hut and lamp were still there when Pappa came home from the workshop, he would repeat the unfortunate facts, double-up the warning, and probably add something even worse – possible fatalities, if the electricity had come back on *after* we were sound asleep. Anyway, in spite of the grim possibilities, to be inside the hut, snug in blankets, stacked up with pillows, reading cartoons in the intimate lamplight, and perhaps with lukewarm pancakes on a plate – it was total contentment.

Eventually, even the furniture covers wore out, but still were not disposed of; new functions were waiting: they were perfect dust covers for something in the basement, or could be ripped up to be used as rags to wipe up fish blood or spilled diesel in the boat.

Now, I lifted one of the covers and saw the naked chair. Immediately, I sensed a kind of wrongdoing in the act, as my father preferred the covers in place, 'just to be sure'. The stripped chair sounded like 'Herb Albert and the Tijuana Brass' and muffled voices intermingled with waves of laughter – the calming and confident soundscape of a party downstairs when you were snug in bed upstairs, with a treat on the side. The naked chair was a memory of the occasions when covers were removed as our parents entertained friends. The living room was totally estranged from us kids the morning after a get-together, our parents still asleep. The faint smell of cigarette smoke and drinks with Brandy, the many unfamiliar glasses that covered the counter by the sink. Naked furniture in the morning was often accompanied by an ample supply of leftover party food: crystal bowls with crumbled wrappings that in lucky cases contained an unpicked sweet, usually liquorice or coconut, the gelatine mould with cubes of ham, cauliflower bouquets, peas and champignons – in times when canned champignons were still party food. Leftovers – that meant we could pick the things we liked best and leave out the peas and tiny carrot cubes.

This was a mundane thing, the inner part of a roll of wool fabric, green with light brown stripes, of minimal value in the tailoring business. However, it could serve a new function in our home, protect Pappa's good chair, make it last longer, keep his kids relaxed and warm. Now, in this setting without him, it was strange to sense how the covers could speak to me, coax forth a wide world of memories, of him, his business, our life in this house, the things we did, what was told.

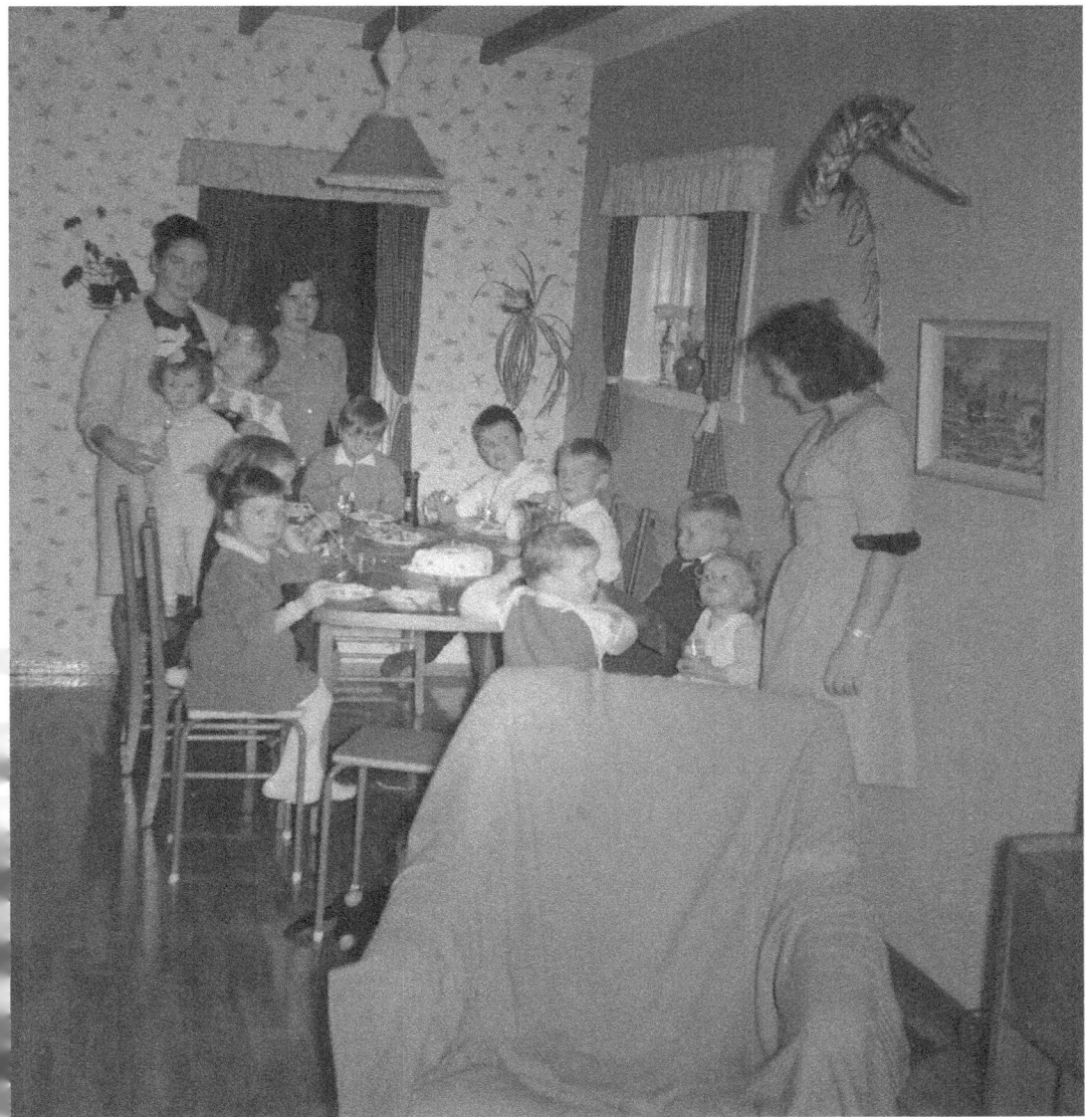

Figure 10. My brother Børge's birthday in the early 1960s. From the left: the cousins May, Marit, Kari, Stig (looking at his mother), Børge (drinking from a straw), me, Gaute and Knut (friends), Snorre, and Dag (Stig's twin brother). Aunt Elsa, Solveig and Mamma (right) are serving and supervising. Note the furniture cover on the chair in front, preserving it from little sticky fingers soon to arrive.

Some 50 years later, Gaute happened to pass on the road and discovered that uncle Faste's home next door was on fire and prevented him from re-entering the burning house to find his mobile phone.

'Bjerck's Garments Everywhere'

Bjercks Konfeksjon was our existential backbone. Not only a family busi-ness that brought food to our table, most of our clothes came from here. My father's father Oluf (snr.) and his three sons Oluf (jnr.), my father and Magne worked here, along with a varied group of seamstresses. The busi-ness defined our place in town. My grandparents Oluf and Mathilde resided in a roomy top apartment, and my mother and aunt Elsa were models in the advertising of seasonal collections in the local paper. We owned a light blue Ford Taunus station wagon with 'Bjerck's Garments Everywhere' painted on the back door. The 'B' in 'Bjerck' was designed (by uncle Faste) as a threaded needle, signifying both the tailoring business and our ever readiness to take on new orders. My mental reference for *one kilometre* is still the distance from our home to the business.

I suspect that this is merely one of many references in my life that comes from Bjercks Konfeksjon. In a tangible and direct manner, the enterprise displayed a way of living: uncle Magne took the car to the harbour to col-lect the shipment from Bergen: rolls with terylene, bright linings, striped tweed, gabardine, and imitated fur for women's overcoat collars. The fabric was unrolled on the large tables in the workshop downstairs, the templates placed to minimise waste of fabric, cut lines marked with chalk, the parts cut and sewn together in reverse. The 'birth' of garments as they were turned the right side out was like watching a perfect butterfly coming out of its cocoon. Upstairs, in the shop, organised and tidy, were orderly racks with costumes for men and women, boys and girls, ordered garments, things mended. There was the ding-dong from the electronic bell at the front door, when a new customer had arrived. The careful assessment from the custom-ers before their purchase, my father's enthusiastic advice, the subsequent hesitant presenting of worn wallets from customers' hip pockets, the metic-ulous money-counting, the immediate recounting of banknotes and coins by my dad, before handing over the box with the nicely folded, silk-paper-wrapped merchandise. The black coffer with separate compartments for banknotes in the office, the calculating of earnings for the seamstresses in transparent bags. Occasionally, I could see that my father collected bills from the coffer for his own wallet, noting the amount in a book – the money we used to pay for things we needed in our home. The chain of operations was transparent and straightforward, it demonstrated the value of joint efforts, how money was made and redistributed, fair and square.

I remember looking with suspicion at the competing Bergen-based man-ufacturing shop in town. I had overheard conversations like: '...they adver-tise far too often and with highly untimely sales campaigns', and, as they only sold ready-made garments, '...what should a costumer do if a zipper breaks – send the whole garment to Bergen?! ...could they even supply a customer with the smallest piece of identical textile if a discreet patch was needed to mend a garment after a bike accident?' To befriend the competing retailer's son was implicitly avoided, even though he was similar-aged, in the neighbourhood and probably good-humoured and likeable.

Yet, in spite of the pivotal role of the business, I cannot recall any expectation for me to grow into Bjercks Konfeksjon. Perhaps my father remembered all too well the unspoken anticipation in how his own future had been decided – far from most of his boyhood dreams, unplanned and casual. He had told me of the moment so many times. My father was fourteen and had been approved for the 'Middle School' after finishing his seven years of primary education. That decisive August morning, the family were eating breakfast – nobody brought up the fact that this was the first day of school. He finished his breakfast, put his plate and cutlery in the sink, and went with the others to do business as usual in the workshop. He never left for school – and his vague expectation of a further education evaporated in the silence of the routines that followed.

Figure 11. My grandfather Oluf, enjoying a day on the beach with his two sons Oluf (jnr.) and Rolf (my father, to the right) in the late 1920s.

In the beginning, the family had very little tailoring experience – it was an enterprise his father Oluf had anticipated could grow into a thriving business. For some years, there was a tailor from Ålesund who taught them the trade; after this it was learning by doing. Once, still in their teens, during one of their father's card-playing nights, my dad and uncle Oluf cut open the lining of an elegant overcoat of one of their father's friends. They studied how the inner pockets were made, memorised details, and stitched everything back as it was. My father eventually became responsible for the shearing and the management of the seamstresses in the workshop down-stairs. His sons were always welcome to visit, to sniff the steam that drifted from the wetted cloth that covered new garments as they were ironed, to sit under the big table enjoying the steady drizzle of leftovers in all kinds of shapes: a triangle-shaped piece of imitated fur was perfect for a troll's beard; I just needed two rubber bands to fix it to my ears.

Figure12. My grandfather Oluf (snr.), the founder of Bjercks Konfeksjon, well-dressed, with slicked-back hair and fresh newspapers rolled up in his pocket – onboard the coastal steamer, presumably to Bergen.

Figure 13. (Top) My father and uncle Magne during a brief break at the table in their parents' kitchen, in their apartment on the top floor of the business. Mathilde's table was set for breaks and occasional visits all day. My father, with the measuring tape around his neck, is busy taking notes (on something to be remembered) with one of his miniature pencils, while also eating a slice of white bread, their favourite.

(Bottom) My father in his workshop downstairs.

Modell «Alice» nr. 185

De får den i denne forretning

Figure 14. My mother giving life to 'Alice no. 185', advertising a model in the spring collection of Bjercks Konfeksjon in the late 1950s. They had even hired the local taxi, a newly washed Mercedes, for her to lean on. Other models were displayed by Aunt Elsa – the wife of Oluf (jnr.) – I guess the brothers were even prouder of their beautiful spouses than of the actual garments.

During the days, my father's workshop was immersed in the pulsing hum from the busy machines of the seamstresses. I had noticed that the sound-scape in the workshop changed each time he left the room. The machines came to a halt, and the seamstresses started talking vigorously, laughing. Once, when I was around five – I still feel ashamed to remember it – I had made myself a comfortable throne of cloth rolls on the table by the window, overlooking the workshop like its ruler. My father left the room for a minute, and the usual small-talk soundscape followed. In the instant his hasty foot-steps could be heard from the staircase, the no-talking, busy hum resumed. Loud and clear from my throne, I proclaimed: 'Now, yes now, you became quiet, as Pappa came back'. The silence in the wake of my traitorous comment said it all. My father pretended not to hear. I could sense that he was not proud of me, not at all. The shame still burns my cheeks.

The shiny red trousers

The house of my father was jam-packed with things that triggered memo-ries, unfolding in a meshwork of associations and sentiments. For every memory, there were many more nearby – the lines of connotations spilled out of the house, to the garden, to neighbours and family, to Firdavegen and other streets in Florø, to friends and foes, to events – the memories seemed inexhaustible. Some memories were loud and happy, even more were mellow and muffled – each of them seemed to evoke five more.

His wardrobe, the windowless closet attached to his bedroom, included his better shoes, suits, shirts, ties, the movie projector and the foldable screen, Norwegian flags for May 17, masks for New Year costumes – it was mainly for the storage of things outside everyday use. Perhaps the intervals between the extraordinary days had increased in later years – the closet smelled stuffy from stored garments. Among them were the outfits he had created for vacations abroad – the salmon-red shirt, the white armless jacket with ample pockets, the safari-like, belted and leather-buttoned jacket in beige gabardine with matching khakis – the outfit he had made for the Europe expedition with Oluf and our mother in 1952. His profession meant that he supplied the family with tailored garments: trousers, overcoats, suits for his boys. Yet his ungrateful sons complained that we never got the factory-made blue jeans like most of our friends. There was a faint sting in remembering this lack of gratitude.

Once – this is a more cheerful memory – I was a teenager, and had asked him to make me a pair of trousers with huge flares made out of a silky shiny red fabric that I had seen in his workshop.

> '...but, this fabric is not for trousers', he told me, 'it is for lining in garments for women, and far too fragile for trousers.'

I did not care too much for his professional advice; all I could think was that these trousers would look like a garment Jimmy Hendrix would ask for, that it would be an eye-catcher at the upcoming Saturday dance in the town's communal hall. He made me the pants, in spite of knowing for a fact that they would be useless. Nevertheless, after my first (successful) appearance in the shiny pants, I accompanied a friend to his shop to ask for a similar pair. However, this time they were made out of pink lining with even bigger flares, and flares lined with orange imitation fur. I still do not know what father thought of the order; he already knew that his professional advice would be in vain. Partly, I came along to watch my friend's disturbed looks as my father made the measurements. I knew what was coming. The length of the inside of his legs, all the way up. If he had known about this humiliation, my friend's daydream of Hendrix-style slacks would perhaps never have been acted upon. To top it off, when my father pulled up my friend's sweater to measure his waist, his oversized white underwear was pulled up above his belt – another comical embarrassment, and to me, a pure bonus. It was one of the perks of my many visits to the workshop, to see customers – especially sincere elderly men – pretending to be cool, but always this awkward, indifferent gaze, staring intensely at the void straight ahead as the imperative distance from the crotch to the ankle bone was measured. It was done swiftly, to diminish the inconvenience, with a doctor's swift precision, carefully mingled in the series of other, less embarrassing measurements. The fact that I was observing with a Mona Lisa smirk on my face probably made it worse.

Anyway, my friend and I both enjoyed a few happy nights in our shiny pants before the seams started to stretch, then fall apart, proving that my father had been right. He was always proved to be right, an annoying fact pertaining to most parents. But that he made me these slacks – I take it as a token of true love. What is the unconditional love of a father if not this?

Now, I could not see any of this ground-breaking garment anywhere in the house. I guess the maimed garment was beyond further use (even for him), and discarded. Nevertheless, it was one of all too many memories of things I could have tackled better.

A conversation by the wall heater

Beneath the big window to the garden, from where we could see and comment on people passing on the road, was 'panelovnen' – the electrical wall heater. The narrow top side was all worn from the thousands of coffee cups we used to place there, keeping them warm as we talked, in the mornings, evenings, or when waiting for the potatoes to be ready. Uncle Faste could come by, or Jostein, his life-long friend, or perhaps Børge who lived nearby. If you added all laughter to the lines of words that were uttered here, you would reach more than half-way to the moon. Usually, I was still in bed when my father would call me from the hall – the coffee was served by the heater. Very often, he was eager to get prepared for the day, to ask his son about his plans, for suggestions to complete the grocery list, what we should have for dinner – he needed time to thaw things from the freezer. Now, the cold, turned-off wall heater made me recall my grumpy responses to his care. Our conversation could be like this:

> 'What shall we have for the dinner today? I have a bag of those tasty fish burgers in the freezer – the healthy heart-shaped ones, you know – how about them? ...and perhaps butter-steamed summer cabbage?', Pappa would ask.
> 'Sounds fine', I would say.
> (Brief pause)
> '...or perhaps, I come to think... I also have those smoked sausages that you like, and mashed potatoes, perhaps would you rather have that?'
> 'Yes, that sounds good, too.'
> 'Helsike (mild swearing), I forgot the single-frozen fillets that I prepared from that fishing trip I told you about, you know... no skin or bone, flat frozen on a tray... all ready for the frying pan. Perhaps you will prefer this instead?'
> 'Okay, let's have that.'
> (Pause)
> '...there is also the possibility of pork chops and sauerkraut, I have both... you can choose.'
> 'My God, Pappa, you are drowning me in all these options, come on, give me a break!!'
> 'Okay – we will have the fish burgers. How many will you eat?'
> '......'

The worn wall heater also reminded me of his reluctance to discuss problematic themes, conflicts and struggles. He would hear me out, even if my annoyance was some new administrative routine at the University. His gaze would wander around the room as he wriggled to find something mitigating, comforting, to lessen the problem:

> 'Well, perhaps they did not mean it in that way... maybe they just thought that... (something less insulting or problematic). I think perhaps you should try to... (do or say something I was frequently too proud or stubborn to undertake).'

Dismantling a home, revealing a lifetime

Some months after my father had passed, it was the big operation of cleaning out the house. A large, gaping waste container was placed in the driveway. The task was a practical one, we thought: deciding what to keep, how to share it, what to give away, and ultimately emptying out the house, everything.

There were the 49 rolls of 8 mm movies that reached from our parent's wedding in 1953 to the summer of 1985, his handwritten index in two miniature ring binders, a blue one for the silent movies, a one brown for the soundtrack movies after he got his new camera in 1976, the German Eumig projector and the foldable screen – all self-evidently in the 'to-keep' division. One evening, we had wanted to see some of the family movies, of vacations, first schooldays, first steps, skating, skiing, fishing, wading in shallow beaches, campfires and blue mussels. Without saying anything, we all knew that troublesome and sad moments were omitted from this patchwork of cherished moments of our time together – as we sat in front of the foldable screen and looked forward to seeing ourselves as our passed father had once seen us. We already looked forward to watching the scene of uncle Faste returning to his red Ford Cortina after bringing us to the coastal steamer in Bergen. There was nothing peculiar about the actual scene. Yet, it had been among our favourite scenes to display in reverse. Perhaps it was exactly this – the total normality of the act, in contrast to the absurdity of the same scene played backwards: uncle Faste in his formal blazer, his slightly stiff and dedicated walking (almost marching) towards the Cortina – then, as he tried to open the car door, dad had switched the rewind button and made him walk backwards across the quay. The same firm dedication, but now with awkward, unaccustomed movements, although his face remained unchanged, just as committed as before. We switched him back to 'forward', this time our dad allowed him to get into the car, which he hastily left for another reverse march, then back again. It was hilarious, we could not stop laughing, least of all our dad, thrilled to be able to control Faste's movements down to the most minute details. If a military tattoo could he performed by a single person, it would look like this. Unfortunately, we could not get the Eumig projector to work. The machine sounded as before, but we could not move the spools; some minute transmission belt had broken or loosened, failed by its own intricate mechanics.

We saved both the miniscule ring-bound indexes, the projector and the rolls of film – they could perhaps be digitised to an adequate format later. For now, the heavy cardboard container of movies was a black box of memories, a thing that withheld its powers. I could not help noticing that the last movie more or less coincided with my parents' divorce. It saddened me to think that the lack of recent movies was perhaps a material reminder of a fading eagerness to collect happy moments. Obviously, this remembering-machine had not been activated much lately. Perhaps my father considered his past more valuable than his future, a past that brought along an uneasy remembrance of happier times. I think this was also around the time that the dishwasher broke – a thing he never took the trouble to get repaired.

Figure 15. Stills from my father's 8 mm movies, recording a trip to Jølster in 1966, where he admired and filmed a field with summer flowers. Later, in the outfit he liked to wear in the outdoors – the beret and the brown suede jacket – he made a fire to prepare coffee.

Figure 16. (Top) My mother Siv and uncle Oluf in the side-car motorbike, on their way to Oslo during their grand European tour in 1952. My father wrote a day-to-day account in a 112-page diary, which most days starts with a note that he had a close shave.

(Bottom) My parents (in the centre) on their return from Europe – their first trip by air-plane – safe on firm Norwegian ground. In his diary, my father mentions a rumour among the party that the tail-end of the plane was the safest. As he also wanted to take a photo of the plane, he asked my mother to secure the seats. Unfortunately, she was unable to keep her place in the chaotic line that occurred, and they ended up in the riskier seats by the wings.

In the photo album, they saved both their tickets, the 'Conditions of Carriage', and a cardboard platter with a handwritten text: 'On this plate we had lunch on-board the plane to Norway. It consisted of tomatoes, salad, ham, French potatoes + a small bag with salt, 2 slices of bread w butter, 2 biscuits, 2 apples, eggs. Later we were served coffee avec.'

Along with the mellow-moments-machine, we saved photo albums, framed photos, a great many books, silverware, paintings, all self-evidently in the 'to-keep' end of the scale – boxes with old newspapers, magazines, instructions for things already not there, worn-out furniture, the broken dishwasher, clothes and shoes, carpets and curtains were likewise easy to place in the container. Even the furniture covers. However, a surprisingly large number of things were in the intermediate part of the keep-discard scale, and involved much debate. Evidently, there were distinct differences among the three of us as to what to keep – as demonstrated by the fact that I ended up with my brother's old wallet containing photos of his many teen-age girlfriends. And what to do with the big sewing machines from Bjercks Konfeksjon, machines that had worked for our family business all those years? As most things, they had outlived their human co-players, the business, but were still able and willing – they were like ship-shape vessels without their captain.

The operation was hampered by our discovery of things we recognised and remembered, things we had forgotten, things that were new to us. All through this we were confronted by the imprints of our dad – his nature, interests and peculiarities, his biography, reflecting the times and places he had been in, the persons that were close to him, including ourselves. Tablecloths with yellow chickens that once had hosted our Easter breakfasts. Christmas decorations (including things from his own childhood), postcards, serving plates, wool jackets, suits and shoes not seen for many years, but all remembered. They all triggered memories that had been laying dormant for years.

Our coffee breaks turned into seminars. My brother was reading aloud from our father's diary, from the legendary 1952 vacation with our mother-to-be and his brother Oluf. Hamburg, Bremen, Amsterdam, Haag, Brussels, Paris and London. Crossing the mountains in Oluf's sidecar motorbike to Oslo where they would join Eva, the girl that Oluf would two weeks later, at the top of the Eiffel Tower, proclaim as his fiancée. Eva – where was our auntie Elsa? The diary's frequent references to the abundance of fruits, fresh or dried, reflected the shortcomings of early post-war times. They were able to buy as many oranges, bananas, figs, dates – even grapes and peaches – as they wanted. We could see signs of complete happiness in our father's notes from 'Peter Vessel', the ferry that would take them to Europe, to the world and to their future:

> 'Now Siv is sleeping with her head in my lap, here on the front deck. On my right side I have dates and figs.'

Figure 17. My father, during one of his journeys in the late 1940s – probably seeing the impressive tail of a peacock for the first time. The scene touches me – his well-dressed appearance (as most travellers were at the time), the concentrated, but relaxed pose – obviously he had studied the remarkable bird for a while. On his return to Florø, he would point to a photo in a book – 'Yes, I saw a peacock myself in Denmark, it was incredible' – as if he had brought a sliver of it home.

Among the many attractions across Europe, they visited the Peace Palace in Haag, where 'the oil dispute between England and Persia was recently heard'. Here, in the very courtroom of the Peace Palace, our father 'nicked a paper clip that was lying on the table, as a souvenir'. This insignificant thing, an object that had presumably once helped to organise pivotal documents in international disputes, was probably still here, somewhere. Without my father, the paper clip's chances of being identified were meagre, and it is now forever parted from its significant history. (Or so I thought. Some years after reading this in the diary, I discovered a paper clip glued in an album with black and white photos from the trip, in my mother's home.)

In the deep part of a closet upstairs we found our mother's heavy-duty three-part hairdryer, a flexible air hose connecting the fan (with shoulder strap) to the perforated hood, an apparatus that our increasingly elaborate teenage hairstyles had also depended on. We joked about the shoulder strap on the fan, as the portable range was restricted by an electrical cord about one metre in length. We plugged it in, and it still worked. I put the plastic hood on my head, and we laughed; I looked like I was being attacked by a creature from the *Alien* movies. Moments later, I was attacked by my own past: the hot air on my head, the humming fan and the sweet chemical smell of the hot plastic evoked a sudden echo of the trembling pre-Saturday-night anticipation of parties long past.

The work came to a halt as we explored boxes containing our own schoolbooks, drawings of dinosaurs and space crafts, wallets with no money but interesting receipts for things we had bought (and since lost) from our hard-earned savings and summer jobs, black and white photo booth portraits of old friends. Stamp collections and herbariums, diplomas. And the now not so shiny silver medallion once given to me on a day of victory: I had proved that I could swim 25 metres, two whole lengths of the minute swimming pool at school, from the easy shallow end to the dangerous deep, and back. I could sense the thrill of the chlorine smell in the stairway down to the pool in the basement of our school. Just being down here meant that I had passed the small-kid stage. It also meant showering without the blue trunks, and the harsh comparing of the diachronic development of our normally hidden parts after summer vacations. Chlorine was also the smell of embarrassment.

All of these things constantly deflected my attention into the never-ending trajectories of my memories. It was like a walk-in-closet of thing-theory, the entanglement of times, things as memory, and how things reveal not only themselves but also their time, the world where they had been active parts; all of the changes that are too slow for the naked eye were captured in Pappa's kingdom of things.

Figure 18. Stills from my father's 'Tunis movie', filmed out the windows of the bus that took us to the outskirts of the Sahara – hasty fragments of sandstorms, Bedouins, camels, Roman ruins, river crossings without bridges – things he had learned plenty about, but had never seen. The film was a method of owning a slice of the strange and unfamiliar. Now, he owned the proofs that he actually had seen these things.

His workshop in the basement of his house – the remains of the closed down tailoring business. If there was such thing as a Black Belt in bricolage, my father would have had one. A small example was the arrangement to suspend the originally-adjustable work-lamp after the table stand was broken. What looked like ropes were superfluous textile bands designed to hold the small plastic suspender hooks for curtains. Below the lamp, his workplace: a desk strewn with countless numbers of products and related materials, fabric, buttons, zippers, thread, machines, the gigantic scissors, templates and crayons to mark the cuts, needles, a horseshoe magnet that would pick up pins that were lost to the floor. After his retirement, he had prolonged the life of many a dear piece of clothing from the town by exchanging broken zippers, making adjustments for a bigger body, and mending ripped pockets.

The contents of his many bookshelves, in the living room or by his bed – a large part of his books centred around facts, an entanglement of entertainment and education: Harry Lorayne's *The Power of the Mind and its Secrets*, books on explorers and inventors, places around the world with all their peoples, animals and landscapes, journeys and expeditions, death and survival. *Among Wizards and Cannibals* – about a Swedish explorer's journey to Indonesia – was the 1952 Christmas gift from his girlfriend, my mother-to-be. Was this related to the choice of deep green rainforest wallpaper for the living room in the house they built in 1957? As we recalled, he had followed this profound interest in entertaining facts into the jungle of TV channels, where Animal Planet, the Travel Channel and National Geographic were his favourites. There was a book in English that I had given him after his vacation in Egypt, *The Rape of the Nile*, on every page were handwritten translations of words he did not know, all the way through, he had read it all. He needed to understand it all, interested or not. In a way I was envious, remembering my own hasty manner of reading, hoping that things I did not understand would come to me effortlessly, eventually. He was the kind who read the complete instruction booklet before turning on his newly-acquired PC – I suddenly recalled him once asking me, halfway in reading the instructions: 'The mouse, you know, do you have to double-click it?'

Another recurring theme among the books was the learning of skills – like handbooks of Jiu-Jitsu self-defence[3] and amateur movie making, *Kinoamatøren*. He had been a self-taught expert in both. However, these things also demonstrated how times change. Take, for instance, the valour of 'amateur', a word that once expressed the self-esteem of learning things on your own, the pride of a creative self-made man. Today, this expression has rather negative connotations, referring to the unprofessional and perhaps incompetent – and certainly no longer a wise choice for a book title.

The illustrated steps in the different self-defence techniques from the Jiu-Jitsu handbook are likewise telling for changing times. Bad guys and ugly situations prevail – but, obviously, the norms of how to meet these kinds of challenges have changed. At present, when at gunpoint, I do not think that this three-step tackle is considered healthy advice:

1) Person A points at B with a gun, and forces B to raise his hands.
2) B strikes fast with left hand at A's wrist from the inside, to divert aiming direction.
3) B grabs A's wrist forcefully, and swings right leg forward and behind A's knee, that is kicked forward at the same time as B hits A's larynx with a hard hand blow.

Similar action is also suggested when a gun is pointed at someone else. Uncle Oluf and my father rehearsed most of these tricks in friendly contests, and were happy to learn that the rumour of their exercises flourished. On the other hand, to remain calm and speak in a contained voice for hours to get out of such a situation would hardly have impressed my young father and his comrades during times of war. The continuous displacement of norms and ideals and their subsequent solutions and actions – too slow to be experienced in real time – came forward as fossils in my father's things.

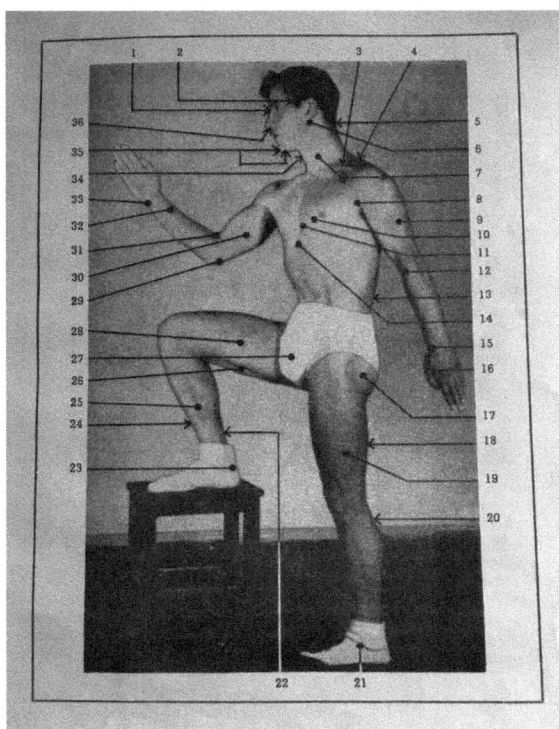

Figure 19. 'The weak points of the body', from the book on Jiu-Jitsu, a self-defence sport practised by my father and uncle Oluf in their teens. I can still remember the unexpected sting from point no. 6, as my father frequently demonstrated. He hissed at his boys to attack him with a folded-up newspaper: 'Come on boy, try to take me, anyway you want.' We knew we were soon about to lose.

Of course, the house-clearing operation involved more than the happy moments revived. Among the things was my father's gift to his older brother Oluf that was never delivered the Christmas before. I recall that we gave the delayed gift to uncle Oluf during the gathering after the funeral, still in its wrapping. I remember Oluf leaving, walking down the driveway in his good suit, still with the unopened gift from his dead brother in his hand. There was nobody to thank for it; it could only add to his sorrow. Our well-intended act was inconsiderate. There was also the still plastic-wrapped shirt Elin and I had once given my father (saved for a better day), the home-made calendar with his photos of his grandchildren among the stacked away magazines.

Now that he was no longer among us, it was easier to see the charming sides of all the things that had been put aside, things that were functional, but out of function, in waiting for some undefined future use: remnants of wallpaper, linoleum tiles and left-over pieces of wall-to-wall carpet, the original packaging for things that may have had to be sent back for repair, plastic bags, pipes, faucets, metal parts of all shapes, wire, ropes of all sorts, exchanged wooden boards, keys for locks that had disappeared, parts from boats that were long gone.

This vast base of 'thing-savings' was accompanied by a substantial collection of old clothes and shoes that were saved for future dirty jobs – there were simply not enough dirty jobs to finish off this increasing number of half-worn garments. I suddenly remembered (and regretted) my irritation at his awkward style of walking the last time we prepared the boat for the winter storage in his garden; he had struggled to curl up his toes to keep the cracked-up shoes on his feet, taking care not to lift the crumbling soles from the ground.

A pencil I found in one of his pockets, a tiny remnant of a pencil, was so small that it could barely be held between the tips of my fingers. Still, it so was meticulously knife-sharpened, we had to sit down in awe after passing it among ourselves. It was yet another telling demonstration of how my father's definition of 'usefulness' entailed that little was wasted. However, the pencil also reminded me of my recurrent irritation over his denial of new (unnecessary) things, his saving of things for others, or for a better time.

This surplus of things reflected his rather annoying reluctance to spend things on himself, like the firewood in the basement that had been there for years, in waiting for an even colder morning. Other things evoked sorer moments – the wedding pictures stacked away in the attic, in a plastic bag from 'Combi', a local store that had vanished by the time of my parents' divorce. However, in the mounting ring of one of the wedding photos there was a length of fishing line, a remnant from a happier moment in my young years, the day I was at home 'sick' and bored, my parents away at work (but still married). I had arranged this invisible line from my room, up through the air valve to the attic, down again through the valve to my parent's room, around a minute eyehook in the corner, all the way up to their wedding photo on the wall. I had worked for hours to set it up. In the end, I unhooked the picture from the nail, and it was free-hanging. I could remote-control its position up and down on the wall from my room across the hall. It was hilarious. I could hardly wait for my parents to go to bed, I think I even went to my room early (but not to sleep) just to speed up the bedtime routines. I waited until the light went out, and hastily lowered the photo frame to the floor – the light instantly came back on, briefly – 'We thought the photo had fallen from the nail, that it could be dealt with tomorrow'. Then, in the second darkness, slowly, along with a faint sound of scraping, I hauled the picture up the wall. The light returned. A moment of total silence followed – a brief, but existential moment beyond the world as my parents had hitherto known it.

Figure 20. One of my father's miniature knife-sharpened pencils, found in a pocket of one of his jackets – a thing I saved as a memory of him, and his notion of what was 'useable'. It now rests in a small box Elin made, on top of my office desk. It is no longer a tool for hasty notes, but still in use as a memory.

The prank was repaid some weeks later, when a sheet of paper that had (naturally) fallen off my desk proceeded (paranormally) to climb up the inside of the closed door. Dad could not keep himself from laughing in the hall outside.

My parents both liked pranks like this; they enjoyed sharing the most minute details of their startled reactions, what was said in the decisive moments – what they had thought when the picture first slid down the wall, and then tried to climb back onto its nail. Family dinners were accompanied by increasingly elaborate repetitions of this and other successful (or particular unsuccessful) practical jokes. The important part was how the stories were told, the expanding and exaggerating of reactions and details; eventually, what had actually happened was of minor importance.

This negligible piece of fishing line proved that at least parts of the family myths were real. I had to check in the attic, and yes, the track of mounting hooks was still in place.

All of the findings and discoveries in the house could only complicate our decisions of what to keep and what to throw away. Why are things made of silver so universally and self-evidently important – and clothes so problematic? The final phase of the process was like finding new homes for homeless pets – all suggestions that could save a thing from the abyss of the big green container were welcomed. The local second-hand store seemed to be mostly interested in first-hand things, and was of little help. A friend of my brother was collecting things from workshops – he already owned the vestiges of a shoemaker's shop and was ready to take on the big machines from Bjercks Konfeksjon. And then there were grandchildren and friends, and also the bright idea to move plates, cutlery, kitchen utensils, paintings and pictures to the family cabin across the fjord.

But still, far too many things were brought to the container. As I threw away an increasingly large portion of his storage of 'may-be-useful-things', I could hear his fatherly advice about things that it was smart to save, and several stories about situations where the strangest of pieces had proved to be decisive. I knew he was right. 'Do you remember that time, when that part of the rudder broke off as we were about to launch the boat?' I did, but he always insisted on telling the full story anyway – it was a privilege in the wake of this success. The part broke off as the boat was lifted to the truck that would put it to the sea. We needed to have this fixed before it was in the water; the man with the car could not wait, nor could he come back for many days, as his schedule was tight. The solution was sleeping in his cellar: 'Right away, I found this metal thing that could be used; it fit perfectly, took me less than five minutes'. The truck man could not believe how my father had managed to find the means to repair the boat in such a short time. 'You even had the right kinds of bolts and nuts', the truck man had exclaimed, impressed – to my father's poorly hidden delight.

Integration into new homes

At the end of the day, two carloads of my father's things arrived at our home in Trondheim. They were mostly things to remember: letters, documents, photos and films, books, the big scissors, souvenirs, vases, some tools and things for the house, suits and jackets he had made, some unsold garments from the store, and for sentimental reasons his First-Aid kit, and (I do not know exactly why) the 'portable' hairdryer. Too little, it seemed, when I was loading the car in Florø. Too much, it seemed, when I was unloading the car at my home in Trondheim.

Serving plates, vases and tablecloths were easily assimilated into their new home. From the last rolls of woollen fabric from Bjercks Konfeksjon, Elin made pillow and daybed covers for the mountain cabin that we later built with the aid of the money I inherited.

I had saved a pair of his jeans. I brought them to Tierra del Fuego, and wore them as field clothes during the archaeological campaign in Cambaceres – I realize now that I wear these pants in the front cover photo of our report from the field study down south. I kept them there, as part of my equipment, in the attic of Ernesto, my Argentinean compañero in Ushuaia. As we ended the project, I wanted to dispose of my field clothes, and asked Ernesto where to put them. 'No, do not throw them away', he responded, 'it is better to give them to the 'bomberos'. The fire brigade usually keeps used clothes in reserve, for people who lose everything in fires, and perhaps do not have any insurance'. So I did, and I am sure that my father would have approved of my decision. Perhaps it was a helping hand to someone in need, a contribution that did not involve any money. I hope his pants are still there, with the 'bomberos', and have not yet found a man in despair.

But most things *have* been difficult to integrate, and seem destined to a future out of place, in the periphery of my material belongings. Their most important quality is that they 'belonged to my father', along with other objects in the museum of myself. They made me realise that my own world of things will end up equally homeless after me, and among them, the remains of my father's things. Where will these things be after my own material world has been rearranged and shuffled in times past me? It suddenly occurred to me – underlining just this point – that the things I had chosen to keep also included all of the things my father had saved from *his* parents. What were the things my father had kept from his parents, and beyond?

In my part of the silverware there is a spoon, still in its cotton bed in a small box, and a card saying that it was for my grandfather Oluf's sixtieth birthday. A silver spoon that my grandfather evidently never used, and probably did not even remember he possessed beyond his next birthday – totally irrelevant in light of all of the victories and losses in his life, meaningless for all he meant to the people around him. What a stupid thing to represent him for future generations. And what about my grandfather's parents, Salomon and Lovise? The enigmatic wooden man? What happened to the belongings of the Iron Age generations of my family?

Figure 21. (Top) My father's rubber boots in my home in Trondheim. I believed they were slightly less intimate than his garments, and thought I could use them around the house, although they leaked a little. Nevertheless, they did not feel all-right, as they had when I had borrowed them before, when he was alive. Besides, I sensed that Elin did not like me wearing them, and was happy to blame the leak in discarding them.

(Bottom) The enigmatic wooden man from my father's things, now in a mixed display in my home – along with a bullet shaped 'belemnite' (a fossil from Svalbard) and artwork from John Roger Holte, on a shelf Elin made out of a teak plant we found in the attic of our home in Trondheim. I believe that the wooden man is a groom that eventually lost his bride, a thing my father probably kept from his parents, perhaps his grandparents. Now, in my home, the figure is deprived of any personal memories beyond my father. As its memory value evaporates, how far in time will the anonymous, divorced groom be able to travel, beyond me?

One of the things I had saved from the green container was a battered and heavily corroded copper vase. Obviously, it had seen better days; its carefully hammered shape and decoration seemed like high quality handwork. I took it, and later coated it with ketchup (like we used to do with copper coins to make them look like silver coins), in the hope that I could clean it. The result was not too good, but I still wondered about its context. I called my mother, and she knew straight away what I was asking after: 'Yes, it is part of a set of three, a bowl and a kettle (my brothers have these), and the vase, which was given to your grandparents for their wedding in 1923'. I had to ask about the reasons for its miserable state, why the heirloom was not kept with more care. 'The reason', she said in a darker voice, 'is that you threw it in the wood stove when you were three years old'.

Down the corridor to the Archaeology Department?

For a while, the copper vase was in the garage, a reminder of the fact that things prevail. Things tend to outlive their human companions, and are always ready to engage in new partnerships, to enter new regimes. But their futures may take many directions. New regimes may include a redefining of their status, different placements, and other standards of esteem, care and up-keep. In some cases, mundane and even ruined objects may be upgraded, as they become parts of prized memories. Or, to the contrary, bright, and shiny things may be put away because they bring unwanted memories. Some are out of sight in safe seclusion long enough to become 'rare', and may enter the regime of antiquities. Others are gradually outdated, falling out of function and style, ruined by the teeth of time, not kept high and dry, discarded, covered, out of sight, forgotten, moving down along the corridor to the Department of Archaeology. Like the copper vase in my garage. When it first entered the series of homes in my family in 1923, it was part of a troika of highly prized gifts. Its value was enhanced by the fact that it was a memory of a watershed moment in my grandparents' lives; it was a child of their new-born home. After their sad and traumatic divorce during WW2 (cf. Ch. 3), the connotations and memories changed – probably a reason why it was handed over to my mother. She loved both her parents and cherished the memory of their wedding unconditionally.

I do not recall any plan or reason for the burning of the vase back in 1957, but the result was that it was no longer displayed alongside its shiny siblings. Still, its history saved it from being discarded, and it ended up in the attic, in the very periphery of my father's realm of things. This is where I found it, after he left us in 2009.

Figure 22. The ill-treated copper vase, now in my garage, formerly a treasured heirloom. Even cherished things may be downgraded as they surpass the horizon of oblivion and lose their grip on personal memories. This is perhaps an important reason why very few objects survive as private possessions through time.

I will do my best, but cannot guarantee that the copper vase will still be within the family after the rearrangement of all things that will outlive me, when I am no longer here to rule my world of things. At the moment, the copper vase resides in my office at the University, a specimen to illustrate thing-biography in my teaching. It plays a different role than was intended when it was once made, and later, when it was picked from the store as a proper wedding gift, when it was left in their daughter's home after my grandparents troubled divorce, during all the times it contained the seasonal flowers in our home, when I burned it, and when the sad thing was saved to the attic. Without question, it has proven its ability to come back, always to different contexts, each time handled in a different way – doing other things – proving that its functions are hard to deplete.

'The charred flamenco dancer was still in his elegant pose, his white shirt turned black, his face disfigured, the shock of the fire imprinted.'

3 Scorched Memories from my Uncle's Burnt Home

February 26, 2013. Why my uncle Faste chose this day for a nice dinner I do not know. There was absolutely nothing to celebrate; it was just a normal grey morning in early spring. The birds were tweeting the season, the buds on the trees and patches of snowdrops yearning for a sunny afternoon to burst open.

My uncle, 85 years old at the time, was in his house amid all his things and belongings, his home. The smell of fresh coffee. The usual programmes and familiar melodies from his radio, a faint rattling from the newspaper, as he read about yesterday's events in town. Just as much as the news, he was looking for imprudent grammatical flaws or funny misspellings. He enjoyed hunting them down, and the rush of the annoyance as he found them. The 'best' mistakes could be conversation pieces when there was a visitor. Little did he know that he himself would be on the front page in the next edition, and orthographical errors would be the least of his worries. But in this moment, it was just another day, a Tuesday, the dullest of all weekdays, neither sun nor rain, winter or spring, a day that would soon sink into oblivion among the thousands of others in my hometown of Florø on the Norwegian west coast.

He was checking out the TV schedule for the evening, marking off the programmes that looked interesting. As he saw something he looked forward to seeing, he perhaps also remembered the nice dinner he had planned, a real treat, Entrecote with Béarnaise and French-fries. He liked the foreign names of what he was planning to consume – they added a certain exotic ring, almost heightening the flavours. Ingredients were lined up in the kitchen, the nice piece of meat already on the counter to adjust to room-temperature.

It was already past noon, and time to get to work in the kitchen. He liked the act of preparing his meals and was quite good at it. The mixture of tempting odours, the tickling anticipation of building up an appetite. He peeled the potatoes and cut them into long sticks, taking care to make them into similar sizes for perfect frying. He fetched the thick-bottomed pan, added the oil and turned on the stove, unaware that the same switch was also the switch for disaster. His mind was on finding the salt and pepper, the skimmer and paper towels to drain off the fries. As he was waiting for the temperature to rise, the doorbell rang. It was the 'Romanian', his new friend in the neighbourhood; an interesting man to talk with, a man who also helped him with this and that. Now, he was heading to the store, and asked if my uncle needed anything. Great, it was perfect timing – he needed some small items and was happy to save himself the walk to the store.

As he closed the door, it was still possible that the day might have ended as normal, a day without any marks in the calendar. However, this was the turning point where fate headed towards catastrophe. Instead of returning to the kitchen, he sat down in his good chair to wait for his friend to return, forgetting his ongoing operation in the kitchen. I regret to say that he waited in vain – he would never receive any of what he had asked his Romanian friend for.

Uncle Faste

He was resting in his safe world of things, the family home since 1936, where he had lived as a young boy and teenager with his parents, his older brother Sølve and little sister Siv (eventually my mother). The all-encompassing turmoil of WW2 had also touched the family. His parents were both teachers, and after the Nazi regime took over, they ended up on different sides and eventually divorced. His mother (my Mommo) stayed in the house while her sons moved out – my own parents were given a lot in her sizeable garden, where they built their new home in 1957.

My uncle took over his mother's home when she passed away in 1991. The house was more or less as his mother had left it. He found his own paths, corners and free spaces on the walls, inserting his thingly regime among the belongings of his mother, carefully adding his home to what had been hers. Her nice coats were dormant on the hangers in the wardrobe, alongside his wind breaker. Her hats were still arranged around the oval mirror in the hall, where he checked his own appearances before his regular trips to town. A mix of his and his mother's paintings and photos were on the walls, their joint books on the shelves, their individual souvenirs jointly on display. His video cassettes with recordings of *A Touch of Frost* with the charismatic Detective Inspector Jack Frost sat alongside her mono radio recordings of Tchaikovsky and Rimsky-Korsakov, tapes with poems read theatrically by deep-voiced actors and classic Ibsen plays performed by the NRK Radio Theatre. His mother's colourful scarfs were still hanging on the inside of the door in the living room. If you brought them to your face, there was still the faint fragrance of her perfume. All things were as they should be, in their fixed positions, a memoryscape embracing the family past in the present.

Figure 23. Uncle Faste, during a fishing trip with his cousin Kolbjørn in Northern Norway, bewildered as to how to unhook a squid. Fishing topped the list of Faste's favourite leisure activities, including making fabulous dishes from the catch. He often included untraditional ingredients, always finding inventive replacements for things he could not find in the Norwegian stores. His 'bouillabaisse' was renowned, a culinary speciality made from ordinary things – topped off by 'canned mackerel in tomato sauce'. He never hesitated to comment on his success: 'You could not have a better dish in the best of restaurants.'

Figure 24. A photo from one of my last visits to uncle Faste's home, his mother's (Mommo's) artwork on the walls, the flamenco dancer on top of the shelves, her scarves still hanging on the door. His home is safe and indolent, inconspicuously framed by a seemingly unlimited array of traditions, everydays, memories. It is a gift to humankind, that we never know how things end.

Bjørn Faste was a man who kept his stuff in ship-shape condition, tending, repairing, deconstructing and bringing things back to new life in new constellations. He owned a bike that he called 'Lespa' (the Lesbian), as it was put together by combining two woman's bikes. In the hall, he could switch on the light by clapping his hands by a self-made sensor. Close by his preferred TV chair, he had arranged a self-made high-hertz amplifier, increasingly useful as his hearing deteriorated – he had also made one for his neighbour Rolf, the ex-husband of his sister, my father.

He prolonged his professional skills into retirement, after a career as an electrical engineer and inventor, a nerd long before this label was commonly used. I vividly recall the visits to him (and his spouse of a short-lived marriage) as a child, along with my family. He lived in Bergen, the big city. Driving through the city streets from the harbour where he picked us up, in the back seat of his bright red Ford Cortina – it was incredible how he could find his way, streets in all directions, similar-looking buildings all over. I loved the fact that this man, our sturdy guide through this inconceivable maze, was my uncle, uncle Faste; it made me feel special. On the way, he pointed at the Fløibanen funicular, one of the city's main attractions. He had constructed the automatic controlling device that steered its track up and down the steep hill. After we reached his condominium in the outskirts of the city, he made coffee for my parents, 'Friele' of course, the famous Bergen brand. He had constructed the device that measured exactly the right portion into each bag, not a milligram too much or too little. He lost us as he deep-dived into advanced technicalities, but he did not seem to care much. Later he prepared the evening meal – slices of bread, butter and bread spread, caviar and cheese spreads from the famous 'Kavli' – he also was responsible for the mechanism that regulated the precise amount of produce in each tube, before it was transferred to the device that sealed the tubes off. The meticulous explanations went on for the whole meal, on optical sensors, piezo-resistivity, potentiometer wiring and transponders – the intensity of his elaborations increased as our questions tapered.

Later in the week, he brought me along to the technical lab where he worked, to see 'Mathilde'. It was some kind of early computer that he took part in constructing – what it could do I can no longer recall, just its enormous size, larger than the biggest of refrigerators back home. It was a technical miracle – there was even a feature story in the paper, the very *Bergens Tidende* itself, that included a black and white photo of my uncle posed alongside 'Mathilde' with his horned glasses and dark slicked-back hair, his name in the caption.

The downside of his engagement with all of these technical marvels, he told us, was that he constantly had to handle 'ill-advised and thoughtless nobodies with exaggerated self-opinions'. He gradually raised his voice as he said this, pounding his hands on the arms of the chair he had, up to now, relaxed in. Directors who had absolutely no technical insight – one would think they would know better – they could decide the most irresponsible things that hampered his work. Janitors who would not let him in to the places he needed to be. Doctors at the big hospital who shuffled him around as some casual technician. Customers who were indifferent to the waste of his time as they had failed to have a place for him to park the car. We could hardly believe it – how he could be so smart amid all this stupidity.

For Christmas, he usually came 'home'; he stayed with my Mommo in the next house from ours, and we visited frequently, listened to more stories that combined technical wonders and ignorant people. His gifts were among the very best – complex constructions kits of war plane models, Halifax bombers, Spitfire and Hurricane fighters, Stuka, MIG fighters. The front side of the box showed WW2 air combats, the model inside in the foreground, and frequently a German fighter further back, heading to a fatal crash, with stripes of black smoke in its wake. Not too long after the gift opening and the coffee, he asked if we wanted to build. He tore open the thin plastic sealing, carefully opened the kit so not to disturb its contents, and lifted out the instructions. The myriad parts were fixed to small plastic frames, numbered to facilitate the sequence of construction that was all explained in detail in the included booklet. I loved to watch him build, to listen to his comments as he did so. 'Have you seen the left rear flaps?... it is supposed to be number 67. Aha, this part goes to up front, you see?' We knew that he would build it to perfection, the propeller would rotate by just a light blow, and the landing wheels could be taken in and out... but you had to be careful. The models we constructed ourselves tended to be more 'solid state': we added glue to the wrong parts, and too much of it too.

Figure 25. Air combat above the clouds, inspired from the many model air fighters that uncle Faste gave – probably a German Messerschmitt, flanked by a British fighter jet and a Hurricane. Their landing wheels are out – I believe now that this relates to the excessive use of glue in mounting the moveable parts to the models, rather than a practise in actual air combat.

Later, I overheard a comment between my parents, uttered in a low voice not meant to be heard, the voice you always strain your ears to grasp. They could not understand why he, as always, had ended up building the kit he had just given to the kids: 'To build the model is the greater part of the fun – or else he could just have given them 'ready-made' toys'. I could not understand the problem. I liked to study his clever fingers, how his face changed in the strain for utmost accuracy, his gritted teeth, his painstaking attentiveness to the instructions, his loyalty to the right way to do it. My good Pappa could do most things, but not this; he was too fond of rough rationality. It occurs to me now that it was healthy for a young boy to see that there were skills beyond what a father could do.

I loved to watch the models suspended by invisible threads in my room, arranged at an angle as if in a fierce battle, and safely out of my brothers' reach. We had found the maimed torsos of the planes in boxes when we cleaned out my father's home, propellers and landing wheels gone, lost in play battles, the roughest of them all. However, in places there were still remnants of black thread from their time in suspended display.

My uncle's last car is telling of both his meticulous care for the things he ruled, and how he gradually lost it as an ageing man. He had purchased the brand new burgundy Toyota Corolla 1.6Xl in 1990. Twenty years later, the same car was parked outside his home; it still hosted the plastic smell from the factory. The car was as ship-shape as all his other possessions, the seats hardly worn, the bumpers slightly duller but otherwise impeccable, and the meter read less than 50,000 kilometres. As advised for car drivers, he always took care to back the Toyota down the tiny private road to the house as he parked. The concrete garden posts and the cast iron gate were not dimensioned for a car – they were undersized and blocked one's sight of the main road traffic – yet he had never bumped into them or experienced any other accident. Well. One rainy afternoon in November, it might have been around 2010, he decided to take the car to the store, to save himself from getting wet, as he told me.

> 'I did not spend too much time shopping, but when I had finished, it was dark, and still raining. As I left the parking lot, I was suddenly confused as to which direction to choose to get home. Soon after, I could not recognise where I was, only dark spaces separated by shapeless light points; it was dreadful. I was driving along in the hope that I would see where I was, eventually. I did not, and kept on driving – a long time. Suddenly, I recognised the place, I was in Fyllingsdalen, just outside of Bergen. But my joy was short-lived – how could this be? Bergen is hundreds of kilometres distant, and you also need to take a ferry. I could not remember any ferry, so I just kept on going. Finally, I saw a sign that read 'Florø'; I must have been well out of town. I followed the directions given, and finally found Firdavegen, but I was so stressed out that I just entered my peewee road front-in, as opposed to my strict routine of backing in the Toyota, you know, and I locked myself in the house, completely exhausted. The next morning, still in my bed, I wondered if this was a nightmare, or a nightmare that I had actually lived. I peeped out of the bedroom window, and there it was, the Toyota parked front-in. It was dreadful.'

Not long after this, he donated the car to my brother's son Erlend, his new neighbour in the former house of my father, in the hope that he would be repaid by simple favours around the house.

House on fire

The car episode was a token of my uncle's gradual failure to care for himself, his home and all other material companions. Nevertheless, if he had, for a millisecond, thought of their possible extinction that February morning in 2013, perhaps the things would have alerted him, and made him remember what was going on in the kitchen. Had even a faint flicker of the thought occurred to him, that this moment was the last he would see of this beloved regime of things, then fate may have been forced to make a U-turn.

Figure 26. The fire in uncle Faste's home, February 26, 2013. To the right is the former home of my father, now the home of Erlend. Note the stranded orange canoe in the garden, cf. Figure 58.

Perhaps this was the core of the problem – that his belongings were invisible in their inconspicuous and normal appearance. Unfortunately, it is the malfunctioned, broken, misplaced or missing that gets attention, a pen out of ink, a tilted picture on the wall, a squeaky wheel. Familiar things in impeccable order and placed as usual tend to be overlooked. In this relaxed moment, all of his stuff was present-at-hand, and so could not speak to him; they were neither broken nor missing – yet. Surrounded by things that remembered places he had been, moments he had cherished, tools and equipment he needed through the days, rows and rows of books with wisdom – all this agency, all this potential, and still this total lack of ability, or will, to act in this decisive moment. How could it have been otherwise? The only thing that this world of material normality could do for him was to make him feel at ease, safe and relaxed... they were dormant things that could only make him sleepy. His attention was on waiting for the Romanian, waiting for the doorbell... and he dozed off.

At first, he thought the Romanian had returned, ringing the doorbell like an obsessed man. After snapping out of sleep, he saw that the room was filled with smoke – the insistent sound was not the doorbell, it was the smoke alarm, '...it was like needles in my ears'. The French fries, oh my God! As he rushed to the kitchen, flames from the burning oil were already up against the wall, the wooden cupboards already burning. He ran for the fire extinguisher in the hall and fought the flames and managed to put them out. But the smoke, he told later, 'was like a cork in my throat, I could not breathe, it was terrible'. It was then that he made his second mistake, as he opened windows and doors to air out the thick smoke. The fire soon regained its strength, spreading with accelerating speed and force – all the while my uncle was busy opening more windows, downstairs, upstairs, the main door.

It was Gaute, who happened to be passing on the road, who saw the heavy smoke from the windows and saw uncle Faste desperately waving the front door to increase circulation, unknowingly fanning the flames. As Gaute arrived to him, he tried to re-enter the burning house for his phone and wallet – he had to be restrained. The fire and rescue squads were alerted, and soon after arrived at the scene. It was too late for the house, but my uncle was saved.

As the Romanian friend returned, the home was already lost, and my uncle on his way to the hospital to be treated for a light asphyxiation. The things from the store I never heard more about. Anyway, he did not need them any longer.

Things remembering the ravages of fire

I learned about the disaster the day after, far away in Buenos Aires, on the way back from fieldwork in Tierra del Fuego. I was relieved by the fact that uncle Faste was okay – but all that was lost kept on haunting me, in glimpses of ever more things and arrangements that I could remember from the home. My mother told me that everything was lost, completely, that it was a tragedy. She had been there only once after the fire, had picked a few scorched items that still held their original shapes, and had put them in the open air to lose the stinking fumes. My uncle never returned to the ruin of his home.

My brother Børge confirmed the calamity, but told me that most things were still there, somehow – and sent photos. Visions of disaster and devastation are normal in our time, but scenes of destruction in places that are familiar are definitely something else. I could recognise rooms and many of the things, but the images were like snapshots from a film noir, or sepia photographs at best – a mayhem of accustomed things deprived of their colours, shapes and order – worse than any of my haunting glimpses. Quite surprisingly, most shapes remembered what they had been, the more recognisable, the more disturbing. Most things were actually still there, in the approximate position I remembered them being in, although profoundly marked by what had happened. 'You have to see this yourself', my brother said, knowing my attentiveness towards the ruined.

On arriving at the scene three months later, I could see for myself, as my brother had advised. As I unlocked the unexpectedly intact front door, the soundscape from my footsteps immediately changed, the brittle fragments that covered the floors making crackling sounds as I moved, adding to the eerie quietness in the silenced house. A house on fire I had seen many times: blazing flames out the windows, the scary crackling roar, the smoke towering towards the sky, members of the fire brigade rolling out the hoses, men running, pointing, yelling orders, groups of on-lookers at a safe distance. But I had never seen this, the muted inside of a burnt home, what was left in the wake of the raging flames. The breath of the fire that had ravaged the house still lingered after so many days. The big oval mirror in the hall was out of service, covered by a layer of tar, Mommo's half melted and disfigured hats hanging on its side.

The living room was in total chaos. Everything was blackened, falling apart, burnt, charred, melted or cracked, but nevertheless recognisable. Things were not only marked by the fire, but also tossed about: chairs turned upside down, the floor covered with ash and charred substances. The green carpet that once covered the floor of the cosy room was only visible in tiny patches. Most books were still on their shelves, their backs all black – like they were copies of the same books in the shop of Satan himself. Skewed skeletons of lampshades hung on the walls, parts of wooden frames from precious artworks, empty, tilted, hanging from their corners, their four sides at odd angles. Scarfs were no longer on the inside of the door to the living room. Layers of charred wallpaper and wall-panels flaked off the walls; in places the old timber construction was exposed, not seen since 1936. The ceiling and beams were totally charred, threatening the basic construction of the house.

Figure 27. The sad remains of the bookshelves in the living room – the scorched books were like copies of the same book in the shop of Satan.

Figure 28. Photos from happier times, in maimed pocket albums that survived the fire.

In the kitchen, the frying pan was on the counter, the wooden part of the handle burnt off, but still, it seemed, awaiting the entrecote amid the flame-resistant remains that had fallen from the collapsed cupboards. The treacherous thick-bottomed pan sat on the stove, but there were no signs of the ready cut potato-strips.

Upstairs, more browned than blackened, was Mommo's artwork in place on the walls. The collage made from flashed-out blitz cubes, the clay placket of Eve resting under the Tree of Wisdom, its once vibrant red apples now in gloomy grey, the painted self-portrait of Mommo's father, now merely a murky rectangle. A few strands of the pearly metal chain curtain hung in the doorway to the bathroom, swaying gently in the air flow from the gaping window frames – the vestiges from one of the most admired self-made details of her home, solemnly referred to as the 'Pearly Gates'. I possess a photo of me as a young father, showing the Gates to my one-year-old son Kyrre, as I later did for Trygve and Helge. And the huge African snakeskin – the former attraction was merely a faint shadow in the wall where it had been hanging.

To me, this horrid sight was mixed with flashbacks of how it had all been before, the cosy home, neatly arranged furniture, the precious things, the photos and paintings on the walls, the colour tones and patterns on wallpaper, comfy carpets. The fact that I had photographed these walls and rooms, as well as uncle Faste in his favourite blue chair, on my last visit enhanced the horror.

Between the two, between the disturbing scene in front of me and the myriad glimpses from my many visits before the fire, I could envision the fierce and brutal moment when the flames had ruled the home.

Initially, there was undramatic normality in the situation, heating oil for French fries, the pleasant anticipation of an extra nice Tuesday dinner. Then the same normality of the doorbell, a minor disturbance, a friend offering a favour. The calamity was born in failing to combine the two trivialities. The oil surpassed the perfect temperature for the fries, a friend turned to foe as the oil over-heated. There were no sounds other than the distant radio in the living room. More and more blue smoke rose, the swirling oil starting to bubble, perhaps already spurting hot oil onto the wall as my uncle next door was slowly dragged into sleep. Then, as if taking advantage of the situation, a sudden blast that was instantly followed by flames, a muffled orange glow in the thick smoke. Very soon, the flames stretched out, licking up to find more combustible things to devour.

They did not have to lick for long. They jumped to the cupboards above, blazing tentacles checking the insides, cracking and blackening all that they could not devour, moving on with accelerating speed and increasing frenzy. In seconds, the heat was intense, making painted surfaces bubble, the smoke like a treacherous scout searching for new prospects for its flaming companion in the next room. What an awkward constellation in the living room, this last moment of how it used to be: Uncle Faste asleep with his motionless hands in his lap, moody melodies about lost love from the radio, the muffled crackling from the flames working in the kitchen, a sheet of smoke rising from the fissure above the door, reaching for the ceiling, slowly rolling and curling, gently, silent, as if not to disturb the sleeping man in the chair below them. The stingy scent of burning must have reached him in his sleep, but it could not alert him – perhaps the stingy smell only triggered a foggy dream of a happy moment by the fire during a successful fishing trip that he did not want to end.

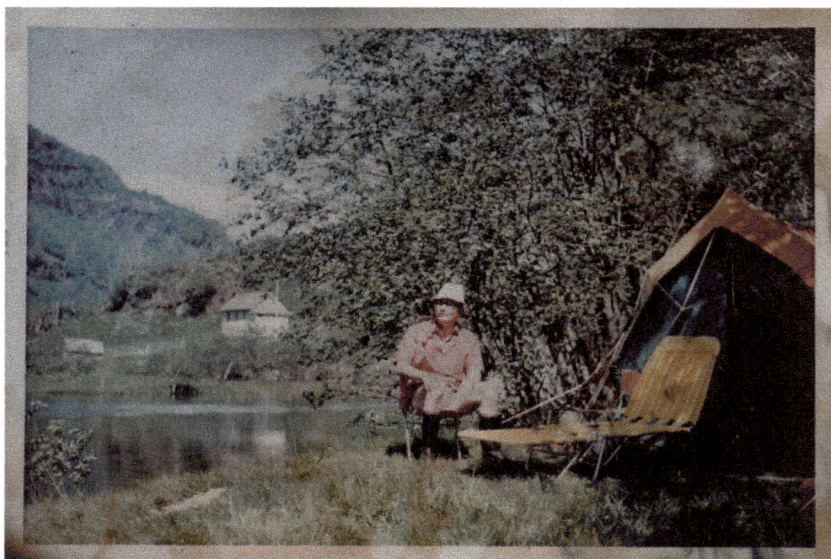

Figure 29. Uncle Faste during a camping trip – perhaps his mind drifted to a joyful memory like this, a morning with a pipe in the corner of his mouth and coffee prepared on an open fire, as the stingy fumes from the kitchen reached him, and eventually stained this photo.

The perfidious veil crept along the ceiling until eventually it reached the smoke alarm. Seconds later, my uncle came to the door, where a tsunami of smoke was pushed at him, met soon after by the hiss from the fire extinguisher, a white cloud that forced the open flames into retreat. Pretending to be defeated, the fire performed its trick from times immemorial – hiding in the embers, hoping for a second chance.

Figure 30. The flamenco dancer, who managed to retain his elegant pose in the flaming frenzy, stubbornly clinging on to his optimistic face as the stack of audio cassettes nearby started melting.

The thick smoke suddenly swirled, as a stream of fresh air from the open windows came into the room. This was what the lurking embers in the kitchen had been waiting for. The fresh air enticed the embers; like monsters in the wall awakened, their red eyes opened and eventually bust out in open flames. The radio, still clinging on to its usual frequency, transmitted an update on the local news, indifferent to the fact that it would not be able to deliver the next update mentioning the fire in a residence in Firdavegen, Florø. The weather forecast was accompanied by the sound of hasty footsteps from the second floor, where my uncle desperately tried to air out the choking smoke, still believing that he had slain the fire. In the kitchen, the flames had already reached the ceiling and followed it to the open door, as they already knew that there were more and better things to burn in the living room.

The flames were lavishly awarded. All things were just sitting there, motionless, indifferently waiting as the smoke, heat and raw flames transformed their surfaces, their very substances. They ripped up the blue armchair, the 'stressless' my uncle had been sleeping in only minutes before, exposing its yellow plastic foam, melting it to facilitate burning. Finding the electrical cables along the walls, they melted the plastic casing. The power cut that followed finally silenced the radio, in the middle a merry refrain. Finally, the fire was home alone and could play its own tune: an unruly beat of bangs, smacks and crackles like a master of bubble-wrap popping gone raving mad, mingled into the ever-louder roar of flames. Huff.

Figure 31. The sad remains of Mommo's artwork in the hall upstairs, next to the vestiges of the 'Pearly Gates'.

I started photographing. Overviews capturing the horrors of it all. I was fascinated by how the flames and heat had transformed familiar objects. There was a perverted aesthetics in it, how things combined what they once were and what had happened. The wooden donkey – the heat had melted its plastic eyes, making black tears run down its chin. The charred flamenco dancer was still in his elegant pose, his white shirt turned black, his face disfigured, the shock of the fire imprinted.

Everything had just been sitting there, as if they had been indifferently waiting to be burned to ash, melted, charred, cracked, blackened, immersed in stinking gasses. The evil of it. The fire had taken no pride or mercy in finishing off its victims. Remember, things are alive without moving. Thus, the scene was a battlefield with still living corpses, marked and maimed, but not dead. They still retained their potential to come back, to be awakened from their dormant state, to recall countless memories of past events, and evoke new action. But they could never come back to what was.

Some months later, the house and everything in it was demolished. Apart from the very few things collected by the family, everything was transported to the town dump, and left even more fragmented and deranged than it had been in the burnt house, left in the open, exposed to accelerating decay. Where the home was, there is now merely a square hole surrounded by a fading drizzle of fragmented things, a few shards of porcelain with familiar patterns, the white side of a slide frame separated from the precious image it had kept for a while.

The boomerang

At the time I was born, in the early 1950s, uncle Faste had been living in Australia for some years – he had even changed his name to 'Bob Bartman' for a while, to save his Australian friends from the embarrassment of awkward pronunciations of his Norwegian name. I found a photo of him that he had sent to his sister, the greetings on the back were in English, and signed 'Bob Bartman' – he was a man of the world. There was a funny story he frequently retold: once, there had been a terrible earthquake in the Balkans, and quite a number of the hard-struck Yugoslavs immigrated to Australia. In Sydney harbour, a Yugoslav presented to the immigration officer a passport with a name of all-too-many randomly placed consonants, that was impossible to pronounce. 'Good Lord Almighty', the officer commented, '...what was your name *before* the earthquake?'

Among the things he brought back was a koala bear made in kangaroo skin. I have faint memories of cutting the fur with a pair of scissors and trying to chew off the black nose that looked so much like liquorice. I could not do it, and neither could my two brothers, who both took their turn after I had given up. I still have the hairless koala, still with his tempting snout – I still do not know what is on the inside of its carefully sewn kangaroo skin.

Figure 32. Uncle Faste with his pilot shades in Australia, from the early days of his 'David Niven moustache'. The photo is partly stained by tar from the fire in 2013.

'Australia' – throughout my life, the very name has been the sound of distant marvels, the big world out there. My uncle's belongings, that during my childhood were kept in Mommo's home, were the hard proofs that the continent existed. On the walls were the photos of uncle Faste in his explorer outfit, with his thin lip moustache, wearing pilot sunglasses and a spotless white shirt, a sun-helmet, drinking from a flat water flask that could mysteriously keep the water cool in the blazing heat. I could not (and still cannot) imagine a sun so hard that you would need a helmet. Umbrellas and coats to be protected from rain and cold – but come on... a helmet for the sun? It was unbelievable. But my uncle had been there, it could not be denied – and the sun helmet was there, mounted on the wall.

In the living room corner, there was a huge snakeskin, reaching from the floor to the ceiling. It was from Africa – my uncle had bought it on his way to Australia, purchased from the black man who had killed it. He had even watched as the man had butchered the huge snake. In my memory of the story, the monster was still moving a little bit.

But, even more attention-grabbing than the snakeskin, the king of the things from Australia, was the boomerang. 'Boomerang'. Just to take this word in your mouth was like tasting the Stone Age. For the ignorant, it might look like a slightly bent piece of wood, a stick that had fallen from a tree. We knew better – it was a fierce weapon that could kill animals. If my brothers and I sat down on the sofa, quietly, without any quarrelling, we could hold it... one at a time. It was a bit heavier than expected, flattened, the edges sharp, but not *that* sharp, and thus even more surprising that it could kill something. But my uncle had seen it with his own eyes: if thrown in the proper way, it would rotate like a propeller and easily crack the skull of a rabbit, or perhaps a small kangaroo. No, our uncle reassured us, they did not use boomerangs to kill koalas as they lived in the trees, protected by the branches. But, best of all, he told us:

> '...if you should miss your target, the boomerang will continue its orbit and return to the hand of hunter.'

The previous owner of this very boomerang in my hand had told a story about a 'boomerang master-thrower'. He had thrown the boomerang without aiming at anything. Then, calmly, he had laid himself on the ground face-down, slowly raising his right foot, just in time for the returning boomerang to land safely on his sole. 'Just as precisely as the helicopter that sometimes lands on the flat roof of the gas station in Florø', our uncle told as he took the boomerang from my hands and hung it back on the wall.

I cannot guarantee the truth of all these details. But my point here is how the souvenirs from Australia affected me, how the stories of my uncle evoked shiny glimpses of the 'big world' that was otherwise only in the black-and-white photos of the five volumes of 'Animals of the World' on our bookshelf. What Faste brought home from Australia made the otherness of the strange and distant real to me. I could take my friends for small excursions to see the things for real, especially the sceptics among them, and thus position myself in the bright and glittery light of my exotic uncle in Bergen, who had lived in Australia.

Later, as a student of anthropology and archaeology, I remembered the boomerang, a real thing from hunter-gatherers, in our own family. This unique instrument from the aboriginal traditions of Australia. Was there a possibility that the boomerang had been more widely used in deep time? Could it be spotted in ancient rock art – in Norway? Could a slightly bent wooden implement from a waterlogged site actually be a boomerang?

Among many of the other Australia-things, the boomerang had in fact survived the fire. Fumes had roasted the wall – it was slightly blackened, except where items had been mounted, which showed as negative images on the darkened surface. In all the misery, I was thrilled. Upon looking at the details, I could see that the boomerang was decorated, long zigzag lines that I had never noticed before. It was lightly charred along its sharp edge, but the exotic thing had prevailed. I decided to ask my uncle if I could own it. A brief moment of joy in all this misery, that I might add this significant piece to the memoryscape of my own home.

This was a Friday. At the weekend, my mother and I visited uncle Faste in his new communal condominium. He gave a brief account of what had happened. The smoke. The chaos. It had affected how he remembered – he claimed that the Romanian was still sitting in his burning living room when he had returned to fetch his mobile phone. I asked about the boomerang, if I could have it. Yes, if it was of interest to me, sure, '...take all that you want, it is all burnt,' he said. He himself did not have anything from his former home. He was dressed in entirely new clothes, in a likewise new home – his present life contained no past, it seemed. I asked him about this, about all the memories in the lost things. Yes, he missed his *Encyclopaedia Britannica*, it was a thing he needed. But memories? His answer was rather puzzling to me:

'No... you see ... I do not need help to remember. Rather, I need help to forget.'

I returned to the burnt house on Monday morning, locking myself in. Immediately, I sensed that something was wrong. Somebody had been there during the weekend. Somebody had gathered a large collection of stuff in the hall, as if ready to be picked up later. Mostly usable tools and equipment not much damaged by the fire. The tools: a hammer, various screwdrivers, pliers, obviously collected from my uncle's workshop on the second floor. The equipment: a gas heater, a rounded-up garden hose. Things in the living room had been shuffled about, as if the room had been searched. Was somebody still here? The place was scary enough – I did not need this. I ventured upstairs – the boomerang was gone.

I could not believe it. How could petty thieves stealing stinking screw-drivers see that this was more than a slightly bent piece of wood? I hoped for a while that it was merely moved, thrown aside in the rubble. But it was nowhere to be found.

After sulking for some time, I chose to be optimistic. The boomerang was not gone; it was still out there, somewhere. For sure, its orbit was wider than usual, but a real boomerang will always return to its master. Or, per-haps even better, it was on its way to Australia, to seek the memory of its aboriginal master, aiming for the sole of his raised right foot. Anyway, I have not seen it since.

The black vase

Even in the burnt and ravaged house, the large ceramic vase was still in its prominent position in the living room. As long as I could remember, the vase had been here, ruling from the top of the fireplace. As it is bigger than most vases, it was only put in use for lavish flower bouquets for major cel-ebrations. On National Day, May 17, there could be fresh birch twigs with spouting leaves and Norwegian flags, on other occasions blooming twigs from the cherry tree in the garden, celebrating the spring. But, for the most part, the vase held a decorative arrangement of dried straws and dead twigs. Comparing photos of the living room as it used to be, I am surprised to find that the very same straws and twigs that were photographed in 2012 also appear in a photo from 1985. Uncle Faste was not much into the artis-tic arrangement of dried-out plants – but he saw no reason to clear out his mother's decorations. Perhaps he cherished the safe and accustomed aura it added to the room.

It probably took less than a second to burn off the dried straws. Nonetheless, the vase was intact, no cracks or pot marks, but it was totally blackened. My wish to keep it was granted, and I took it to my mother's home to clean it. What I believed was a layer of soot or tar was in fact a last-ing change to the surface of the vase. Washing with all kinds of detergent, from 'Zalo' to 'Vanish', and vigorous scrubbing revealed a faint pattern, but the colours were different; I did not recognise them. My mother came to see how I was doing, and commented:

> 'That is the vase Sølve gave to our mother to celebrate the final formalities of the divorce from father in 1948.'

Although intended to mark a happy moment as it arrived in the home, its relation to my ill-fated grandfather was completely new to me. It was likely not among the proud and happy memories that are most frequently rejoiced in and passed on along the generations.

I only saw my mother's father Nils, my grandfather, on one occasion, as he was passing through Florø on board the coastal steamer. I was three years old, and faintly remember a man sitting at our dinner table; he was a stranger, and I was shy and hid behind a chair. I also vaguely remember a blue and white paper bag with sweets – it obviously helped me to find the courage to face him. I am told that I invited him into the tiny cot that was my playhouse upstairs, and that he crammed himself in there with me.

He was referred to as 'Grandfather in Nordland', a long-winded name that denoted his position as a distant figure at the periphery of the family, although I always sensed that my mother loved him dearly. She frequently exchanged letters with him, and also visited him in the north on a few occasions. But none of my brothers ever met him. I cannot recall that I ever sent him a letter or a Christmas card, nor a single drawing of a boat or a dinosaur. I never talked to him on the telephone. He was never there during big celebrations, not invited to the weddings of his children, nor to the birthdays and baptisms of his grandchildren. What were his misdeeds to deserve this ill-fate?

The calamities dated back to the turmoil of wartime – Nils had enlisted as a member of NS ('Nasjonal Samling'), the Nazi-controlled Norwegian party that ruled Norway during the occupation. Mommo, his wife, strongly opposed his decision, and demanded he leave the home immediately. In post-war times, his membership of NS was labelled high treason, which called for lawful punishment. He was sentenced, detained, divorced, and deprived of his children and profession. The stain that the incidents inflicted seeped into innocent family members as some kind of unstoppable capillary force – shame. I vividly remember my own sense of unspoken disgrace in my relation to my troubled grandfather every April 9, the date when the Nazi regime occupied Norway in 1940. On this date, the normal school agenda was put aside, and the class were immersed in a self-evident dichotomy of heroic deeds and cowardly atrocities. I knew that my teacher knew my family story well – although he never wronged me, I sensed that I did not deserve to belong to the right side of his yearly retelling of the brave and empathic endeavours during the war.

This thing, the vase that for all my years had been a decorative thing in the living room of Mommo, revealed itself as painful heritage. It was as if the fire had finally caused the troublesome stain to come to light, as if it had been there all the time. Now, with more time, and as a grown man, I could distinguish better the differences between unspoken inherited shame and done deeds that deserve disgrace. However, this dark memory evoked an interest in this man, my grandfather in Nordland, a nearing to his presence, and I kept the vase as it was. The stubborn blackening suddenly appeared to have a meaning, perhaps originating just as much from the vase itself as from the fire. It was absurd to imagine how uncle Sølve must have searched the store for something nice to support his mother, not to comfort but to celebrate this moment, the formal divorce from his father. In this instant, as he paid for the vase, he must also have remembered his recent letter to his father, as he tried to move back to the town after completing his prison sentence. Nils had attempted to return to his family, but was informed – in clear words – that he was not wanted, and needed to leave town within 48 hours.

Now, what had been a thing to celebrate his exclusion from the family could only draw him closer, evoke further questions to my mother about him – how he was as a father, the circumstances that ended in his enlisting in the Norwegian NS. He was a teacher – teachers were forced to choose between membership in the Nazi-controlled teacher association, or to resign from their position. As he needed to support his family, he chose the former, in opposition to his wife, also a teacher, who chose to be out of work. But there was more – his brother and father had also enlisted, and there were other signs of support for the nationalistic political ideals. Did he know and approve of all the atrocities that are common knowledge today? Some of them, obviously – but also the gruesome 'industrial' killings? Was he responsible for bad deeds – did he do anything to hurt anybody, was he responsible for sharing information with the Nazi occupants? We did not know – although there were no actual signs, it was something we feared.

On the other side, I learned about misdeeds by the winning team – grown-up people calling my quite innocent 12-year old mother a 'Nazi-child' on the street, uncle Faste being forcibly taken out of the parade of victory through the town streets in 1945, quite contrary to his own self-image – he had obstructed the occupants by partaking in illegal radio communications. There was my own fear of being placed on the wrong side of the pan-world conflict – why had my parents chosen a name for me that sounded German?

A few years after the fire in the house, in May 2017, it happened that the National Archives declassified the documents from the post-war high treason trials. We decided to apply for access to the files of Nils Liseth, and by June, my mother, her husband Gunnar and I were allotted an appointment to see the files. There was a solemnity to the visit that I did not expect. The formal appointment, the identification card, the mandatory placement of bags and jackets in the wardrobe, the archivist who led us to the room – everybody whispering, shelves all around, the clean green tables where documents were presented. We had to be seated before the box with the files could be unfolded.

My mother was tense as we opened the container, as we caught sight of the letters in her father's pen, his original signature. He was arrested only days after the capitulation of the Nazi regime; there were the records of his interrogations and the testimonies of others that could enlighten his case, as well as the formal juridical accusation: the most serious being that he took part in a training camp, wearing the Nazified 'Hird' uniform, and received training in handling weapons. He had agreed to these accusations, but explained that the weapons training was 'oiling a gun and shooting three times with cork training ammunition.' Afterwards, he had left the NS and returned his 'Party book', as he claimed he could never aim a weapon towards a fellow Norwegian. The formal sentence was one-and-a-half-years of imprisonment, which also denied him the right to teach. There was a later letter with a request for a pardon – he claimed the responsibility of support-ing his two sons in their education – which he was granted after one year in prison. Actually, there was little that we did not expect – the most surpris-ing was the orderly and fair process he had undergone in the trial and pre-scribed atonement.

We left the archives with relief and proceeded with a lunch in the open, Gunnar and I both needing cigarettes – 60 years after the vase was presented to 'celebrate' Nils being barred from the family. In the wake of our relief, there was sorrow... and shame. This time, the shame was different – it had turned into a shame of my own passive neglect. The poor man – he had not been an evil person responsible for other people's misfortune, but it could not be denied that he had failed in taking the right decisions, and by this supported a regime that had brought terrible things to many. The year in prison must have been the least of his atonement.

He spent some years as a butler in the home of a renowned ship-owner in Bergen[1], where Alma, the woman he later married, was the private teacher of the ship-owner's children. After a time, they moved to Northern Norway, where he was allowed to continue his profession as teacher; he also admin-istered the municipal library, and was the organist in the local church. My mother had kept in contact with letters on birthdays and Christmases. He left life at 68, in 1969. One of his last actions, as he was fatally ill, was to write a letter to my mother for her birthday. My kid brother Snorre, when he learned the reason for her crying, had commented that he thought it had been much worse when the cat had died.

In 2019, Elin and I enjoyed a summer vacation in Northern Norway, where her home place is. We travelled around, visited friends, and happened to pass not too far from where my grandfather Nils had spent his last years, and where his grave was. My youngest son Helge had already visited the grave some years earlier, as he was spending time in the area. It touched me that he had bothered – apart from uncle Faste and mother, he was the single one of Nils's now 22 descendants to have honoured his grave, chil-dren, grandchildren, great-grandchildren, even great-great-grandchildren. I felt tense as we approached the settlement in the inner part of his fjord – it was mid-summer, sunny and hot, and the landscape was magnificent. It struck me that the scenery resembled Western Norway, 1500 kilometres further south, where Nils had come from.

His home could be recognised from explanations from mother and from photos I had seen. There was the church where he had played the organ

– but the cemetery was much larger than I had expected, and it was not easy to locate his grave. I called my mother. No, she told me, it was a long time since she had visited, and she could only give vague whereabouts. As Elin and I were searching, an older women arrived to tend one of the graves. I asked if she knew the area of graves from the 1960s, to narrow down the search. She was not sure but asked who we were looking for. As I told her the name she exclaimed:

> 'Yes, of course, I remember Nils very well. He was my teacher in school. He was the best teacher, I recall he was teaching history, the lessons were so good that we did not have to do any homework, he had explained it all too well in class. He was married to Alma, wasn't he? He lived right below the hill here. Yes, I remember Nils. His grave is closer to the church, in the lower part of the cemetery, go and look there.'

It was so unexpected – to run into a person who had actually known him without any shame, who knew him not as a traitor, but as a normal person of good memories. The friendly lady probably never understood how deeply her mundane gesture moved me. On her advice, we soon found the over-grown grave:

Schoolmaster
Nils Liseth
17.5.1901–9.2.1969

Thanks for good memories

Beside his was the grave of his wife, Alma, who had outlived him by 28 years. She must have witnessed his profound grief of being so far, physically and emotionally, from people he very likely cared much for. I suddenly remembered that I was told that Mommo had excluded him from my mother's birth certificate, as she had changed her children's surnames from Liset to Bjartmann, to distance them even further from the stain of their father after the war. Perhaps they were good intentions, but, in reality, it was more an act of self-protection than of doing much good to her children.

We tended the graves with bare hands, laying down fresh flowers that we picked nearby.

Later, I discovered a photo of grandfather and his class – 'Tennevoll school 1958–1959, Class 6B' is in his handwriting on the blackboard, and I keep wondering if the helpful lady at the cemetery is among the smiling girls sitting in front.

There was also a letter from him to his daughter, dated June 1956. The intimacy in seeing these mundane sentences in his own handwriting – it was as if they were spoken, his voice gentle. It touched me to see him referring to me:

> 'I guess Hein has become a big guy now? Already more than two years.'

Figure 33. My grandfather Nils proudly standing with class 6b in 1959. Is the helpful lady in the cemetery 61 years later among the girls in the front row?

In this moment, already more than 60 years later, it felt like being touched by someone close, whom I never got to know – and never bothered to relate to. Did he ever receive a clumsy drawing of a dog, or a note with misspellings and reversed letters telling him that 'we went to a beach on Sunday'? It is a pity that you have to have become a grandfather yourself to recognise the value of such humdrum things.

The black vase now sits in my living room, on the windowsill with the best view. The stains from the fire could not be removed with soap, a fact that now has its meaning. I have stopped looking for alternative detergents. The colour is right. It is painful heritage, but also a thing to be remembered.

A letter never answered

The flaming frenzy did not reach uncle Faste's bedroom on the second floor. However, its forerunner certainly did – blazing heat and the sickening, sepia-tainting fumes roasted most things in their way, preparing the ground for flames and destruction. Fortunately, the fire squad managed to circumvent the burning bonanza downstairs.

There was sawdust and a chainsawed rectangle from the wooden ceiling lying on top of the bedclothes, evidently from the fire men searching for lurking embers. The bedclothes were rumpled – it touched me that they also retained a faint shape of the man who had slept here in blessed innocence, unaware that it was the last night of the house as a vibrant home. How unthinkable it would have been, that last day, that he would never more warm his cold feet beneath this duvet, this most intimate place of his places. Now, it was an incommensurable combination of things, 'matter out of place' – the very definition of filth. On top of the pastel-coloured flannel bedclothes (and the rubble from the fire fighters) was a free-standing electrical heater and a number of ripped open boxes and suitcases with documents and photos, that had evidently been dragged from under the bed.

The home was lost, clearly, but a substantial number of things were still present, marked, useless, not considered worth keeping. It occurred to me that there were ethical dilemmas here. The unworthy and useless status of this thingly realm was not synonymous with 'unowned', and not open to all for scrutiny. Things still had a 'face', a face with a name, Bjørn Faste Bjartmann. Keeping documents under the bed normally means that they are important to the person who owns the bed – even if it is abandoned. To others, the under-the-bed things would probably be of minor interest – but could just as well be things intended to be withdrawn for others to see, family members and outsiders alike, friends or foes. This was looking behind the scenes, into the private – lifting the bedclothes, literally speaking. I had sensed this – the uneasiness or talking with my uncle about things that had survived the fire. The uneasiness was a token of ethical dilemmas in the rubble. That rampaged things are depreciated and rejected by their master does not mean that they are open for everybody to study. Certainly, I would not like my own things to be rummaged through and inspected when I eventually leave my possessions – independently of if sordid secrets exist or not.

They must have originated from here, the documents I was offered by my mother. Evidently, someone had been rummaging in the house. Surely, the intentions had been the best, as it was known that outsiders had searched the lost house for things that could be of 'historical value'. Mommo had been renowned in the town: a teacher in the primary school for decades, and a popular *causeur* in jubilees for all kinds of societies, she had made prologues to openings or celebrations of institutions, and her artwork was occasionally on display in the high-status exhibition window in the town's bank. Quite a few town members could remember her practice of rewarding achievements – she would put a gold star in your algebra notebook, and was renowned for rewarding the best tan among her pupils after sunny Easter holidays. Likewise, after moving to his home town in his retirement, uncle Faste had been engaged in the local radio station, and had been writing memoirs of highlights, and articles in the annuals of the local historical society or town paper. Yes, there could definitely have been findings of general interest. Nevertheless, searching the ruined house was crossing a line, and the things were returned to the family – and now rest with me.

Figure 34. Mommo, entertaining in her father's top hat in the 1960s, reciting a poem by Karl Rolf Øygard during the broadcasted celebration of Florø's centennial. Her father had bought the hat as he witnessed the solemn crowning of King Haakon VII in the Nidarosdomen Cathedral in 1906. The hat is currently hanging from a nail in Børge's garage, still struggling to rid itself of the stench from the fire in 2013.

The things were as various as they were harmless: bills in foreign and outdated currency, 'Banque de L'Algerie', 'Vingt Francs', a photo of my uncle in front of his tent during holidays, another of him in his khaki-coloured shorts, a leisurely cap with sunshade, fishing pole in one hand, two good-sized trout in the other, an enigmatic smile on his lips. There were professional photos of a number of his technical constructions, a detailed account of his installations in the Fløibanen funicular. A notebook, slightly charred in its margins, contained his elegant handwriting, sketches of details, descriptions, notes-to-self about slit controls, photo multipliers, Golay detectors, Holmium filters – all far beyond me, well behind the scenes of 'Bjartmann Spektronikk', his enterprise. I knew he was good – yet I was surprised that I failed to find any second-thought alterations or corrections, not a single one – remembering how my own work-sketches look.

As everywhere else, the documents illustrated the mingling of things from two homes. There was a notebook with a few of Mommo's speeches – the 'Gentlemen's speech' for the local gymnastics society in 1957, preformed in 'Fram', the town's community hall – the first draft in her very recognisable pen, with inclusions, small pieces of glued-on paper with alternate phrasings, over-crossings, underlinings – the familiarity in her elegant cursive writing held a faint echo of her vocal sound. In a sentence she referred to the 'sound wall' – the phrase underlined in red. At the bottom of the page, in the same red pen, in uncle Faste's handwriting, the expression had been corrected to 'sound barrier (typical mother)'. The added words in brackets indicated that the correction was no comment on her active preparation to complete the speech – obviously it was a remark in retrospect – another sign of his keen interest in tracking misunderstandings and misspellings.

There was also the typewritten version of the same speech – I knew that this version was for herself, to rehearse and memorise.[2] A manuscript would hamper her performance, she needed both hands free for her generous gestures. I remember how she rehearsed in her living room, always standing – taking care to position her feet correctly – and using voluminous arm gestures to underline her main points. My son Kyrre discovered that he could earn money by visiting during her rehearsals. He would be paid a coin for being completely silent... his bonus was to listen to his great-grandmother's strange oratorical voice and study the rehearsed motions. Along with the typed manuscript, there was also her backup, hand-sized notes with key words in bold capitals, small enough to be hidden in her hand, so as not to obstruct her movements.

Again, there was the mixing of times and contexts. A colour photo print had been enlarged to A4 format – uncle Faste amid installations, cables, speakers and sound mastering equipment, still in his wind breaker, looking seriously towards the camera, as if photographer had said 'look to me'. Imprinted in the photo was a text, 'Bjørn Faste Bjartmann visiting Capricorn Studio'. There was even a Christmas card from Elin and me. I was pleased to see that he had had it lying around for some time – on the back side of the envelope were three circular coffee stains (from cups) and some hasty handwriting: 'DO NOT TOUCH! for evening meal NB! Spagetti!'

Figure 35. Uncle Faste during a professional visit to one of his many and varied clients, Capricorn Studio.

There was also an unaddressed pink envelope, tainted by age, corners and edges worn, discoloured. The envelope flap held an inscription in the unmistakable pen of my uncle, obviously a memo of things he needed for some technical thing he was constructing: '5m plastic cable, 1 socket, 1 holder, 3 sewing machine [lightbulbs?] 30W'. This mundane list was apparently added to the envelope at a much later time than the actual letter, indicating that it had been in the open for some time.

The letter was in a child's pen, with self-made lines to support the writing. It had a top text, 'Burn the letter as soon as you have read it...' I realised that I held the hard proof of a story uncle Faste had repeatedly told, and which I also later found in his written memoirs.[3] In the initial days of the Nazi overtake of Florø in 1940, they feared that the town might be bombed. As with so many others at the time, Mommo and the three kids were evacuated to a community further inland. The host of their refuge had similar-aged children who became good friends; they enjoyed happy summer days amid the commotion of war, and Faste – he was 14 – had fallen in love with one of the daughters. In early fall, they returned to the town, and not long after, Faste received a letter. His older brother Sølve saw that he had received it – the anonymous pink envelope bore all the signs of juicy content. Faste hardly had time for a hasty reading before his brother demanded to see it, and chased him as Faste refused. He ran upstairs and managed to throw the letter to the loft in the hopes that his brother would not find it. Sølve caught him, he was 'held down and tickled' to force him to reveal where the letter was – but he defended it with his life. Now, he had to wait for a chance to retrieve the letter, the thing in the loft was burning a hole in his heart. When he finally got a chance, he could not find it anywhere in the darkened attic. He wondered if his brother already had found it, and had to wait to see if he would be teased. As this did not happen, he went back for a closer look without any luck. Days and months passed; his pain faded into oblivion.

Figure 36. The secret letter that was never responded too. Its curled-up state relates to Faste's hasty hiding of the letter in the attic, where he could not find it afterwards. The temporary loss meant that young love faded – yet another opportunity in life that evaporated. One thing I cannot understand – how can it be that the anonymous pink envelope is *not* crumbled?

Years later, when he returned from Australia in the mid-1950s, he needed to place things in the loft, and remembered the letter. He found a flashlight and located the vanished letter in a small space between the beams. Finally, he could read it thoroughly, his hands shaking:

> 'Burn the letter as soon as you have read it and do not show it to anybody. Answer in silence and let nobody know.
>
> Dear Bjørn-Faste. I must write a little letter to you, I really think so. I really do not think anybody loves you as much as me. But Ingerd has said that you do not love me. Faste loves me and not you, she has told me. I did not believe her, but Ingerd stuck at what she had said. He has said it, she said. And she teased me and said that you had blown her kisses and given her apples many times when I did not see it, all this she said and more too. I could hardly believe her. I have had no peace since I heard, day or night. I could not forget what you said to me at Jeila. Now I must write to you and have an answer. If you love me or not. You must answer me if you love Ingerd or me.
>
> Cordial greetings from Oddrun XXXXXXXX.'

The poor girl. She never received any response to her fair request, and eventually she was probably convinced that her 'friend' had been right, that she had to forget Faste. It was terrible – he could vividly recall how much he had liked Oddrun, and now it was all too late; the young love had turned to yet another chance in life that had not been realised. In time, the flaming affection became a sore and mellow memory, a story to be told – even to Sølve, without forceful tickling.

And now, by chance, the actual letter was in my hands – it had avoided being burned, but nevertheless retained the flames of young love.

The scrapbook

I found an interesting album in the scorched rubble, on the collapsed shelf close to where the dining table had been. It was the remains of a scrapbook belonging to Mommo. I could not recall seeing this album before. It was singed along the sides, but the insides were intact, except for its moist and stinking state. At the front there was an index, one line for each year, describing key facts throughout her life. In the pages that followed were more details, almost year for year. I decided to take it out in the open to check it out and take photos of its contents.

The first page was about 1919 in Kongsvinger, where Mommo went to school. In handwriting, she had added: 'Here, my heartbeats were for Georg Erdmann.' From 1928 was a paper clip about the May 17 celebrations that mentioned her speech. There were obituaries, invitations, many newspaper clippings, increasingly more detailed as time went by. For 1945 there was a photo of the miniature steam engine that Bjørn Faste had made, only 17 years old. He had won a well-earned prize for it, 100 kroner, which he had given to his mother as a gift for Christmas – the envelope in which the gift had been handed to her was glued onto the page. His prize-winning steam engine was still in his workshop upstairs; the fire had not managed to do much damage to its metal parts. In later years, it had been one of the main attractions for kids during visits to his home. Instead of steam, he applied his own body weight to run the engine – he filled the inner plastic container of a wine carton with air and tubed it up to the engine, before simply sitting himself on the air-filled container – making the engine run flawlessly, to the astonishment of the on-lookers, time and time again.

Obviously, the initial part of the scrap book was a collection of retrospectively happy memories – there was no mention of her married years in pre-war times, or the traumatic times around her divorce from Nils. I was reminded of my own memoryscape – of the unspoken censorship of things that could remind you of the darker phases in life.

On the pages that followed were things she had collected as they happened, notes on gifts she had received, gifts she had given, to whom, prices, dates, from which shops things had been purchased. The scrapbook contents constantly mingled with things I remembered, and objects that could still be traced in the scorched rubble. There was the invitation to my parents' wedding in 1953, and from 1958, when she had her first telephone installed, I could still remember her ivory-coloured phone. She loved this fancy phone – she even treasured her phone number, 2226. I recalled her pointing out the beauty of the three '2's in a row, gently kneeling, like angels. A woman who could see the beauty in her own telephone number – how would she have wrapped her mind around seeing the burnt ruin?

There was the funeral announcement for chief machinist Harald Jacobsen in 1961, where she had added in handwriting: 'Flame number 1.' Then the first TV: '(black/white). February 27 1964. Big day!!!. Siemens-Norge. Kr. 2700. Delivered by Asbjørn Hatlem.' An invitation on which her name was misspelled, and her comment: 'How could they send this out!' Newspaper articles from when she resigned from her position as a teacher after 41 years of service, in 1965. In the 1966 pages, there were two cigar-bands, 'Sorte Mand' (Black Man), and the text: 'Marks from a 'visitor' who watched the Laja-movie with me.' I was starting to wonder if there actually *was* a reason why I had not seen this scrapbook before.

The moon landing in 1969 was marked by a paper clipping: 'The first stroll on the moon this morning', where she had added: 'I cried of joy' over a drawing of 'My Earth'. What the scrapbook did not mention was that she was riding on the same wave of joy at the next moon landing, when she came all the way to my school just to give me a plate of chocolate. It was a caring and kind thing to do, but I recall that my gratitude at the time was a bit reserved. It was the main break and I was at the far corner of the school, probably smoking with my buddies. I could see her down the road, waving her arm with the chocolate in hand. From a distance of 30 metres, the perfect distance for everyone to hear, she yelled:

'Heein!! Hein... they have landed on the moon!'

For months after I was teased – my buddies mimicking her distinct voice:

'Heeeiiin .... have they landed on the moon again??'

It was how she was, generous and enthusiastic, but perhaps not always with the best nose for the situation. Like the mending of my shorts. I was about to visit uncle Faste in Bergen – I was eight or nine years old. She had discovered a tear in my favourite shorts, and as I could not go to the big city like that, she offered to mend them. I had my worries, but did not anticipate anything even close to what she ended up doing. She had found a piece of fabric from a dismantled sun chair – stripes of very bright colour, bright yellow, red, green. The patch was shaped like a house, a house with an embroidered joyful face, windows for eyes, and a happy smile below them. Minimalism was not her style. To accentuate the artistry of the garment she had also added a similar patch on the left side, where there was no hole – she had thought that the design needed symmetry. It was a catastrophe. I took the pants to Bergen; I did not want to be ungrateful for her favour. I was hoping for rainy days, but no – it was brilliant sunshine from day one. As I ventured out on the street by my uncle's apartment it did not take long before I was tailed by a mocking crowd of Bergen-rascals, yelling 'houses in your ass!' My humiliating return to my uncle's, walking sideways like a crab, trying to hide my fancy butt against fences and hedges – I would have been better off naked.

The scrapbook also held the menu from my brother Børge's confirmation in 1973, a memory of fine-dining at the time: 'Asparagus soup for starter. Mains: pork roast with Brussel sprouts, sauerkraut, carrot cubes and peas, pea stew and crispy potato chips. Ice cake for sweet course. Coffee and six types of cakes.' The invitation was glued to the page: 'Dress code: The nicest thing you have.' Below, Mommo had noted: 'I took: Spanish dress w/grey complet w/orchdé.' In the upper corner, she had added: 'Weather: Cloudy w/ drizzle.'

There were accounts for new things in her house, renovations, who did the job, when, the costs, photos. There was the remake of the kitchen, a photo of Atle Rundereim as he exchanged the burners in her stove, July 22, 1985, the very same stove that started the fire 27 years later. The album went all the way to 1987, all the way to her last years and her increasing health problems.

It was a family treasure. But could it be saved? It was in a terrible state. Soaked, the ink washed out, in many places the interesting handwritings were barely readable. The glue that had kept everything in place for all these years had been dissolved by the water from the firefighting. The clippings were loosening as I was moving the pages, and very often they stuck to the opposite page. I had to reconstruct pages as I was taking my photos. I would have to dry the pages one by one. They would crumble. I would have to do a considerable amount of re-gluing. And still, the stench from the fire would linger.

Figure 37. A page from Mommo's scrap book, which I photographed but could not save. Its contents are highlights from Mommo's life: a new lamp, a window, a kitchen table – dates, prices, who did the job – the plumper Jarle Brandsøy and his son, Alfred Skudal, the carpenter. On July 22, 1985, Atle Rundereim changed the burners in her stove, the stove that would burn the house down 28 years, four months and 27 days later. The ever-present vase rests on its throne on the fireplace. Merry memories make me mellow, and sad memories just the same. What good do they do to the world?

I could feel that a turning point in my study of my uncle's burnt home was nearing. I was getting sick from the fumes I had been breathing in for many hours, my head was aching, and there was a sting in my throat, like an early stage of influenza. The boomerang had been stolen. The unpleasant fact that the house had been scavenged by outsiders breaking-in made the whole thing even more sordid. The task to save the scorched things was too big for me. Everything was marked by the fire: tar-covered, charred, crumbled, and immersed in unhealthy fumes that were hard to get rid of. The scrapbook was only one object among thousands. Besides, as a memory-scape, the tragic event of the fire was now added to what the things remembered – a filthy veil that covered everything. It could not be washed away. And what would I do with these dismembered objects even if I *could* manage to save them? Build a museum?

Figure 38. My mother sleeping on the couch in her mother's living room, probably around 1950.

At a deeper level, something was growing in me. The last days of heavy engagement with all of the memories had made me mellow and sad. They were plenty of good memories, but they also evoked a strong feeling of loss, of good times that were now the bygone past, of homes lost, of good peoples no longer alive – the atmosphere of safety and belonging was fading.

In a personal, cognitive memoryscape, there are bad memories – I don't think that I need them. And there are good memories that evoke a feeling of sadness and loss. The memories that the things in the house could offer would forever be marred by these latest sordid circumstances. In this mood, I could see it differently, why my uncle had not asked for anything from here for his new home, and his words that he needed oblivion more than remembrance. Perhaps it was exactly about this, that bad memories and happy memories are alike, they do not bring forward much happiness to the present.

My knees were turning sore from squatting over the scrapbook while photographing, my back aching. As I stood up, I remember I said to myself, not very loud:

'(swearing)... it is lost. I cannot do very much about it. This is beyond me...'

In the wake of these words, I felt strangely relieved. I took the scrapbook back to where I had found it, walked out of the house, and locked the door. It was the last I saw of the place.

A man without things

A couple of days after the calamities, my mother visited Faste in his first of many temporary homes. He was wearing a brand new, comfy jogging suit that smelled of 'unused garment', something in-between factory and washing machine. They were drinking coffee from cups that were new to them, in chairs that were comfortable, but unfamiliar – the view from his window was scenic, but strange. On a neutral plate he was served sandwiches that were tasty, but different. Yes, he was lucky to have survived – but not happy. After a moment of silence, he said dejectedly:

'...that smoke alarm certainly did not do much in helping me to save the house.'
'Well...', his sister responded, a bit distracted, '...the alarm certainly saved your life.'

For the first time since he had been a new-born, he was no longer immersed in familiar things. Now, he was a man without things, deprived all belongings – if not vanished, they were certainly useless. Even the shirt and sweatpants he had fought the flames in that other day had been thrown away. It may seem trivial, but nevertheless, they were among the very last things that he possessed. Do not worry, he was told. He was insured, and would get all his material needs reimbursed, and also money from the house. Money-wise he was a wealthy man, but he was poor in what money could buy. Nor was heavy-duty shopping something he looked forward to.

After some time, he was allotted a small municipal apartment. It was a bit ironic that it was situated on top of the town's rebuilt Fire Station, but it was placed in the town centre and included some help with cleaning and cooking. My mother and her husband Gunnar assisted him in buying new clothes. He needed everything: a complete wardrobe, toiletries and furniture, sofa, coffee table, pillows, a blanket for afternoon naps, bed and bedclothes, slippers, TV, complete white goods, stove, fridge, washing machine. The shelves in the kitchen were filled with salt and pepper, his favourite crispbread ('you know, the slim ones that don't make a steady drizzle of crumbs on your chest'), milk and eggs, vegetables, pork chops. Cupboards, plates, milk glasses, coffee cups, pots and pans, drawers with cutlery and kitchen utensils, a water boiler, coffee machine – it adds up to more than you would ever think. Anyway, all his material needs were cared for – he did not miss anything, it seemed.

However, and perhaps not surprisingly, the assortment of flawless and complimentary material helpers could not make him a happy and confident man. Even the irritating annoyances he could occasionally find in the town newspaper were overshadowed by some kind of accelerating bewilderment and confusion, and also difficulties in assessing the value of money. He would offer a large sum of money for some help with shopping, and in the same day complain about the cost of a taxi when invited to dinner at his sister's home. Not long after moving into the condominium, he would report that, on occasion, there was an unknown woman sleeping on his couch. She had tucked herself in under his blanket – how could the municipal administration allow her to sleep here, in an apartment he paid for?

My mother tried to convince him that this was not the case – that it was something that he had envisioned, that it was just the shape of the blanket on the sofa. He both was and was not convinced of this, and proceeded to complain about the difficulties in keeping track of time – of distinguishing night from day, and especially mornings from afternoons, which were both suffused with the same half-light:

> 'What I really need in this apartment is a 24-hour clock', he grumbled, in his usual confident tone. My mother corrected him:
> 'But Faste, look, you already have a 24-hour clock – look at the display on the kitchen stove!'
> 'Oh, come on Siv... the display on the stove is not a clock, it only shows the electrical voltage, it does not tell time', he answered, similarly confident.
> 'But how about the display below the screen on your TV – that is also a 24-hour clock.'
> 'No, I cannot trust that, the television transmits reruns all the time, every day, all day, it is useless.'

'But how about looking out the window, and seeing the position of the sun and the shadows?'
'How could the sun and shadows tell me anything about time!!? I am not familiar with this place and its whereabouts, and the position of the sun tells me nothing', he exclaimed loudly and frustratedly, pounding at the arms of the new chair.

Later, he had been watching the respected academic Frank Aarebrot speaking on TV, on *The War in 200 Minutes*. It was a program to his liking, interesting, quite accurate, although he had noticed that Aarebrot in fact needed 215 minutes. Everything was well enough, until he suspected that Frank Aarebrot had moved into his bedroom. There was light emitting from under the door, shadows of moving feet – evidently from Aarebrot. He dared not enter, and slept on the sofa.

Obviously, he possessed the mind of an increasingly ageing man, and was naturally and gradually losing the ability to orient himself. An important sign of this, I now believe, was his growing mistrust in his material surroundings. More and more, as time passed, he could not rely on them to guide him through the days. The fact that he lost his home by forgetting a detail that turned to catastrophe proves that he already had problems coping without assistance. But could the total loss of his accustomed material world be the reason why his disorientation accelerated?

That he did not miss anything was true enough – every necessary and needed object was at hand. But the wealth of new things lacked the links that could adhere them to his long row of familiar, well-proven everydays, his past, his skills in coping. I do not question the quality of his new chair, but it was not his good chair that could also remind him of his former home in Bergen. His new TV-arrangement was without the self-made hertz-amplifying speaker that he was proud of, that allowed him to grasp the finesses of the charming dialect of Detective Inspector Jack Frost. He had many mugs for his morning coffee, but not the one that could evoke memories of the friend who had given it to him. The picture on the wall was decorative but hosted no memory of the day he had bought it, the arrangement of colours could not remind him of the charming smile from the lady in the shop. Pots and pans contained no memories of past successful meals – the ones he used to have always had the faint odour of his previous culinary victories. The tiny scoop to size up coffee measured differently. The temperature intervals of the new stove were different; the pork chops did not develop the tasty browning as they used to – they altered between turning out burnt and dry or soggy and grey, boiled more than fried. The tin can opener worked in a different manner. His new slippers, they kept his feet snug all right, but failed to produce the accustomed sound as he moved around. His well-organised boxes, ringed folders and notebooks, archived in the lost workshop, that would have adhered him to his professional past, were missing – not to speak of his tool-ridden work desk. His new thingly realm was devoid of most of the recollections that old things entailed – the fresh belongings could do almost everything, except communicate with him. His things could not meet his hand as accustomed, make him remember skills, and were no longer able to guide him through the days. His new stuff was unable to support his confidence and well-being where he was.[4]

I believe that this is yet another pivotal dimension in how humans engage with things – that is more than remembering events and happenings. Dealing with familiar objects is also about keeping in touch with safe routines, about helping humans to repeat their actions as accustomed, in short, about coping with the world. Of course, eventually uncle Faste could have become accustomed to the new scoop to measure coffee. The problem was the massive scale of the changes, which, combined with his aged status, imposed a troublesome strangeness on his material realm. A man without his things as he knows them is disabled.

His distrust and frustration decreased, I think, as he lost more of the world around him, when he was moved to a single room at the Furuhaugane care centre. He said that the food was excellent, and that the personnel cared well for him, that they were his new friends. His disorientations became less frustrating, more drawn towards cherished fragments of past times. Like Australia, where he had not been for 60 years. One day, in the living room of the care centre, as told to me by my mother, he was sitting beside a woman reading the paper. He looked at her – his thirst for local news and wrong spellings had evidently been quenched – as he asked her:

'Tell me, is it a map of Australia you are looking at?'

When the woman explained, he excused his mistake by the fact that he had *just* returned from Australia himself, that he had lived his *whole life* in this country. Of course, the urge men can feel to impress a woman is unrelated to age. However, I do not suspect him of boasting on false premises – memories from formative years tend to grow on you in parallel with old age, as the mind is freed from the more recent trivialities. One day, as he learned from his sister that his driving license was no longer valid, he suggested redeeming the loss by buying a motor bike. To me, he once explained that he was about to present a lecture at the care centre, next Sunday to be exact, but was secretive about the contents – it was going to be a surprise. Before I left, he revealed with a smile that his subject was the artificial kidney he had (in reality) constructed, and was rightfully proud of.

There are also heart-breaking moments that bear witness to how a man who no longer has a grasp on reality is responded to, not considered trustworthy, ignored. It is yet another episode I learned from my mother, from one of her many visits during his last year. He grabbed his well-worn wallet – there was a pocket shine to it, developed from following him around in his active times. The wallet probably owed its existence to the fact that he had wanted to give money to the Romanian friend in the hour before the fire six years earlier. It was chubby, hosting strange, dog-eared bills from around the world – most of them no longer valued as currency. Now, he pulled out a 200 crowns bill and asked his sister if the bill was valid money. As this was confirmed, he said that he had presented this very bill time and time again the day before, when he had wanted to buy a 'villa'. He was ignored – nobody responded to him. Of course, they had been thinking that this old man was out of his wits, thinking he could buy a whole villa, a house, for 200 crowns. In fact, he had simply been thirsty, and wanted to buy a drink from the machine in the hall, a bottle of 'Villa Farris'... in reality he could have afforded many. For the most of us, this trivial misunderstanding would have been cleared up immediately – we would have laughed about it. To him, the aged man who was no longer ascribed a sane relation to things, his domain no longer responded. It saddens me to know this.

On the fringe of the archaeological record

Perhaps it was not the fire that blew apart the memoryscape in the home of my grandmother and uncle. Perhaps it is more correct to say that the fire parted things and humans, and thus deprived the things of their memories. Burnt or not, the larger part of the memories is not in the objects themselves, but in their relation to a cognitive mindscape of a human being. Thus, is not possible to inherit a memoryscape, impossible to hand it over to another person or a new generation. My uncle could not identify the insignificant objects his mother had perhaps kept as a memory of Georg Erdmann, as little as he could know what memories this imaginary thing had evoked in his mother. Many days, every day, in the years he had lived in the house, my uncle would have seen the flamenco dancer on top of the bookshelf; it was an object to remember his mother's trip to Torremolinos in southern Spain in the late 1960s.

For myself, the item evoked a memory of rubbing my grandmother's legs with 'seltzers' – Mommo believed that the minerals would enhance a tan; she was desperately sunbathing *before* she went to Spain. When she arrived at Playa Blanca, she could not have legs like Sølve, she told me – they were as white as maggots. Likewise, uncle Faste could never know how the miniature flamenco dancer related to his mother's memoryscape. Perhaps it was not the thing in itself but the attraction to a man she had met at the terrace that day that she remembered, perhaps a hot day that ended with a heavy rainstorm, both of them happy to be trapped under the canvas shelter as lightening ruled the sky. As little as I could know my uncle's memories, he could know little of mine. Probably, not even Mommo remembered my vigorous seltzer-rubbing on the occasion.

The memoryscape elaborated on in these pages is first and foremost my own. I have acquired information about things, stories I have been told, but still this memoryscape is my own. In fact, one may say that the fire was a disruption that broke open this world of dormant memories, that perhaps the fire evoked even more memories than it took away, eventually.

Perhaps this constant loss of memories as people and things depart is one of the reasons why nobody seems to possess very old memory objects – the ephemeral nature of things as memories. The memory value of a heirloom object tends to evaporate between the generations, and new memories that are added through the next generations are not strong enough to keep them safe, to keep them remembered, to be recognised when people depart from their belongings. Perhaps this is why there were no Bronze Age pins in the family jewellery, in the black box that Laurent Olivier received after his mother had passed away, his elegant example to illustrate the past in the present in his book *The Dark Abyss of Time*. The dynamics of how things remember is elegantly formulated by Henry Glassie, quoted by Bjørnar Olsen:

> A German couple buys a carpet in the Covered Bazaar in Istanbul. It becomes a souvenir of their trip to Turkey, a reminder of sun and beach, and it becomes one element in the décor of their home, a part of the assembly that signals their taste. Their son saves it as a family heirloom. To him it means childhood. Germany replaces Turkey. The weaver's memories of village life give away to memories of an ageing psychiatrist in Munich from whom the carpet recalls a quiet moment when he lay upon it and marshalled his bright tin troops on a rainy afternoon. Then his son, finding the carpet worn, wads it into a bed for a dog, and his son, finding it tattered in his father's estate, throws it out. It becomes a rag in a landfill, awaiting its archaeologists.[5]

As Glassie points out, things persist. As parts of homes, things are owned, domesticated, and not available for everybody else. As things break loose from humans when homes are disrupted, they are freed, become faceless, unowned, wild. It is a rudimental process in the formation of the archaeological record. They will enter future presences – like the Turkish carpet, the boomerang and the blackened vase. They are forever blocked from re-entering what they came from, but they retain their potential to re-emerge, where they will be related to other memories. They may reveal a much wider and deeper range of events – memories that never were activated in my uncle's home.

As part of the archaeological record, perhaps memories of a much wider world of events have a better chance to come forward. The flamenco dancer in the store, before it came to the hands of Mommo, was still part of a Spanish family's business strategies, linking it up to the workshop that made it, and beyond. As objects in the rubbish dump in Florø – in line with Harman's OOO[6] – things are both smaller, and at the same time bigger than they were as members of the memoryscapes in my uncle's home.

Perhaps these inherent memoryscapes are better seen in objects without faces, the things that deep time has cleansed to complete anonymity, the archaeological record.

'Nothing of this found its way into my scientific report, of course.'

4 A Home from the Deep Past

On returning to the long since deserted settlement, the barren cliffs echoed the faint but unmistakable and ever distressing sounds of a screaming baby. I stopped to listen better. It had to be the local policeman's baby that was crying. For once, the familiar squeals were not disturbing; the sounds did not trigger the basic instincts, the urge to act, to find out what was wrong, to make it stop. There was something else to it, equally attention-grabbing. It was the timelessness of the soundscape that embraced me, how the rock faces around the long-silenced Stone Age camp added a reverb to the sounds of the upset baby. There is no reason to believe that a Stoneager infant sounded different. I listened to the soundscape of unhappy newborns of all times – the eternal ring of baby squeals resonated from the equally timeless shapes of the cliffs. It was a primeval soundscape, a soundscape I shared with the people who had once resided at the encampment almost 10,000 years ago.

On that occasion, I had been down to the car to fetch some more gear for the excavation. I no longer remember what – it has sunken into oblivion, like so much else that has happened among these cliffs. It was back in the late 1980s – I had arranged a field course for the locals on the island of Vega off the coast of Northern Norway, and a group of 15–20 people was now excavating the remains of a house from the newfound Stone Age encampment of 'Åsgarden', abandoned some 9400 years earlier. A very mixed group of people had enlisted for the excavation: local enthusiasts, teachers, an artist, a mother with kids, some elderly tourists, an 11-year-old boy who travelled from the mainland every day. And the local policeman and his family, who had brought a small tent for their baby to sleep. At that moment, the poor thing was not happy – as occasionally all of the infants who had resided in the 'live' encampment in ancient times must have been.

In the reverb of the baby squeals, the soundscape widened. Although nobody could be seen, I could hear my eager crew working up there. It was as though the ancient settlement had unfolded itself, revived. Words could not be distinguished, only the unmistakable reverb of human speech, commenting, telling, consenting. There was a brief laughter. Somebody was calling out a question to a person who was not near. There were the sounds of people doing things, somebody banging at something, the *tjack-tjack-tjack* of vigorous washing in water. I knew that the sound was from washing out the sediments we were excavating in a small pond – but it was also the ageless sound of somebody vigorously washing something in water. There was a sudden whiff of smoke. I knew it was from the fire we used to make coffee for lunch. But it was also the eternal smell of fire, the timeless scent of humans nearby, preparing something, resting, getting warm. Suddenly, the place was more than an archaeological site – more than an arena for scientific calculations of settlement area and assessments of age, accurate positions of house pits, their diameters and depths, a reservoir of lithic objects. It was a tangible echo of how the site had sounded in the time when it had hosted Stone Age inhabitants.

I stood there for quite a long time, taking it all in, *the past in the present*. It was a timely reminder of all the things humans share through the times, as creatures of an all-encompassing planet Earth – Stoneagers and supermodernists alike. Like my past fellows, I could sense and sort out the entanglement of sounds. The blue sky was above me, the sun shining like all sunny days were one, warming my back, casting shadows in the exact same manner as in all the days of the past. The mild breeze in my hair, the pleasant chill, the gentle motion of the grass on the ground – the breeze acted in the only way it could, as if there was no time. Whimsical flies flew before my face, as annoying in this moment as in deep time, seagulls' squealing, the outline of the distant island out at sea. The eternal shapes of vibrant birch bushes, sweet scents from summer flowers – winter was as distant in this day as it is in all summer days. It was a happy day for me, such a day as the ancient dwellers must also have enjoyed – perhaps the embers of a pleasant dream from the previous night still lingered inside me, alike with the Stoneagers, sometimes.

Perhaps I talked about this revelation to members of my crew as I returned, but perhaps not. Certainly, I would not risk my scholarly reputation. Nothing of this found its way into my scientific report, of course. I was eager to excite my scholarly elders and knew that none of these sensed trivialities would thrill them. It was way-off limits, far from what we were expected to record – it was neither hard data nor tangible observations that fitted the format of the A3 millimetre sheets. It could not be put in the accustomed tables to be compared to observations from other sites. Nor could it be fitted in any appendix format. Still, my encounter with shared things throughout the times that morning was neither false nor speculative; it was reality. However, it was a reality that is considered irrelevant to scholarly archaeology, self-evident and yet well beyond the limits of prescribed observations.

The past in the present

The materiality of the past resides in the present.[1] Nothing of what the past was built of has *remained* in the past. The silenced Mesolithic things are just as real today as they were during their days in able Stoneager hands. Even though there are no known faces attached to the hands, and every bit of personal memory has been washed away by time, the things can still *remember on their own*, as they bear memories of events that they were part of in the past.

Figure 39. Excavations at the Stone Age encampment in Åsgarden, in 1990. Excavations are like moving into the site, in a way you 'own' it along with its past residents. They decided what to look for and where, but very soon you have (like them) 'furnished' the area with designated locations for things and doings: where to dig, the screen-wash gravels and store findings, and also where to keep tools and gear, to have breaks, places out of rain and wind, where to find water to drink, viewpoints, and where to put a tent for the baby Isa, as Aud and Hårek needed on occasion.

It seems as though archaeology is biased towards a focus on 'differences' between now and then, 'changes', what was and has now become. My imagined Stoneager friend from the beginning of this book would probably be very surprised if he was told that his time would, in some distant future, be named after mundane and minute lithic tool parts rather than his much wider and more significant engagement with the world. But 'Stone Age' denotes dissimilarities to this remote time that has become our present, a time when tool parts made of stone are a rarity. Of course, it is also a question of preservation. Stone tends to endure weathering better than most of the many other materials past peoples used to carve out a living, and thus it dominates the remains that have survived the millennia. Nonetheless, the term 'Stone Age', and how we speak about it, obscures the simple fact that most things in the world are similar throughout the times – things that are perhaps self-evident, but nevertheless also imperative to human existence.

Admittedly, raw materials for most tools have changed, as have sea levels, ways of dwelling, how people have joined in social constructs, how words are spoken, mobility, values, beliefs. There were no phones and electricity in the past, no items that contained parts produced in other corners of the globe. Average lifespans were shorter, bacteria and viruses never seen (but surely experienced). The 'Stone Age' and everything therein is usually looked down upon, ridiculed, to stress that the 'now' is better than the dark bygone times, a celebration of the victories of humankind.

On the other hand, like our Mesolithic companions, we possess two ears allowing us to detect sounds and from where they originate, two coupled eyes in front that produce 3D vision, a mouth for tasting, eating, shaping sounds and communicating, the two-legged interplay with gravity that enables movement. We share clever fingers to create, the need to sleep, and brains that allow for sentiments, remembering and resonating, making plans for coming days. Likewise, things in the world that humans share are mostly the same – gravity, night and day, the amount of time in days and nights, the number of nights between full moons, and the configuration of stars to the north. How the winds and currents shape ocean waves, the rolling of waves, and how the shapes of shorelines affect how waves collide with beaches. The mountains at the horizon, even the shapes of receding snow patches on their sides during spring. Where the sun rises and sets, the early signs of a threatening storm on the horizon – when there is still time to seek safety. The soundscape of heavy wind that usually brings cold, what winds can lift and toss around and what stays in a stormy night. The habits of animals, the flavours of bait that fish cannot resist, what floats and sinks, what burns and what does not. The feeling of safety in being close to mother, the fear of losing your father, the competition between equals, being jealous, the sweet appraisal from someone you care for, the beauty in a smile as it conquers a face.[2] These are all things that we have shared throughout all times – they are not post-war inventions.

Figure 40. The materiality of the past resides in the present. Most things in the world are shared trough the times, a fact that is under-communicated in archaeology, a discipline that focuses on changes and what is different. From today's shore line in Vega, with a harbour for small fishing boats.

Evidently, how all of this was understood, combined and weighted is mysterious and unknown to us, and problematic to sort out – the main point is that all these myriad circumstances unite us with people from the past, hipsters and hunters, fishers and feminists alike. 'Each archaeological present is a compressed and coextensive past formed by myriads of mixed and accumulating deposits of stranded and useful things', as Bjørnar Olsen has formulated.[3] The already-mentioned notion of 'Presentism' reminds us of these factual trivialities, banal perhaps, but not unimportant – they are the basic building blocks of our very existence as humans. Hence, all of this is relevant to our engagement with the memories in things left behind by people of the past. The question is how to elaborate, include and make sense of all that is obscured beyond the horizon of scholarly archaeology.

An island remembering its past

Perhaps my attention to the effects of the baby-soundscape in Åsgarden that morning evolved from the joy of discovering the ancient encampment some years earlier. It was back in 1985, as part of my first real project I conducted as an archaeologist, 'The Vega Project'.[4] Vega, this island off the coast of Northern Norway, was already famous for its abundant prehistoric sites: a large coastal flat and a myriad of smaller islands and shallow seascapes surrounding the ca. 800-metre-high Vega mountains. At present, the island hosts around 1500 inhabitants – the number of separate islands outnumbers the inhabitants four-fold. Since the first settlers in early post-glacial times, 11,000 years ago, it seems that this prosperous seascape has never been abandoned.

However, most of today's lowlands were submerged throughout the Stone Age. The earliest camps are found at fossil shorelines that are, at present, elevated more than 80 metres. When they were inhabited, the distance to the mainland was ca. 20 kilometres of open sea, meaning that settlers had to arrive in seaworthy vessels. In fact, boats were also imperative for most other transport within Vega, as steep cliffs and rocky shores would have made walking slow and complicated. What existed of Vega with this elevated sea level were the mountains and the unsheltered shores at their base – an environment that was as bountiful as it was hazardous for the Stone Age inhabitants.

The Vega Project was about securing the heritage from the Early Mesolithic settlers, exploring methods of locating settlements, and finding out if there were different types of encampment. The research strategy was simple; I trusted how the island itself remembered its own past. For months, I scrutinised the elevated former shores from above, studying the terrain in black-and-white stereoscopic aerial photos and contour maps. The crustal rebound since the Ice Age in this region is quite pronounced, as the sheer weight of the massive ice shield had lowered the land. As a result, the oldest shorelines are found close to 100 metres above the present sea-level.

The island still holds the memory of how it was at that time, after it was freed from the ice. A distinct notch along the steep sides of the Vega mountains marks where the sea level was back then, when icy ocean waves pounded at approximately the same level throughout perhaps as many as fifty Pleistocene Ice Ages – almost three million years of ocean swells hammering and constantly spraying the naked rock faces, maximising the frost weathering, breaking waves undercutting the rock faces, causing rock falls and screes, cleaning away lose material, exposing fresh bedrock for more frost action – it is like the forces cooperated in their effort to devour the whole island. Above this sea-eroded notch, the bedrock is still steep and rugged – sea cliffs lifted out from the sea. Below, the bedrock is abraded and smoothed by wave action, between stretches of rough cobbles that denote drained ocean beaches. The cobbles remember the power of the waves – their round shapes are memories of being tossed around by the seas, their size proportional to the magnitude of the energy that hit them. In the most exposed places, the average size is akin to the biggest of pumpkins – all smaller particles have been washed out.

After the ice, as the island was relieved from its weight, the gradual crustal rebound produced a succession of shorelines, gradually younger in time, all the way down to the present beaches. As marine resources ruled the Mesolithic lifestyle, the settlers presumably chose places close to the shore for their settlements, following the receding beaches through the generations. Thus, the land rise produced a 'timing device', in that the oldest settlements are found along the higher shorelines, and then gradually at lower elevations through time, thus hinting at their relative age.

This means that the island remembers how it was at a specific time, as each shoreline around the island remembers its detailed shape. A lucky legacy from the past to an archaeological study, it implies that most Mesolithic settlements from a specific time relate to the same shoreline: I could explore how the people had adapted to a past seascape at a certain time, where they had settled, and the internal arrangement of their settlements by surveying a specific shoreline – that is, a specific contour line on a modern map.[5]

Drained seascapes

I chose to explore landscapes and seascapes adjacent to a shoreline elevated sixty metres up, corresponding to a beach line that geologists suggest existed ca. 9500 years ago. The preparations were simple: contour maps and a red marker to enhance the visibility of the 60-metre contour line. It was like a journey in a distant time, the red marker my boat along the ancient shoreline. In parallel, I studied the black-and-white aerial photos at hand, the stereographic viewer my drone, its flight guided by the red contour line on the map beside me. Above the red line was the landscape, the sea cliffs, sheltering knolls, bays and beaches, points and small islands. Below the marked line, there was the Mesolithic seascape, the depth of bays, skerries, wave breakers, shallows, channels and deep waters.

It was the most exiting tour ever, looking down at the emerging Stone Age world, a seascape that had since lost its waters. I stopped to scrutinise smooth bays and beaches that had once offered good landing places for fragile boats, and searched for flat, sheltered patches suitable for their encampments. This was what Vega had offered its human companions; these were the places they had to choose from in their quest for places to rest, for operations that needed a firm ground and warm fingers, to keep their families fed and safe. My simple methods had evoked a low-resolution memory of the physical environment that the Mesolithic foragers[6] could see as they paddled along the shoreline of their time.

Of course, today there are digital data and tools that could do this work in five mouse clicks – the tedious manual marking back in the 1980s is not at all impressive. Digital tools are fantastic and highly potent and ought to be welcomed and cherished, however I do not think that any digital device could have evoked this vibrant excitement in the wake of my slow travel at the tip of the red marker, the scratching sound of it, even the tantalising fumes. The digital fast track could never have evoked this quivering anticipation of what was around the next point, of arriving at the places to do the fieldwork, of seeing for myself. I supposed that the expected Mesolithic campsites would be ridden with abandoned lithics, literally blankets of dormant waste material from the production and maintenance of instruments and equipment, things that were ever-ready to come back to the hands of humans – to re-emerge as truth-bearing hints to an ancient riddle. I could hardly wait to get out there, to cut open and look below the obscuring carpet of soils that had accumulated since then.

I wrote a letter to my field crew, Berit, Lisa and Mart.[7] They were all students at the time, but already trained Stone-Age hunters, experienced in hunting down forgotten settlements. They all received big envelopes that held copies of the maps highlighting the 60-metre contour line. My request to them was simple: 1) pick the six best places for settlements along this shoreline; 2) range probabilities; and 3) present a rationale for your choices.

In the meantime, I prepared for scientific tests. The lost shoreline was cut in numbered segments of equal size, 500 × 500 metres. Random sampling was the mantra back then, in the 1980s. In addition to a hypothesis and defined criteria of where to locate settlements, we needed an antithesis, a basis for 'falsifying'. Still in the office, I picked from my hat a selection of areas to test in the field, to balance the hypothesis. The result of the 'lottery' did not please me, to put it mildly. All random test localities happened to fall in the most impossible of places – steep faces of bare bedrock and talus slopes that were just as demanding for archaeological surveys as for Stone Age settlements. Another 'random' test was similarly disappointing. To survey these locations would be a mockery to our Stone Age companions, as well as to our limited budget.

Figure 41. The crew that rediscovered the Åsgarden encampment in 1985: Berit Gjerland, Mart Hauglid, Lisa Bostwick and Trond Steinbru.

Although I managed to reassure myself that the second random test was also 'only preliminary', the third senseless blind test brought on a sense of cheating, a need to shut the office door. How many times can you do a random test before it is not random any more? Besides, would negative results from field testing teach us anything beyond the fact that Mesolithic people shunned terrains that did not permit them to stand upright, or places where ocean swells would tear their brittle vessels to pieces, even on the best summer days? The random-pick-kit was never brought to the field.

On the other hand, I was pleased to find that the field crew's sane responses were quite coherent, both regarding the sites chosen for field testing and the internal range between them. Their arguments for probabilities were also similar. The single most prominent factor was the presence of 'natural harbours', favourable landing places where the red-marked contour line revealed bays, wave breakers or other factors that permitted reliable access to the seas where the people earned their livings. This decided the plan for the fieldwork, after which we began checking out the chosen places, starting with the sites that we had rated the highest.

Discovering the Åsgarden encampment

Now, we had finally reached the place called 'Åsgarden'. Truly, it was the gem of our selected test areas on the drained Stone Age shoreline along the 60-metre contour line. On our way up from the road we had studied the present-day sea-less seascape in the wave-abraded landforms, up the small valley that had been a large bay facing west. In the mouth of the bay was a large knoll that had reached up to the ancient shoreline; it must have served as an effective wave breaker that protected the inner part of the bay from treacherous ocean swells. To top it off, the isthmus of such high expectations could also be accessed from a wide bay facing north – yet another memory of a safe harbour adjacent to the place. Now, as well as then, big waves may arrive from any direction, but, as in the past, wind and heavy waves can only hit from *one* direction at a time. Thus, the alternative landing places meant that the site could be accessed safely at most times, no matter wind or wave direction.

At first sight, the isthmus where we had anticipated a settlement did not meet our expectations – it was straightforwardly disappointing, a rocky place between steep cliffs, a mix of barren bedrock and patches of beach cobbles covered by sparse vegetation. We could not trust our immediate dis-enchantment. We needed to find something, or at least document the lack of cultural remains.

Our strategy was to dig the traditional 'test pits' – small peepholes dug into the underground, ca. 40 × 50 cm in size. What we were looking for were remains of worked lithic material, usually flints or various quartzites. Unfortunately, cultural remains from organic materials were expected to have decomposed throughout the millennia. We had to rely on finding the stone components of their material realm. However, even the smallest pieces of worked stone were sufficient to confirm their former presence. To be sure not to overlook anything, the subsoil from the test pits was scooped up in buckets and carefully washed out in fine-meshed screens in a nearby pond.

Our first test pit was negative, as was the next. Our high hopes reluc-tantly dwindled. The third pit was even less promising: as we lifted off the topsoil, large beach cobbles were exposed, large as melons, and between the cobbles were voids – all sand and gravels had been washed away by ocean waves at the time when the sea could still reach the isthmus. However, if tiny flints had been dropped here at a later time, they would surely have drizzled down between the cobbles and ended up deeper down, where there would have been gravel and sand to contain them. The test pit had to be enlarged to lift out the cobbles to access the gravels below.

It was Mart who first spotted the shiny flints down below, the hard, unmistakable proof that we shared this place with the people of a distant past, as evidently they too had found this very place in their quest for a campsite.

In a way, it was a reunion through the times – members of the past and present had arrived to this place by more or less the same reasoning. The Mesolithic foragers had studied the qualities and capabilities that the place hosted as Vega was in their time, still surrounded by its bountiful marine resources and rugged seas. They had found this exact spot worthy of the investments needed to establish their major land base. Nine millennia later, we had rediscovered the place, not by chance, but by the careful and attentive sensing of how Vega remembered itself, by analysing how the island still retained memories of its lost seascapes. The Stoneagers had arrived in their very tangible canoes, riding along the ocean swells – we, the second newcomers, in our imagined boat at the tip of a red marker. The place was common ground for two groups of people separated by millennia – we owned this site together.

We looked into each other's pleased faces, proud of our joint efforts, like a team that just had won a tournament, a band that just had performed their best gig – the feeling of being part of something that are more than the sum of our individual efforts. We were not musicians or athletes, but had just experienced success alongside our Stoneager co-players – they were equal members of our winning team, past and present joined. It was a cheerful moment indeed – there was an aura shared trough the times, between the foragers who had initially spotted the place and the four archaeologists who now celebrated that the long-forgotten settlement had been awakened after its long sleep.

On the side was the simple freedom of dirty field clothes, of throwing yourself to the ground without looking. The place was our best friend, and we were confident parts of it. Coffee from our flasks – it was debriefing time, a moment to elaborate on and ridicule our bygone doubts, what Mart had thought as he first spotted the flint, what we had thought when he told us. We laughed about how he had told us, how he had tried to obscure the bubbling joy in a serious tone, like he had spotted something insignificant. We handed Mart's shiny pieces between us, commenting on the ample space for more test pits – what would they bring? This addictive feeling of finding, this hunger for more, this quivering lust so hard to satisfy – it is high-octane fuel for further efforts.

Of course, nothing of this was included in how we reported our discovery. The report was reserved for what was believed to be 'scientifically relevant'. By the end of the week, we had covered the isthmus with test pits, plotting them on millimetre paper, marking the number of artefacts from each test pit. Pit by pit, the settlement had been growing before our eyes, alongside a rough map of the site.

If arriving had been a joint thing, what we now did was also departing from them, the Stoneagers. We had brought a new language to the site, other measures and point of interest – steadily translating the encampment into our terms: artefact densities, artefact concentrations, negative or positive test pits, find-bearing areas, chronologically-significant artefacts, percentages of diagnostic artefacts, micro chippings – all measures to be able to report observations. It was yet another paradox: our translations of past arrangements into an archaeological language unwillingly alienated us from the things we were most curious to learn.

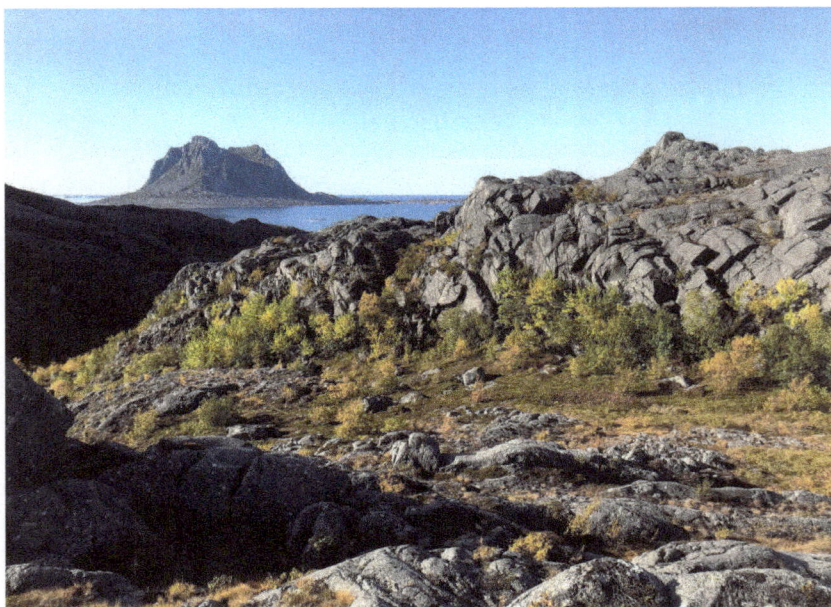

Figure 42. The isthmus (foreground) that hosts the remains of the Åsgarden encampment, with the outermost island of Søla in the background. The photo was taken in 2019. The Stoneagers had to relate to numerous things in this landscape – I like to think that a great many of the shapes seen today had Stone Age names – the enigmatic Søla for sure.

Anyway, the encampment was huge – the area with positive test pits on my plan came to cover more than 2000 square metres. If the densities of lithic artefacts in the pits were representative (a mandatory academic reservation to include in the report), the Stone Age dwellers had left a total number of around 280,000 lithic objects at the site, comprising the ample amounts of lithic waste from their toolmaking. This was plenty enough, but there was more: a number of vague round pits, three to four metres in diameter, surrounded by low walls. Could they be remnants from houses? We could hardly believe our eyes – house remains this old had hardly ever been reported from Norway. After adding more test pits and adjusting the visual detection in more detailed surveys, it was confirmed that the depressions were in fact house remains – perhaps as many as 20.

A place of future prospects

In the weeks to come, we explored several more of the chosen places along the designated shoreline around Vega. Each time, we approached the places from below, walking at the bottom of the ancient submarine seascapes and ascending to the imagined shoreline 60 metres up, to study the places that the island had offered to its humans at that time. How many times had I wondered how it was, the landscape below the surface of the sea? Here it was, in a way, before our eyes, without the water and the marine fauna, but still with the shapes that had defined the ancient seascape, the landing places, how the ocean swells had hit the beaches, the shallows where fish and seals would have thrived.

It occurred to me that there must have been a Stone Age name for the place that had long since fallen into oblivion, along with all their other names, spoken language and traditions. What could that name have been? What would it have meant? Place names are about organising space, a necessity in the exchange of all kinds of information about our immediate surroundings – and Mesolithic Vega was probably no exception. Place names are ascribed by people *for* people, and normally host some kind of relation between the place and the name givers, straightforward or subtle. Names can refer to the physical shape of the place, or something that the shape resembles – thus making it possible to recognise the place simply by knowing its name. Names can also relate to accustomed actions, or something that is experienced at the place, things that can be found or achieved, a reference to a person or event that was remarkable. Names can relate to animistic beliefs, whereby everything in the surroundings was considered a living entity – something that can still be found as fossils in modern names, in the frequent references to witches and trolls in names for caves, cliffs and mountains. As demonstrated by the myriad traditional place names around the world, names can even be different depending on whether you are coming or leaving, or if you arrive from sea or land, north or south – and thus connect you to the place directly. The list of possible names has no end. The only thing to be completely sure about is that place names are never random configurations of sounds – they always host some known (or forgotten) rationale – perhaps this is another human tradition shared across the times. Could the initial Mesolithic place name of Åsgarden have been something that could be spelled out like 'Northern-Landing' or 'Twin-Bay'? 'The-Landing-that-Saved-Someone', 'Place-of-Spouses', or simply 'The Base', or 'Home'? Vega itself bears a name that is similar to many other major islands in Norway – short unexplainable names that end with 'a', perhaps meaning 'island' ('øy' in modern Norwegian): Sotra, Hitra, Leka, Dønna, Aldra, Træna. Are they faint echoes of ancient mental maps?[8]

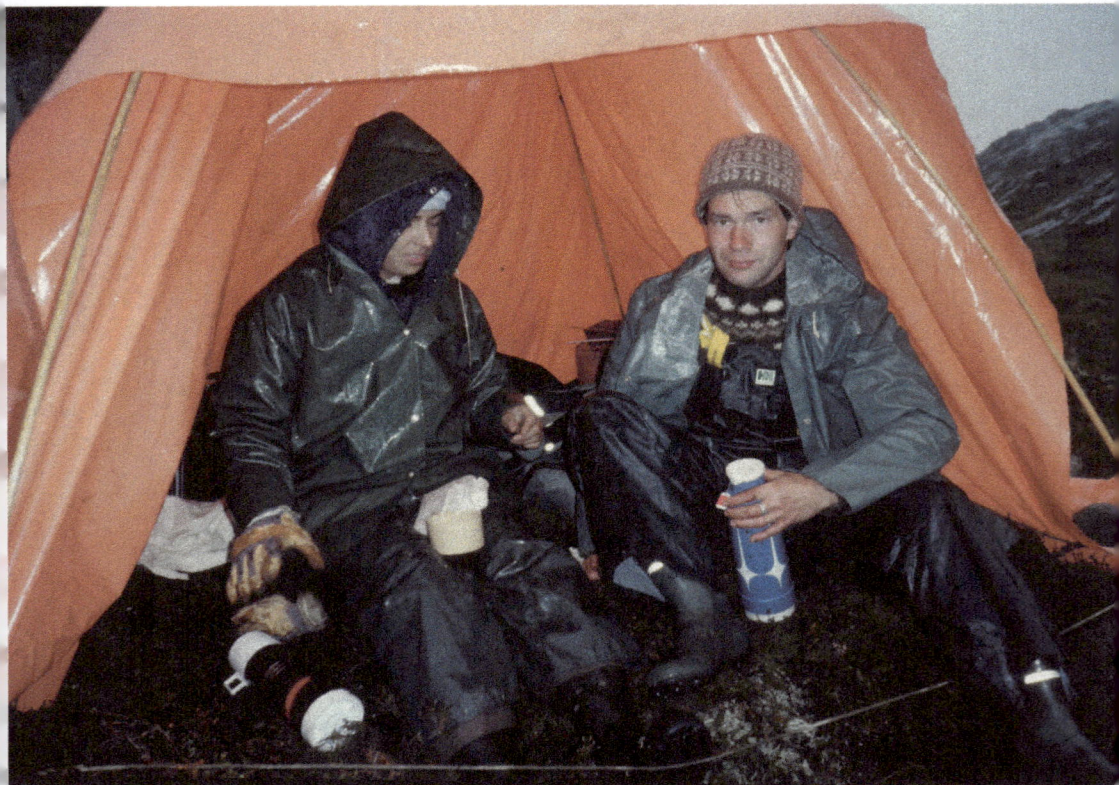

Figure 43. Kjersti Schanche and Mart Hauglid, trying to enjoy a break under a tarp during excavations in Åsgarden in 1987. During the cold and rainy September days, we envied the people who once had been snug in the heated house we were excavating.

Of course, it is impossible to recollect the Stone Age labels for different locations around Vega. Nevertheless, I liked to think about the abundance of shapes that could still be recognised in this landscape, that had been mentally marked by names now forgotten. What is now a nameless low hill, unimportant to most in our time, was a sub-sea formation back then, a shallow for plentiful fishing, an advantageous wave breaker that made seafaring safer, or perhaps the opposite – the location of treacherous wave falls, where somebody perhaps capsized and perished. Of course, this place would have had a tag in their spoken language. To think of this brought me closer to the place, and made me more attentive to formations I had hitherto not noticed.

One evening during fieldwork, we had invited locals from Vega to see our newly-discovered Stone Age settlement in Åsgarden. Many showed up at the meeting point by the road. Among them was an elderly man, a fisherman who had roamed the seas around Vega for a lifetime. He did not look too interested – perhaps he was thinking of how cultural heritage repeatedly hampered the clearing of new land for cultivation, roads and gravel-mining. We stopped several times on our way through the lost seascapes, pointing out and discussing formations. As we approached the inner part of the drained bay, where we could see where the encampment had been situated, I showed them the map with the 60-metre shoreline, and pointed out the past shores with their shallows, points and bays.

I noticed the elderly man looking up and around, mentally comparing the map, shapes and formations around him, and all that he had sensed in his life-long engagement with seascapes. He could now see what he had, up till now, only 'seen' indirectly, from studying the shapes of waves, how deep his line would go before the sinker hit the bottom, the right depths for nets and fish traps. Now, perhaps he envisioned being immersed in the half-light of blue-green water, a baited bone hook jiggling amid a group of hastily nibbling fish, the line connecting to the cigar shaped shadow from the vessel on the surface. He nodded, and briefly commented: 'Yes, indeed ... this was a good place at that time.'

His approval of the site warmed my heart, and apparently he was surprised that his own long experience at sea was actually useful in grasping an understanding of his distant ancestors. I regret that I did not ask him to suggest what the name of the place could have been.

I was pleased to be able to show, talk about and discuss the qualities and particularities of our newfound Stone Age encampment. It was like showing off your new car – perhaps a parallel of how it once was for the group of hunter-fishers, pointing out this place of future prospects to their elders and spouses for the first time – the place they had eagerly bragged about. For us, as for them, the site had potential for future prospects. For 20th-century archaeologists and Stoneagers alike, the place had potential for building futures – independently of whether it was considered an 'archaeological treasure' needed for the building of academic careers, or a suitable position for prosperous living in the Mesolithic. In a way, we shared the site between us. Time prevented a rivalry between us.

The dwelling remains

It must have been a troublesome surprise to the Stoneagers, this big flat-topped boulder that emerged as they were digging the pit for their new home. The boulder in question had not been visible until the pit was nearly finished. It was too big to be removed. The Mesolithic constructors could have chosen to give up the nearly-finished pit for their new house, relocate the pit and start anew. Instead, they chose to include the protruding rock as part of their inventory. Perhaps this is yet another thing that has not changed much throughout the ages – the reluctance to leave investments.

As we excavated one of the house-pits, some years after discovering the Åsgarden settlement, this boulder was exposed a second time. Evidently, the dwellers-to-be had chosen to go on with the house as planned. Perhaps the flat-topped boulder was useful for placing things that needed to be elevated above the damp floor, or to sit on... it may have been a favourable reservoir of heat if the fireplace was placed near-by, a place to dry things, or to place something that needed to be lukewarm, to soften the resin that fastened a damaged projectile point to a shaft in order to exchange it. It was probably a normal thing for them, to make the best of things, to adapt, to live along with most things in the homely environment. All of their traditions, experiences and efforts could not have prevented unexpected things like this from happening. They had kept on removing cobbles for their house, all the way down to the gravel layer below, that would soon become the floor in their heated shelter. As they finished, the flat-topped boulder protruded almost to knee-height from the floor. And they placed a hearth adjacent to it, to the south-east.

The field of large beach cobbles that we had initially taken as a disadvantage was actually a perfect match for semi-subterranean houses. Perhaps the difficulties in digging test pits in this rugged sediment was the unspoken reason for our misreading. Anyway, using the cobble field as a construction site for houses would have had several favourable benefits. To prepare a pit for the house allowed for lower roofing, perhaps a dome-shaped superstructure of saplings covered by skins, maybe bark, and heavier patches of sod to pin it all down. The lowered construction would have made it more resistant to heavy winds, the stormy nights when the house was needed the most, or perhaps to periods of absence when the house could not be tended. To lift out cobbles to make a suitable pit would have been easy, much easier than digging in fine-grained soils. Even during lengthy periods of heavy rain or melting snow, the surface water would have drained into the voids between the stones and been sucked up by the gravels below. Also, the airy layer of cobbles would have allowed for an ample supply of air for the fireplace, preventing the interior from being filled with smoke.

The house foundation that was before us now remembered these basic advantages, how the well-functioning house was when inhabited all those years ago. In all its simplicity, the house was a 'machine' that provided a snug refuge from rain, wind and cold, an inner core of that could contain heat, security and relief, a place that was designed for meeting another day.

We carefully exposed the gravels that were once their house floor – gleaming chips of flint and quarts were visible everywhere. We acted as a cold-case-team, fixing strings to mark out a grid of 50 × 50 centimetre excavation units that allowed us to record the approximate positions of things in the lay-out of the abandoned house. The finds were put into plastic bags, marked with the coordinates and the layer of the excavation unit they belonged to.

It was a memory bank – remnants of used tools, waste from tool production, chips from the shaping of details, nodules of prepared lithic raw material (or 'cores') for things that never came to be, things that never came to pass the border between prospects and manifestation. Nevertheless, the shapes of the lithic cores occasionally gave a hint of what these prospects had been, what the stone smith had aimed at, proving that the maker had been capable of intricate planning ahead. Some of the tool remains suggested what they had been used for – cutting, perforating, scraping. A flat beach cobble, broken in two, had pronounced pits on both sides – we could not find the other half. We guessed that it might have been part of a fire-starting kit, the top weight (or handle) used to position a friction stick in a bow drill, that could have produced enough frictional heat to generate embers to be blown into flames.

It was like a digital photo gradually getting more pixels. Pieces of charcoal were scattered around the floor. A fireplace emerged adjacent to the boulder in the centre of the house. The hearth was not immediately visible, but revealed itself in a concentration of fire-cracked flints and tiny pieces of charcoal. The charcoal, that for a time had kept the interior heated, had long since cooled – but could still tell us the number of years that had passed since it had been part of a living tree, probably very near the time when they fuelled a warming fire inside the house.

It was from here that we collected the sample that we hoped would indicate the age of the house. Well-equipped laboratories and sharp instruments were (and are) needed to develop this faint but highly-informative memory of age, based on the gradual but constant loss of the radioactive portion of carbon (^{14}C) found in all organisms. When still a part of a piece of burning wood, crumbling apart to glowing embers, the sample had surely witnessed talks about a 'future' in what today is the past – plans for the next morning or after the storm, strategies for the forthcoming season, perhaps how to avenge a cowardly raid from a neighbouring band the previous spring, or a mother teaching her offspring a way of doing. How absurd, that the cooled embers also could bear witness to how many years had passed since this mundane instant. And even more absurd, when seen from this past instant, that these humdrum embers could measure the time interval to when the hearth was rediscovered in a distant future. Around 9400 years, the ^{14}C-laboratory would later inform us.[9]

All of these things had been left in the house, dormant for this great length of time. Once, they were handled with the utmost ease, for cutting, engraving, perforating. The ill-lit floor was once regularly searched for a piece with just the right shape for a specific need. The things did not vanish with the people who handled them back then – they are just as real in the hands of archaeologists today as they had been in the hands of Stoneagers. In a way, we owned them together, as if there was no time between us.

The things had demonstrated their ability to come back, awaiting new action. But now, they were not handled to cut and pierce as they used to. They came back to something different, human actions that treated them otherwise, as objects to scrutinise, compare and learn from, to build local identities, or academic careers. Nevertheless, the things were the same, and did not seem to care much about the difference. They seemed just as willing to be handled now as then, proving their inexhaustible capacities. They had never been gone – they had been there in all those presents since then – awaiting new challenges. How many more times will they return to the hands of humans, and what accomplishments will they contribute to?

The recovered remains were integral to the meshwork of lived lives, were fragments of incidents throughout times, chunks of machines that once co-worked. These silenced fragments retained their ability to communicate, but depended on skilled attentiveness, our ability to interpret the messages they carried. Very little spoke to us directly – some things were revealed in the most minute details, others in large-scale patterns, like our knowledge of stone-tool production traditions in general.

Memories in stone

In the evenings, in the cosy old house we had rented for accommodation during fieldwork, after putting our damp rubber boots by to dry, after hand-washing and a quick dinner – it was time to look closer at the artefacts found during the day. We carefully rinsed the flints in the kitchen colander, distributing them to drain off on strips of paper towels, carefully marked with their coordinates.

How can rocks remember? Rocks remember very well, actually – literally, the embedded messages are written in stone. They are, seemingly, insignificant shapes of stone. Like metal components from car engines, for most people they are no more than any other piece of metal, while in the hands of an experienced mechanic the same piece is a meaningful machine part – he or she could perhaps even read its function and the details of the machine's capabilities. Archaeologists are trained to understand machine parts in stone, and how they co-worked in bigger machineries. The things were as present in the light of our kitchen lamp those evenings as they had been in the flame-light of a deep past – the things did not linger in the bygone.

But how does rock-remembering work? As said, the selection of rock types is one strand of how rocks remember. Rock types were not selected for their ability to be knife sharp or needle pointed alone, but just as much for their willingness to be shaped by an able hand. Most stone implements were shaped by percussion, the splitting of stone into desired forms by strong and precise hammer blows. Accordingly, stone-tool makers depended on rocks of homogenous internal structure to be able to control the fractures, to ensure an outcome as close as possible to their intentions. It seems that various qualities of flint and chert topped the list, along with quarts, quartzite and glassy rock crystals – there was an optimal balance between their willingness to be shaped and their ability to form sharp points and cutting edges. In most places, suitable rocks for toolmaking are hard to find – Stoneagers must have directed one of their two eyes towards the ground constantly, scanning for a lucky piece of the right stone. It is very likely that they were able to judge quality merely by appearances, and could assess how a rock would react to their blows. Nevertheless, as found elsewhere, lithic nodules worth bringing to the camp were often tested by a few fractures, as if to put in a 'window' to assess internal qualities – yet another token that 'securing investments' is not a modern phenomenon.

I liked to think that the raw material in most of the worked flints that we now found in the house had been evaluated, found worthy, carried along in bags or baskets, and perhaps brought to the camp by boats, where they had been kept as precious things, future prospects of successful toolmaking. Occasionally, we could spot minute pieces of outstanding quality, worked with the uttermost care – still emitting a faint memory of the moment of joy and admiration when first spotted – for us, as well as for our Stone Age companions.

Most of the rock objects from the floor of the ancient house were small chips flaked off during operations to obtain specific shapes. The pieces remembered every blow they took, the blows all embedded in the stone in the form of 'percussion marks' and 'fracture faces'. In fact, the rock still witnessed the precise point of impact where a bone hammer had hit it 9400 years ago – the adjacent 'bulb of percussion' imprinted in the stone in the millisecond of the blow. The shock wave of energy from the blow had shot through the homogenous stone and caused a fracture, inflicting a slightly curved shape. The energy of the blows was captured in ripples in the fractures – the marks from the inflicted blows instantly fossilised in the stone.

These shapes are as visible today as in the split-second they were imposed by the stone-tool maker. Each and every one of them remembers the very instant of the action that was repeated again and again to produce the basic sharp, hard and durable parts of the tool repertoire. A certain configuration of repetitions suggests that the stone smiths aimed at specific shapes – these repetitive patterns are hints to his or her intentions in shaping the stone.[10]

On the Stone Age side of this object, the stone smiths were trained to do this, to know how the stone would react to the blows from their hammer, to find the exact percussion points, to decide the force and direction of their hammer. On our side of the object, archaeologists are trained to read the sequences of percussion scars, to read how they chip into each other and reveal sequences, to read the shapes of the percussion bulbs to decide what kind of hammers were applied – hard direct blows with a hammer of stone, softer bone-hammer blows for higher precision, or even indirect percussion by antler chisels, for even greater accuracy. It is like studying past technical skills in a movie played backwards. Our professions met in these tiny pieces of rock as if we acted in the same movie.

Figure 44. A stone tool experiment during our fieldwork at Vega – an experimental flint blade fastened with heated resin to a sheep rib turned out to be an excellent tool to procure fish. The knife's edge suffered barely any damage, and the few that occurred at its tip were similar to the use-wear in blades that we recovered from the house in Åsgarden.

There were also sections of smaller chippings (retouch), to blunt sharp edges to support a better finger grip or to shape a dulled edge that would be suitable for hide scraping, or miniscule chippings to enhance a point to a needle-sharp projectile point. I cherished the thought that they had a specific name for doing exactly this – as for several other stone-handling actions. Perhaps we share the lithics, but the way we talk about them is surely different. If there was a way to find out, I would not be surprised if the

Stoneagers had talked about these things as their active co-players – what they could *do* – as opposed to the common archaeological focus on inactive morphology – what they *are*. The lithics on display had listened to both languages – seemingly indifferent to whatever they were called.

A few of the lithics bore the marks of actual use as tool parts: sharp corners or edges with minute chips or crush marks from working whatever had needed to be cut, scraped or pierced – bone, wood, leather, meat, sinews, plant fibres.[11] Only rarely, and contrary to popular belief, were stone tools shaped by reducing a piece of rock down to one single tool, as we would carve out a wooden object. Most stone tools were composite – intricate applications of sharp edges and points – produced by varied methods of fracturing, and equally wide-ranging methods of hafting. We had learned about the innovative application of lithic edges from well-preserved instruments, that combined lithic parts with hafts from bone and wood, from outside Vega.[12] Evidently, the abundance of sharp-edged lithic waste material was also a deposit of potentially usable parts. Several odd pieces displayed use-wear – we could envision how they had occasionally fumbled among things on the floor for a piece that could solve an immediate need. We could identify the piece they had found, but not what it had been needed for.

In the light from our kitchen lamp, we handled these tangible messages from the past, turning them to scrutinise them for details. The faint, broken-glass-like ring that escaped from the lithics as we handled them – the same ring heard when the lithics had been fumbled around for on the floor of the Stone Age house. We felt the sharpness of dormant killers, solvers of problems that had long since vanished.

Sometimes, we applied a quick tongue-licking to wet a detail to enhance visibility, occasionally checking for minuscule use-wear through a one-eyed optical magnifier. These tiny pieces of stone were a common ground between us, the Stone Age hunter-fishers and we Anthropocene archaeologists. To us, the things originally shaped by them as tool parts to meet their daily struggles hosted memories of bygone actions. To them, they were mundane products of recent actions, and the shapes of lithics could easily be related to ways of production. To us, trained to read the language of stone-tool shaping trough experiments and observations, the same shapes remembered the actions they were part of before their big sleep. To Stoneagers, they were part of tools that permitted successfully hunting, procurement, the obtaining of equipment, garments and other tools. To us, after waking them from their long sleep, they were building blocks to enhance our understanding of past actions, and also to shape our very own academic careers. How absurd to them, that the mundane by-products of their daily struggles would be activated as able players in some distant future. Likewise, how absurd to us that our own things will be included in new contexts in an even more distant future – in ways we have no way to foresee or comprehend.

A special artefact shape in the masses of lithic remains caught our attention. In our time we label them 'blades' – they are basic tool parts that surely had a specific name among their makers, a name that fell into oblivion as their tool tradition disappeared. As we could see, this specific elongated shape had been copied again and again, and also had marks from being uses in various tools – this particular shape had surely been intended as a basic building block in their tool-kit.

Blades. Their shapes are as beautiful as they are effective, and were a hallmark in the tool tradition of the Åsgarden homes. It took special skills to make these long slivers of stone, several centimetres long, with parallel razor-sharp edges along their smooth sides. Blades could be further modified by chipping or snapping them to fit as cutting edges in a range of tools, fastened in resin. The flint smiths used specially-prepared cores to produce blades. Some blade cores were reduced beyond further use – others could still produce; they became prospects turned to stone. Here, as in other sites, their quite uniform formats indicated that they were partly intended for the manufacture of standardised edges in composite tools with exchangeable parts – indicating that shafts and handles were frequently re-tooled. There is a certain rationality to this, as shaping various hafts of bone or wood would have involved a lot more effort than the minutes it took to produce and exchange a worn lithic blade. A standardised shape allowed for the replacing of damaged parts with new, so that the machine could continue its function as before.

Occasionally, glimpses of this rational renewal of tools could be observed. Every now and then we found blades that had been snapped – thus producing new pointed corners at the end of a sharp edge. Often, the pointed corners showed use-marks, indicating that they had been used as knives – the upper corner was being the knife's point. Small, seemingly useless segments of blades occasionally also bore similar use-marks. Initially, this was a puzzle to us – how could this use-wear have been inflicted to pieces that were far too minute to be gripped? Eventually, in rare cases, we were able to see that these minor blade segments had been snapped off the tips of worn knife blades. By snapping off the worn tip, a fresh 'knife point' was produced – just as we renew the points of our wallpaper (or Stanley) knifes.[13]

Lithic remains are merely a diminutive proportion of the Stoneager machine, which also included ample components of materials that have long since decomposed. However, these missing materials appear as myriad phantom parts in how Bryant envisions 'machines'[14] – including the well-greased co-function of items of bone, antler and wood, dried grass, lines and lashings, skin and leather, ropes and roofing, garments, baskets and boats – all available materials that were carefully explored, administered and adjusted according to the Stoneagers' knowledge and skills regarding resources and their capabilities. All of these invisible parts of their lifestyle must also be envisioned and accounted for, however obscured.

Structures of encampments – echoes of logistics...

Presumably, the excavated pit in the Åsgarden was a house that had once played an active part in a Stone Age machinery. However, what are my reasons for labelling the house a 'home', and not just another occasional shelter for needy hunters? The assumption of a home is grounded in the overall pattern of camps discovered along the shoreline at the time, as explained in more detail in the following.

Over the course of the next years, we surveyed and tested other of our designated locations along the 60-metre shoreline, and also made a similar survey along a slightly lower shoreline elevated 50 metres above the present sea level, believed to be close to 1000 years younger, but still safely within the Mesolithic, at 8400 years old. All of the sites found were similarly tested, and a few were excavated to attain a rough idea of their contents, of vestiges, camp areas and visible hut remains.[15]

In brief, we found clear similarities between the camps along the 60- and 50-metre shorelines, indicating more or less the stability of logistics and encampments throughout more than 30 generations of Mesolithic hunter-fishers. However, nowhere else along our selected 60-metre shoreline could we locate a huge settlement like Åsgarden, although many other of the selected test areas turned out to have been visited. What caught our attention was a series of minute settlements. Test pits indicated that the amount of lithic remains numbered merely a few hundred, and that campsite areas were limited to 10–20 square metres – that is, only a fraction of the large Åsgarden site. At first sight, the smaller camps looked like the remains of casual places to rest, clean fish, butcher a seal, or mend or renew broken tools. However, some of the minor sites also included remains of a dwelling, where charcoal and fire-cracked flints remembered warming hearths, similar to the houses observed at Åsgarden. A semi-subterranean house was an investment that indicates a clear intention to return to the same place, a camp to be relied on in upcoming times. Thus, the hut remains bore witness to the fact that at least some of the minor encampments were part of a planned layout of encampments. Obviously, these insignificant sites were more than casual stops – they were permanent stations in a 'built' environment.

After looking closer at the lithic remains from all of the encampments, the contours of a pattern emerged. The finds from the large Åsgarden settlement were dominated by lithic waste: more than 90% of artefacts were small chips (flakes), reflecting the ample amounts of lithic waste produced in the making and maintenance of stone tools. Remains from actual stone tools were clearly outnumbered, numbering less than 5%.

At most of the minor camps, this was different: we found considerably less lithic waste and fewer cores, and a markedly higher number of tool-remains (20–50%) – that is, a tool-ratio five to ten times higher than the

Åsgarden settlement. Furthermore, it seemed as though the composition of instruments also differed. The minor camps contained a more confined range of instruments, mostly knives and scrapers – tools that seemed to pertain to the basic procurement of prey – hunter-fishers *in action*.

This is unlike the wider range of tools from the large Åsgarden settlement, which seems to have embraced tools to make and maintain a more widespread assortment of material necessities. In additions to knives and scrapers, Åsgarden included awls to perforate skin (indicating the making of holes for seams, skin garments, boat hides, bags), burins (for the shaping of hard materials like wood and bone, handles and shafts, boat frames, houses, racks), a broken drill bit (for the drilling of holes in wood or bone), lithic blade cores (from and for the production of various cutting edges and points), and flint edge inserts ('microliths', signifying the assemblage and maintenance of projectiles). Presumably, the Åsgarden tool assemblage points in the direction of the basic manufacture and upkeep of a wider array of material things – that is, *preparations for future actions.*[16]

... and a Stone Age 'home'

The combined observations of the lithic remains, dwellings and encampments evoked the skeleton of a mobility pattern that included qualitatively-different camps that in sum provided the basic resources necessary for the hunter-gatherers 9400 years ago. The large Åsgarden settlement was a communal base with several separate dwellings, a place for the greater part of their people, families, relatives and neighbours, a place that also allowed for the procurement of most of the material necessities for mastering their daily challenges along these harsh shores. It is very likely that the dwellings corresponded to households. It was perhaps the main place for people and things, a place of frequent returns where they spent the most of their time on firm ground, a collective that provided social security, a place from where a new day could begin – a proper nave for the machinery that produced their livelihoods – in essence, what could be labelled a 'home' in deep time.

Additionally, their home base was surrounded by several smaller camps that served as support points for task groups, stations for hunter-fishers in action, for fishing, the hunting of sea mammals and the gathering of eggs, shells, and all other resources that they craved. Some of the found sites might be vestiges of casual chores, places to await better weather, for mending or procurement – others, as the occasional house remains indicate, were planned, permanent and reliable land-supports. They were already-prepared camps that reduced the need for daily returns to the home base, places of relief, to prepare food and get warm – in short, places that allowed for longer stays when operating far from the base. In fact, the network of reliable camps also reduced the risk involved in roaming the large bays of open sea, they were alternative places to seek refuge in situations when winds changed for the worse. The lithic tool remains could very well be the sole survivors of a wide range of things that were needed at the station – dry garments, needles and thread to mend things, perhaps a storage of harpoons, lengths of fishing line and spare hooks, remedies to kindle and fuel a fire, covers to ensure a good night's sleep, a place to talk, compare observations and catches between boat crews, exchange advice and amusements.

Very few of things the stone age dwellers fabricated were inert end products. They were more than the sterile inventory lists that regular archaeological reports may indicate. As with things from our own time, they were most often *for something else*, wider and bigger, they *did* things, implied further actions, as Levi Bryant's machines help us to visualise. These wider implications are hard to prove in direct, observable data. Nevertheless, it is not far-fetched to assume that an awl was more than the formal, static artefact category 'awl' – that the awl *did* something along with all other things, humans, non-humans, animate and inanimate, that engaged in holistic collectives. All of these *verisimilitudes* – things resembling truths – should not be neglected in order to purify scientific conclusions. Without the verisimilitudes, this chapter would have ended many pages earlier, after a few maps and concluding tables of artefact inventories.

Will their future surpass their past?

I will risk the claim that the 'now' is thought of as some kind of paramount moment, as a measure elevated above both past and future. Past moments seem to dwindle, to become increasingly unimportant in parallel with their distance in time, as moments melt into days, years, decades, millennia and eons. The future seems to be a similar melting pot of time – but the timescales of past and future are not symmetrical.

It is a paradox perhaps, the many scholarly disciplines that address the past, from yesterdays to enigmatic eons. The opposite direction, towards times to come, intentions, agendas, plans and prognoses, have a considerably smaller time-range, 'the future' rarely exceeding the century. Yuval Harari's bestselling *Homo Deus*[17] is an interesting exception, extending trends that are observed today into millennia to come, debating their consequences. Interestingly, he foresees that archaeology is one of few professions that will prevail unchanged – saved by the discipline's complexity and marginal economic output – that is, as a necessary discipline not worthy of much further development.

As with the 'deep past', we must recognise the 'deep future'. This involves acknowledging that a very large part of our thingly realms will survive us, perhaps not only as things in the garage, or items stowed away in basements or lofts – we also have to count all material things that will eventually be engulfed in the archaeological record. Surely, there are components that will prevail in the faceless conglomerate that is the archaeological record, as more or less biased representatives of what today is the 'now'. Their future effects, and the otherness they will encounter, are beyond comprehension. We can only rely on the fact that it does not stop here, that material vestiges will continue to be unfolded and affect what is the future.

Antique remains are implicitly seen as being captured in the 'now', laid to rest in reports and museum storages, as vestiges finally brought to still-stand after their long travels. However, as the remains from the ancient Stone Age community at Vega demonstrate, the same things may fall in and out of human attention time and time again – periods of oblivion broken by episodes of reappearance. Each time, things reappear in a world that has changed; each time they enter new actions, machines that may produce new effects.

There are good chances that the Stone Age vestiges from Vega had been rediscovered (and forgotten) many a time before we brought them to light in the 1980s. I like to think that in the millennia that followed the abandon-ment of Åsgarden, in times when the stone-tool manufacture tradition still lingered, lithic instruments were constantly stumbled upon and recognised as remains from past peoples. The 'accidental stumblers' probably read the memories in the things they found with far better accuracy than us. However, they were presumably also able see some 'otherness' in the things – a different choice of raw materials, manners of manufacture and use. In turn, such observations are likely to have evoked speculations and the oth-ering of what came before, of time and mythical origins – and hence affected their present and future.

I recall a peculiarity from another excavated Mesolithic site, Locality 52 from the extensive Ormen Lange project on the coast of north-west Norway, some 400 kilometres south from Vega – presumably around 11,300 years old.[18] The site produced thousands of flaked flint artefacts, all within their tradition of Early Mesolithic lithic manufacture, as expected. That is, all except for one single instrument, a well-shaped and polished Early Neolithic adze. There was also a scattering of charcoal at the settlement that was sam-pled and dated. The result from the two ^{14}C dates matched the typological date of the Neolithic adze, around 5700 years old. A brook that happened to cut through the settlement at the place would certainly have offered visibility and access to artefacts from the much older encampment in the Neolithic period. Neolithic peoples' daily flaking of stone would surely have made them recognise the things they found as 'man-made', and probably also made them notice alien modes of production. Inevitably, their finds would have suggested something that had been, a past, mythical or mun-dane – that perhaps called for actions that included fire and the deposition of their well-shaped adze. This incident took place in the middle of the time-scale between us – the original early Mesolithic settlement was as distant to them as the Neolithic event was to us, the archaeologists. Coincidences may not be ruled out, but nevertheless, it is a fact to be trusted, that past people were engaged in landscapes that were ridden by unruly heritage from their own past times – and that they had the skills to identify it. The recollected past vestiges are very likely to have affected their conception of the world.

Similar accidental findings of ancient stone tools also seem to have occurred with Iron Age people, long after stone-craftmanship dwindled and vanished. The Norse myth of Thor, who rides in the sky and produces blasting lightning as he swings his 'hammer', was probably influenced by accidental observations of peculiar and perplexing Stone Age axes found in the ground – believed to hammers from past lightening events. They are commonly found embedded in Iron Age constructions, grave cairns or stone walls, perhaps to protect those places from future 'bolts out of the blue'. Who knows – our present saying that 'lightening never strikes twice in the same spot' may very well relate to prehistoric beliefs, as indicated by the fact that stone axes were labelled 'thunder bolts' in early antiquarianism.

This constant mixing of presence and absence is fascinating – past things brought to attention again and again, each time to something different, each time having new effects on the humans they encounter, indifferent to whether the effects are good or bad, true or false... or verisimilitudes.

Nevertheless, this time, after some time in oblivion, the Åsgarden remains were rediscovered by actors who had learned to embrace them in the archaeological way. Again, they returned to something different and proved their ability to engage. Myself, Per Morten[19] and others have undertaken hundreds of excursions to the abandoned encampments. The Stone Age findings have contributed to a vital local identity among modern residents. More now than before, as archaeological knowledge increases, the sites are viewed as valuable and worthy of protection. The antique settlements were important leverage in the establishment of the Vega archipelago as a World Heritage site[20] – along with the vibrant traditions of tending nests of eider ducks and the subsequent picking and processing of valuable eiderdown. It is hard to prove, but this symbiosis of birds and humans may very well have its deepest roots in the Mesolithic machine.

Now, decades after the fortunate rediscovery of Åsgarden, it is easier to admit what earlier was subtle and unspoken, but surely hinted at between the lines of this book. Obviously, the discoveries along the shores of the drained seascapes at Vega have assisted in the trajectories of my own professional career.[21] They made it possible for me to be invited to conferences and guest lectures inland and abroad, to evoke attention and make publications, things to elaborate on ideas in my teaching – all in all, decisive building blocks in my eligibility for academic positions. Even if my capacities were tenfold, they could still never compensate for the effects of what Stoneagers presumably saw as useless remains on the floor of their abandoned home 9400 years ago. Thus, they too, unknowingly, affected a future beyond their imagination.

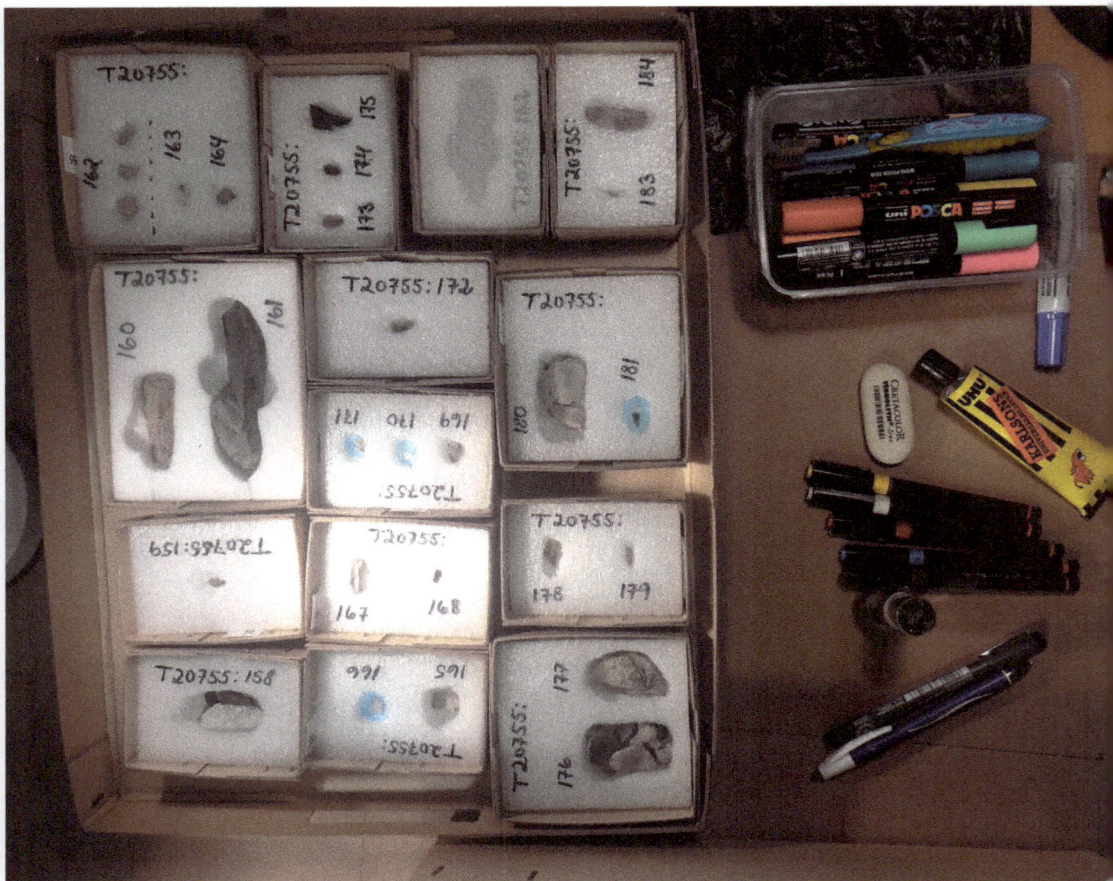

Figure 45. Birgitte Skar's workstation during the examination of lithic artefacts from Åsgarden, in 2020. The things that once readily co-worked with Stoneagers' hands are just as willing to cooperate with Birgitte and her tools today – a thing Stoneagers would struggle to comprehend. Still, the things are the same, as if no time has passed.

However, things do not end here. In recent years, Magnus Holen, a young student, reopened the bags we labelled in the 1980s and examined the production details of blades – focusing on their detailed technological traditions. His study is based on observations in similarly-aged pan-Scandinavian contexts.[22] The study demonstrates that the Vega dwellers were well included in new technological trends that occurred within the Mesolithic – in indirect percussion with bone chisels, and even in the use of pressure techniques to acquire higher precision in the making of lithic blades. His efforts were awarded with an excellent grade, and a recent scientific paper of his study are good prospects for his future career.[23]

At the moment, the lithics from the home in Åsgarden are on display on large tables in the backrooms of our museum. My colleague Birgitte Skar is trying to refit the individual lithics in their production sequences to understand more about Mesolithic technological skills.[24] She is noting differences in colour and texture in raw materials, to narrow down the 'mother nodules', and is scrutinising for shades, lines and shapes that may lead her to find the exact link between fractures. Each lithic among the countless flakes still remembers its nearest relative, like a penguin mother in the myriads of chicks in the barrens of Antarctica. In theory, it is possible to track the whole lithic assemblage back to the original raw material nodules that were brought to camp all those years ago. In fact, even the missing parts may be traced – the parts that were taken from the house and left in other places – their shapes linger in the voids of the refitted material. One may even hope for the retrieval of missing objects at other encampments, matching the shape of the voids – thus proving ancient communication. The technology to produce digital models of 3D shapes already exists, but the large amount of information in mass recordings hampers comparisons and subsequent matching. When this obstacle is passed, probably in the not-too-distant future, the identification of holistic signatures of production and skill will be possible – including how lithic instruments were distributed among encampments in the Stone Age.

Last year, Jo Sindre Eidshaug and Ole Risbøl[25] brought their drone to the site, making a 3D model of the settlement, including the exact surface shapes and layouts of dwellings. Heidi Mjelva Breivik[26] brought her sampling gear to look for the possible presence of ancient DNA, which may detect the origins of the decomposed organic matter of what was brought to the camp. We are awaiting the results – nevertheless, they constitute efforts to further expand the limits of the archaeological vision. The claim that 'the future advancement of archaeology will be in the labs more than in the field' is far from irrelevant.

These are all current projects in which things from the Åsgarden encampment play a role. As mentioned, and as already shown by the retrieval of these ancient vestiges, it does not stop here. However studied and scrutinised, the objects will forever keep something in reserve – details that hitherto have not been discovered. They have proven their ability to survive their humans, as already shown by the long-gone previous generations, and in time, eventually, we will be among them. Sooner or later, our studies and the lines here will be as forgotten as the Stone Age conversations that occurred in the moments of their making. The things, however, will be persisting memories – may be studied by scholars whose great-grandparents are not yet born – and even further, as they too become part of the past, inevitably. The durable lithic heritage from Vega and elsewhere has the potential to be forgotten and rediscovered in times we have no means of foreseeing or understanding.

Nine thousand and four hundred years Before Present. If we flip the age of the Åsgarden encampment towards the future, we reach to the year AD 11,421, adding on the two millennia since the more recent moment of the birth of Christ. This is the amount of time the Stoneager vestiges have proven able to survive. Suddenly, this distant future become a reality. Independent of all unknown effects of the present climate crisis and shifting political regimes – we can rely on the fact that this year will arrive (although we cannot know if BC/AD will still be valid time references). Days will surely be different in AD 11,421, but they will also still be within the frame of the planetary constants. In thinking this, my home suddenly changes – what things here may be part of these distant days? A brick from the chimney, a metal part from my scooter, or the spark plug in Elin's chainsaw? In an even more distant future, as the millennia steady and surely mingle into eons, we, Stoneagers and supermodernists alike, will be joined in the same past. The time that today divides us will be too minute and insignificant to mention – alike with our present neglect of the difference between happenings in the centuries before and after 9400 years ago, or between the one-million-year intervals within the Devonian era.

The vestiges from ancient Vega may very well have more future than they now have past.

'– they are all entanglements of things and people that lived for a while, up to moments when people and things departed – becoming material vestiges on the threshold to the archaeological realm.'

5 Things, Memories, Life and Time

Undeniably, the things and contexts elaborated on throughout these pages are intimate to my own individual and quite personal experiences. The home of my deceased father, who left all his things exactly as they were on his last day in life. The unfortunate home of my uncle, who lost all his things in a fire, just as abruptly. The two homes were both instantly terminated by these ill-fated events. Nevertheless, the circumstances were kind of opposites.

When my father left this life, his abandoned things were just sitting there, ship-shape but bewildered, as if awaiting to be included in routine actions that were never to be repeated. Their master had left the building. His things did not seem to realise that they no longer belonged to a 'home' – overnight they had turned to 'things in a house'. Soon after, their collective partnership was broken apart by his sons – divided between the communal scrapheap and new homes that could never include them as before.

In the home next door, uncle Faste managed to escape from the decisive destruction of his home, but his realm of things could not be rescued. They had not vanished, but were maimed, unable to function as before, their scorched and stinking state adding something to their memory value – they had become dark heritage. After the fire, my uncle became a man without things. Admittedly, the insurance company compensated him for the monetary value of his loss, but his new, unfamiliar things never managed to provide a new home that could sustain life as he knew it. They were unable to connect him to his past, his skills, his routines.[1]

Despite their differences, the two cases are both instances in which humans and their material things were split, their entwined and long-lived liaison ended. This is also the case in the myriad archaeological assemblages around the world, from deep time to the recent. They all meet in this – they are all entanglements of things and people that lived for a while, up to moments when people and things departed – becoming material vestiges on the threshold to the archaeological realm.

On the other hand – and this is the very backbone of the archaeological discipline – things are ever-ready to return to attention. However, each time they reappear to something else. The world has changed during their dormant state, humans handle them differently, the instrumental values they used to have are no longer valid, their intended functions rarely accompany them through the times beyond the horizon of the archaeological. Their loss is partly compensated by values that were added in their lengthy absence.

Figure 46. The emptied house of my father – a house without things, ready for a new owner to furnish.

Now, they return as objects to be studied, they are things that 'remember' how things were before, how they took part in, assisted and decided routines and actions. Still, they are able to be things of importance: building blocks in a general understanding of an ever-changing world, instrumental to insights into how human-thing entanglements work, vital entities in the constitution of memory and identity.

These ever-present entanglements encouraged us to explore yet another situation in which humans and things had split, this time a case from a distant past. Although the circumstances are in the dark, the former Stone Age home in the Åsgarden encampment was another human-thing assemblage that was terminated. All three of these homes may be seen as little 'machines' that were once maintained and worked well, with machine parts put together by things of their time, tended to and lubricated by practical human competence and social skills, producing 'home outputs' on a steady array of 'home inputs', as Levi Bryant suggests.[2]

In most ways, the recent and the ancient human-thing collectives are similar, independent of whether things or humans left first. They are the basic parts of what eventually constitutes the archaeological record. In all their ill-fate, and however tragic to me, the closure of my father's and uncle's homes marked the very moment when they transformed from livelihoods to archaeological contexts. Perhaps I held on to a strand of professional curiosity to lessen the loss in the traumatic incidents, but I do not know for sure.

The house of my father is now the home of his grandson Erlend, rearranged and refurnished, repainted and retooled. My father's things are currently divided between the city dump and the thingly outskirts of new homes – on display as cherished memories, or in boxes in the attic. The blue jeans that were handed to the 'Bomberos' in Tierra del Fuego have perhaps already made a difference to an ill-fated person in the far south, or may (hopefully) still be kept in reserve.[3] I do not know.

Some months after my study in 2013, the vestiges of uncle Faste's home were demolished by mechanical digger and reduced to a couple of truckloads taken to the town's garbage landfill. Erlend sent me photos from the quite organised destruction, all within the regulations of sorting and recycling. At a certain moment in the demolition, there appears a transverse section through the house – a transect that was always there, but never seen before. The transect may resemble something that an architect may draw up to visualise a future prospect. Unfortunately, I know that it is completely the opposite, a vision of post-mortem. In one of the gaping doorways, the last strands of Mommo's 'Pearly Gates' may be glimpsed. Her scorched artwork is still on the wall. In the basement, in chambers not seen since I was a child, the colourful drawings from her schoolchildren are still hanging on the chalked walls. The minute triangle-shaped loft can be seen, where Faste once searched for the letter of lost love. There is an

Figure 47. The orderly, but quite brutal demolishing of uncle Faste's (and Mommo's) scorched house – that at some stage produced a transect that was always there, but never seen. Currently, the place is merely an overgrown hole.

absurd detail that haunts me: amid the rubble outside is Mommo's beloved pink bathtub, perhaps the most intimate of the things in her home, still with remains of the pipes for hot and cold water – it is like a heart ripped out. The vision brings about a sense of deep loss. Hopefully, the vestiges were deposited not too far from my father's things, as they were before, joined in a pair as recent additions to the masses of material remains from their time in the world.

Where the home of uncle Faste once stood is now merely a rectangular hole with unruly weeds. My mother recently sold the lot, after he passed in 2019. Most of the trees have been cut down – the garden will soon have new paths, and before long there will be new generations of kids to worry about the 'risk of bumping into foxes'. Fresh homes are under way – there will be apartments for sale, advertised as 'close to the town centre'. It is ironic to know that the initial owner of the house (it was a wedding gift to a woman called 'Pusen') sold the house to my grandparents Nils and Ruth on the grounds that it was *too far* from the same town centre.

The ancient home in Åsgarden – it is a fact that it once lived for a while, and that things and humans split at some moment, a moment that transformed the benign and heated home to the remains of a house with things. The circumstances may have been just as traumatic as in the two recent cases, or perhaps not – nobody knows any longer. Anyway, how the vestiges re-emerged from their long sleep in the depths of the Stone Age was definitely a happy moment. It is a moment I witnessed and was an active part in. Maybe most of the fortunate archaeological findings have a dark twin in the bygone – in the circumstances when humans and things split up.

Ironically, it is the oldest of the three homes, the one that predates the homes of my father and uncle by some 9000 years, that today is the most intact. Already ancient as the first of the Egyptian Pharaohs were embalmed, the slight depression between the sheltering rock face and the pointed boulder at Åsgarden persists, still visible to the trained eye. The surviving elements of its original inventory were painstakingly 'lifted out' and now rest safely in a stable climate in their individually-shaped Styrofoam beds at the museum, their numbering and coordinates presenting a low-resolution image of their original position.

One may rightfully argue that my intimacy with the homes of my father and uncle (and grandmother) are beyond what is possible to study with an objective professionalism. On the other hand, memories are difficult to explore from an objective distance, and I did not even try to. In fact, perhaps my project here is attempting to do the exact opposite – to enhance and nourish a subjective 'auto-archaeological' nearness. Indeed, there is perhaps a similar (albeit unspoken and less obvious) intimacy in what is supposedly handled *with* the prescribed professional distance needed to meet scientific standards.

Figure 48. Excavation of the home in Åsgarden in 1987, with Mart Hauglid and Kjersti Schanche. Ironically, perhaps the oldest of the three homes is today the most complete. The house pit is still visible, and the items that survived through the times since the Stoneager residents have been painstakingly lifted out, marked, and stored in separate Styrofoam beds in climate-stable storage in the museum.

To discover and excavate, study details and trends, and present and publish archaeological data also involves a considerable amount of this personal 'amongstness' in what is studied. As archaeologists, we were active parts in the rebirth of one of the Åsgarden homes, acting like mid-wives assisting in its release from the murky womb of the past. As with most other successful deliveries, it was a moment of prospects: not only of the benefits of qualified, professional knowledge to scholars and the general public, as frequently argued – we also had the privilege to shape some sense into how things were interpreted (for a while), how the things we found related to the unseen, the missing human companions. What we chose to promote as reasonable was forged and tainted by our own preferences and experiences of being members of the contemporary – by some sort of 'parental guidance' for the things in their new context.

Archaeologists like to appear altruistic. However, perhaps less outspoken is the fact that the reborn material is soon integrated as vital parts in individual or collective prospects: they are objects to be talked about, things that call for attention, gems of conference presentations, essential parts in publications to come, in positions to be gained, in regional identities and politics. The ancient objects prove their ability to return to the hands of humans, and they are still usable in the now, albeit for different purposes than before.

An existential 'amongstness' through time

Perhaps past and present are not as different as we are taught to believe. In fact, all attempts to bring rationale and meaning to material remains from the past, from simple functional interpretations to elaborations of overall societal trends, depend on involving what humans share throughout the times: the general and lived experience of a shared planet – what burns and what doesn't, what floats and what sinks, the sequence of seasons, the familiar trajectories of all that shines in the night sky, how cold water drains heat from a body, the interplay of gravity, the balance organ and the two legs in walking and running, the appearance of a slippery surface, the affordances and hazards of the sea, how insulating capacities change when garments are wet, the chilling effect of strong winds, the ability to please or insult someone, the frisky smell in the morning after a rainy summer night.

The list of shared, timeless experiences in the world is hard to exhaust. Admittedly, exactly how all these existential things were conceived and embedded in past lives is in the dark – but it is a fact to be trusted that they *were* sensed, administered and involved in human strategies and actions, in how lives were lived – back then, as in the now.

The multitudes of experiences from this shared, timeless 'Earthly existentialism' evoke a subtle 'amongstness', an intimacy between past and present. Although largely unspoken, scientific archaeological research is likewise dependant on this general experience of the same planetary amongstness. To make sense of Stone Age heritage, we constantly bring in elements from our own basic knowledge of how the world works. I cannot think of any scientific elaboration that is not based on shared fundamentals like gravity, temperatures and vegetation, seasonality and expected life-spans, the need for sleep, food and oxygen. Nevertheless, these are self-evident beyond what is worthy to mention, and are eluded and silenced as trivialities.

As advocated in the perspectives of 'Presentism', these banalities should perhaps be more explicit in how we discuss and relate to past people. In my opinion, this is exactly what theories like Levi Bryant's bring forward, in seeing the entities in the world as interdependent, multi-scale machines that actively co-work, operating in a symmetrical amongstness (or flat ontology) that embraces humans, non-humans, the animate and inanimate alike.[4] What matters is what things *do* in their co-working wholes – not the static descriptions of the separate machine parts – what things *are* – that all too often are given priority in archaeology. As Harman formulates in his introduction to Object-Oriented Ontology (OOO) in *Immaterialism*, emphasising a stance towards the mainstream Actor-Network Theory (ANT):

> The track record of ANT in dealing with objects is decidedly mixed. In one sense it already incorporates objects into social theory as much as anyone could ask for. ANT offers a flat ontology in which anything is real insofar as it *acts*, an extremely broad criterion that grand equal initial weight to supersonic jets, palm trees, asphalt, Batman, square circles, the Tooth Fairy, Napoleon III, al-Farabi, Hillary Clinton, the city of Odessa, Tolkien's imagery Rivendell, an atom of copper, a severed limb, a mixed heard of zebras and wildebeests, the non-existent 2016 Chicago Olympics, and the constellation of Scorpio, since they all are equally objects: or rather, all are equally *actors*. OOO could hardly be more inclusive of objects than ANT, and in some respects, it is even less so. Yet in another sense, ANT loses objects completely, by abolishing any hidden depth in things while reducing them to their actions. After all, you and I or a machine are not just what we happen to be doing at the moment, since we could easily be acting otherwise, or simply lying dormant, without thereby becoming utterly different things. Instead of replacing objects with a description of what they do (as in ANT) or what they are made of (as in traditional materialism), OOO uses the term 'object' to refer to any entity that cannot be paraphrased in terms of either its components or its effects.[5]

The contemporary domain does not offer shortcuts to definite answers, but could certainly expand our understanding of the wider contexts and dynamics of existential entities, and has a potential to narrow the gap between past and present. However, the supermodern notion of the gap between past and present is constantly kept open by the archaeological promoting of the *dissimilarities* between what was and what is – the intricate alterations in social systems and roles, gender and labour, consumption, stone vs. metal, analogue vs. digital.

Of course, the discipline of archaeology, with its fine-tuned attentiveness to materiality, its accumulated knowledge, theory and methods, makes and has made major contributions in expanding our vision of bygone times. What is the archaeological past is what things remember, the marks that are embedded in things from actions and happenings they were part of. In what way the fractures in stone tools bear the marks of how they were shaped. How comparisons of recent experiments and archaeological material reveal trends in work processes, the practical use of experimental instruments – the cutting, scraping and piercing of different materials – producing wear-marks to be compared to antique use-wear. How symbolic values or inscriptions of settlements and monuments can be read in landscapes and seascapes. Insignificant pieces of organic material may reveal significant chemical or genetic signatures that may reveal provenance, isotopes that tell of the approximate time that they lived, like the radiocarbon dating method. This is merely a faction of the archaeological toolbox, designed to read and develop what objects 'remember', those objects being both more (and less) than their *components* and *effects*. I could also add a wide knowledge about observed human dynamics in societies around the world from ethnography and anthropology – practices and rituals, social and singular, theoretical models – but I think the point has been made. Nevertheless, even the most elaborate archaeological tools can only manage to shed light on fragments of what once were machines in lived human lives.

Home is something we are so close to that we do not see

What, then, are *homes*? Actually, the more I think of it, the harder it is to reach an all encompassing definition. As soon as I have formulated something that I think circumscribes this all-too-common thing, something different pops up that is also a home. What a home is is self-evident to a point that it escapes any simple delineation, like 'time', in parallel both universal and specific.

First, I tried to seek a general understanding from the internet, and bumped into a wide range of wall-art definitions:

Home [*hohm*] noun
A place where love resides, memories are created, friends always belong, and laughter never ends.[6]

A place that feels like a tight hug: where time stands still for just a moment, where the noise of the outside world is blocked out and where you can breathe it all out after being tense all day. From the moment you enter the door, you are safe, you are warm, and you are loved.[7]

'Home is where your Wi-Fi connects automatically' is found on T-shirts that may be ordered. A more general set of definitions are found in *The New Penguin English Dictionary*:

Home /homh/noun
1 the place where one lives permanently, *esp* with one's family, or as a member of a household. **2** a house, flat, apartment, etc. **3** the social unit constituted by a family living together: *She comes from a broken home.* **4** one's native region or country: *I regard the Midland as my home.* **5** the social of professional environment to which one belongs: *The stage was my home from an early age.* **6** the place where a certain object is kept: *I must find a home for the new picture.* **7** the place of origin of something: *Welcome to Oxford, the home of pressed steel.* **8** an establishment providing residence and care, *esp* for children, the elderly, or those physically or mentally unfit to look after themselves. **9** the finishing point in a race. **10** in board games, where you are safe from attack. **11** in computing, the beginning of the line or file one is in.[8]

Although the definition is intended to be general and all-encompassing, I find that something is below the radar: *things*. Definitions omit the fact that homes are entanglements of people and *things*, more than 'the place where a certain object is kept'. Clearly, the social dimension is allotted a dominant role in the general understanding of 'home'. Admittedly, a home could very well be a place for love and eternal laughter (although this sounds like a bit of an ordeal to me), but a home with problems will still be thought of as home, even if there is more warmth and love at the pub or the place you work.

Et hjem: Der alle vil deg vel.   1947.

Figure 49. 'A home: Where all wish you well.' Mommo added these words to this peaceful photo of Faste reading the paper in her cosy living room.

Homes are often thought of as places for families – but there are millions of well-established homes that are not for families. People may choose to reside alone, with friends, in collectives to share costs, and still may have worthy homes – in fact, homes for single persons seem to be increasing in number, and may be just as good as any other home.

Many would say that home is about 'identity and roots', the place where you were brought into the world with parental guidance. But most people eventually establish perfect homes in new places. The phrase 'my home is my castle' hints at a place of safety, but many are also known to be the opposite, as places of domestic abuse indicate. You may rest, sleep and eat well in hotels and restaurants, but even the best of them are not counted as homes. Your fridge could be emptied, your bed could be merely a sheet of cardboard, and still, the place would be spoken of as home. Even most homeless people have a place that they think of as home, a place that they return to, a place that contains belongings, lavish or sparse alike. Most people move around as life passes, and have many homes in a sequence – I count that I have already had 22. Homes are related to places, but are not necessarily fixed positions. They could be tents, boats, vans – mobile homes.

Nevertheless, it strikes me that it is the *social aspects* that foreground what is thought of as 'home'. When someone tells that there is 'trouble at home', I guess that your first thought is that a household member may drink too much, that a teenager may have been expelled from school and now is grounded, or that there is a father who spends his rare moments at home in unpredictable rage, or similar mischiefs among the *human* household members. Your first thought is hardly about the multitude of material components of a home – a plumbing deficit, that a leg of the favourite chair has snapped, a problem with the TV or coffee machine – or a broken hammer for that matter.[9] Similarly, on learning about 'a happy home', your first thought is probably not about well-sharpened kitchen knives, or that the light bulbs have been exchanged with LED, that the garage workshop is finally organised to perfection, that new warming carpets have been installed, or that there are no squeaking doors. Your initial 'happy home' association is healthy social relations between the human members of the home. However, if asked, most people would agree that a place without things can rarely be counted as a home. Things that are present and well-functioning tend to be taken for granted, as are most things that are near to you.

'How are things at home?' This is a normal and acceptable question from close friends and relatives. The same question from a person behind the counter in the hardware store, or an electrician (who actually *is* a professional in things in a home), would be taken as impertinent, a violation of the private sphere. Again, the myriad actual things in a home are not what is addressed here.

Obviously, the social is given a prerequisite role in our understanding of a home. The imperative material parts of homes are taken for granted, not counted – like the afore-mentioned 'unsupported solo expedition to the South Pole', or Heidegger's 'broken hammer'. Homes may be poor, wealthy, elegant, disorganised, joyful, short-lived, cosy, cold, or creepy – nevertheless, there are none without things.

Perhaps your thingly home is best seen when you are not at home, as the novelist Karl Ove Knausgård observes in how he sees his home on returning from a vacation abroad:

> There was a distance in the homely then, as if it was familiar and new in the same instance. The house smelled like before, but there was a smell that I usually did not apprehend. My room was slightly estranged, as I suddenly saw what I usually did not see. The orange bed. The shiny ball shaped lamp on the desk, the green motley pattern on the linoleum-covered floor. The school rucksack that leaned on a leg of the desk. The poster of 'Wings' on the wall. This strangeness also rested in the slope of the street outside, which I shortly ran up. All the houses lined up, the cars that were parked in front of them, glistening in the greasy light from the setting sun where it hung burning above the treetops in the west. After some hours it was gone. Then, everything was like before. It was there, it surrounded me completely, it was my world and my life, but invisible. And it is home. Home is something we are so close to that we do not see.[10]

What a home can be and what a home does for people reaches far and wide. Homes constitute starting points for meeting new days and provide bases to return to after days have come to an end, to meet another night, rest, sleep. Homes are bases for possessions, materials, equipment and tools, and grant various kinds of ownership rights. Your home provides that your next day starts among the same things that were routinely employed the previous day. Basic skills are closely related to these objects, practically and mentally. The co-residence with things evokes a certain stability – actions may be different, but things are handled more or less as they were the day before. Thus, there is an intrinsic 'gravity' in the thingly realm that produces a certain repetition in how humans act out their days, and plays an active role in shaping futures. Additionally, homes frequently accumulate things from many yesterdays, and produce configurations that reveal the traditions and lifestyles of past days. Thus, things that furnish homes are more than their daily presence – they also embrace past and future. To quote Bjørnar Olsen:

> Our active cohabitation with things regulates and routinises our behaviour, making it repetitive and recognisable; we repeat certain actions by habits, by bodily skills instructed and impelled by the things themselves. Through this interchange actions become standardised and predictable, producing what we like to think of as (social) structures and institutions.[11]

'What is remembered correctly is never up to you to decide'

I have this habit, alike with most, I guess, to blend the scholarly, novels, movies and news with the things I sense and experience from my being-in-the-world. I cannot decide if it is a problem. If this mixture reduces perspectives to a particular subjectivity, that hampers my ability to perceive the general. Or perhaps, more optimistically, it brings on a receptive and constructive openness. As with most other things, impressions probably mingle into something that is hard to sort out in detail. Indisputably, 'nothing floats into the world from nowhere'. The struggle to sort out where it all comes from, to decide if things are (objectively) valid or (subjectively) dubious may make you lose the point. Right or wrong, I will risk proceeding along this blended, blurred and constantly furcating path.

As argued, even as my memories from the two recent homes have 'faces' and relate to the lived lives of people I know well, the memories that are evoked are my own. Events may be partly told, partly experienced, but full knowledge of the personal memories in things is exclusive. Memories depend on someone remembering, as Marie Persson states.[12] I can never know my father's memories of things, not even his memories of the frying pan that he used to prepare his last supper, still with faint residues of the actual meal. Neither could my uncle know his mother's full remembering of the black vase on top of the fireplace, or the miniature flamenco dancer. I believe that even my own fluctuating memories of things are impossible to deplete, like the furniture covers in our living room. The associations they carry are always related to sentimental, practical and social contexts that may vary beyond what it is possible to explore.

Remembrance is no reliable measure. The reason for this, once again according to Karl Ove Knausgård, is that 'remembrance does not prioritise the value of truth. Remembrance is pragmatic, it is sly and cunning, but not in a hostile or evil way – on the contrary, it strives to please its host. Something is pushed towards the empty void of oblivion, something is twisted to inconspicuousness, something is gallantly misunderstood, and yet other things, and these other things are close to nothing, are remembered sharply, clearly and correctly. What is remembered correctly is never up to you to decide.'[13]

Thus, memories are always subjective and individual – even collective memories are not the same for all. More than 'collective', collective memories are beliefs that are agreed upon, mixed with personal engagements, experiences, what is told – the outcome is as unique as your fingerprint. What things may remember is closely connected to the experiences of being a member of the world – phenomenology. In Bjørnar Olsen's words, phenomenology is 'concerned with the world as it manifests itself to those who take part in it'. He proceeds to point out that 'the phenomenological approach to human perception implies our relatedness to the world as entangled beings fundamentally involved in networks of human and non-human beings'. Furthermore, he argues, 'we relate to the world not (only) as thinking subjects but also as bodily objects – our '*being-in*' this world is a concrete existence of involvement that unites us with the world'.[14]

For obvious reasons, the phenomenological experiment that is laid out in the famous paper 'What Mary Didn't Know'[15] has never materialised. It is about Mary, a woman who has lived all her life in an isolated chamber without colours, equipped, however, with all possible sensual information of the world. Would she, on the day of her release, experience colours as she had envisioned? Or would she exclaim, flabbergasted by seeing a banana for the first time, 'but why is it blue?'

In parallel, memories are closely related to phenomenology. Memories cannot be understood in a void – their connections to experiences from lives lived in the world are imperative to their ability to speak. This is the basics of memory – the associations of our sensing of things (seeing, listening, smelling) with certain places, persons, shapes and surfaces, evoked in associative chains and labelled 'memories'.

There is a passage in *Tyven* (The Thief), one of Göran Tunström's novels, that I like to remember – it illustrates how humans (and probably many other organisms) constantly link things and experiences in associative chains. It is about a man travelling in the Scandinavian woods. He arrives at a lumberjack camp. It is totally silent, but there is smoke rising from the cabin's chimney. As he enters, he sees all the lumberjacks occupied in wood carving. After a brief welcome, the cook explains that they have engaged in a task that they all believed was easy – to make a 'kofes':

> 'And what is a kofes?', the traveller asks.
> 'There are two simple rules to what a kofes is', the cook explains. 'Firstly, a kofes may be anything. Secondly, it must not resemble anything but itself'.[16]

In spite of all their efforts, all the things the men struggled to shape, it was always something else that the object would resemble – a face, a horse's back, a crocodile, a beetle, a swimming bird, a cloud, a boat, a pebble, a ladle. Nothing could qualify as a 'kofes', no object could be made that was free of any likeness to something else.

This is an example of how simple and self-evident things are – and also illustrates the complexity, the ever-present ability of things to relate, to be many things in the same. Evidently, memories are closely connected to associations with materiality. Nevertheless, as in the referred dictionary definition of 'home', the social dimension is likewise emphasised in explanations of 'memory':

> **memory 1** the brain's or an individual's ability to remember experience in general or to recall particular experiences: *She was endowed with extraordinary powers of memory.* **2** the store of things learned and retained from an

individual's experience: *I searched my memory for his name.* **3** an image or impression of somebody or something stored in the brain: *She had no memory of the incident; It brought back many happy memories.* **4** the time within past events can be or are remembered: *The event was within living memory.* **5** commemorative remembrance: *The townspeople had erected a statue in memory of their previous MP.* **6a** a device, esp. in a computer, into which data can be inserted for storage, and from which it may be extracted when wanted. **6b** the capacity of a device for storing information. **7** the capacity of a material, e.g., metal or plastic, to show effects resulting from past treatment, or to return to a former condition.[17]

Again, the imperative role of things and materiality is eluded, and explanations amplify the role of the mental, the intrinsic conceptual trajectories within human brains.

Paradoxically, popular wall-art posters are more precise – at least the table is brought to the fore:

The fondest memories are made when we gather around the table.[18]

In any case, the imperative role of things is clearly downplayed. Most often, it is our engagements with things that evoke memories, as the latter are, in a way, stored in the former. It is a well-known fact that things often trigger lively and precise memories and conversations about past events and experiences among people with dementia who are otherwise utterly confused about most of their present surroundings. Even jokes – I have been searching my repertoire, and struggle to find jokes that are free of things that bring forward the absurdities, the surprises, the funny misreadings and illogicalities that we normally laugh about. Jokes need a quite a lot of shared understanding, but, in detail, the associative trajectories are always subjectively unique. Perhaps this is why jokes are not funny for all.

Although difficult to prove, the proximity between objects and memories, and how things hold remembrance was probably very similar for most Stoneagers. There were other objects, their experiences of the world were different, associations took other flights, but it is unreasonable to believe that bodily necessities and intellectual capacities have changed much during the last millennia. In assessing deep past remembrance, we need to acknowledge the 'global sameness' in how the world responds to us as bodily humans.

Learning about the world is a mixture of things that are told and learned, and others that are experienced by interacting. It is hard to prove, but even harder to disprove, that the Stoneagers observed, made sense of and acted upon a similar materiality. What burns, what doesn't. The difference between a rising tide and its ebb. The abilities in materials – how they may be shaped, what they may be used for. The differences between up and down, cold and warm, salt and sweet. Thus, our own experiences of the world are always engaged in our visions of how past lives were lived – authorised researchers and laymen alike. These basic, ever-present existential 'planetary facts' are involved without us even thinking about it.

Tim Ingold addresses something similar in the introductory part of his book *Being Alive*,[19] where he advises the reader to 1) wet a stone and watch it dry, illustrating the complexity of materiality; 2) to sense her/his whereabouts and connectedness to the world by walking without shoes; and 3) to saw a plank in two to feel the intricate interplay between bodily action, tool and materiality in even the most mundane of operations, things we just do without second thought. The awareness of the shared things in being alive on this planet is also what Åsgarden is about, as the adjacent cliffs offer the same ring to 'baby squeals', independent of time – these are among the plentiful phenomena we omit to cleanse our scientific reporting of the 'irrelevant'.

As little (but also as much, to be more optimistic) as I can relate to the individual memories in the homes of my father and uncle, can I relate to Stone Age memories. According to my own memories, all sensing and remembrance relates to the masses of banalities from observations and what we have learned about how things work in the world.

Rhythms of temporality

Allegedly, Franz Kafka once described 'art' as a clock running too fast. I hesitate to compare archaeology to a clock running too slow, although I sense that a lifetime in archaeology has accentuated a feeling of continually being too late – as if seeing things in a blurred rear-view mirror. I should have studied things before decomposition had taken its toll, or when ancient traditions and skills still were alive, before the layers of dusty oblivion had settled.

Elin and I once came close to catching up with past times when travelling along the Pacific coast in southern Chile in 2001. It was during a study trip in the wake of the famous American archaeologist Junius Bird and his *Travels and Archaeology in Southern Chile* in the 1930s.[20] Bird and his wife Margret had travelled by car to Puerto Montt, sold the car to buy a boat, and continued through the archipelagos to the south, exploring and excavating along the way. Elin and I followed the tracks by the coastal steamer to Puerto Edén, where the Birds had anchored almost 70 years earlier. The 'hospidaje' where we stayed was situated on top of the ancient shell midden, lithic artefacts strewn on the beach below. Junius Bird had photographed the place, inhabitants and dwellings in 1933, when the Kaweskar Indians still resided in their traditional huts, and still added shells to the midden. 1933 was the very the year of my mother's birth – time was narrowing in. Gabriela, a similar-aged Kaweskar woman we got to know, was born in just such a hut. She made us whale-bone harpoons and basketry from grass in her garden.

I scrutinised what Bird had reported of the Kaweskars in the settlement, but was surprised to find that Bird had been preoccupied with seeing details of their equipment, comparing traditional mountings and lashings – all the time he had had an unlimited opportunity to ask directly about so much more of the hunter-gatherers' lifestyle. Maybe Bird had lived the problems I only was able to imagine after bringing my imaginary Stoneager friend to my home.

At school, we learned about a woman who always managed to make perfect soft-boiled eggs – the white always firm, the yolk smooth and runny – every time. As she had no clock, she was asked about how she managed to time the eggs to such perfection. The woman had replied, 'I'm not sure, but I think that God is assisting me. When I put in the eggs, I start singing this psalm to praise the Lord, all the verses, and I take out the eggs as the psalm finishes.' As we listened, and without saying it directly, the class was led to believe that the spiritual atmosphere spilled into the eggs, somehow. Perhaps it did, but the fact that the timing of singing the song and boiling the eggs were a perfect match did not occur to me until later, after the spiritual message in the story had had its intended effect.

There is a passage in *The Christmas Oratorio* of Göran Tunström. The main character has returned to his little home town. The town is the same, but different, as are its inhabitants, and as he is, too, as he has become a celebrity since he had lived there. The situation accentuates the natural focus on what was before and what is in the now. On strolling the main street in the afternoon rush, he happens to stop in front of the exhibition window of jewellers' store, looking at the swarm of clocks, in the window and on the many shelves inside the shop. The clocks and watches are in all kinds of shapes and colours – tiny and elegant women's arm wrist watches bordering on pure adornment, and similar ones for men, oozing subtle masculinity. There are alarm clocks in many shapes, larger clocks for wall mounting, smaller ones that can be folded in boxes and suitable for travel. Some are clearly in fashion, with digital displays, others with hands, some of them plainly old-fashioned, as if they can barely keep up with their own time. There are bombastic clocks to be placed on mantelpieces or prominent shelves, classy, showing time hastily moving forward in an aura of timelessness. It suddenly occurs to the man that none of the clocks displays the same time. One of them shows 10:12, the adjacent one 15:16, another past six, and others that have already reached evening – a myriad of different times are unfolding, ticking along at their own pace. A few have stopped – clinging on to their ability to show the right time twice in every 24 hours. Included in their asynchronity is also their destiny to be synchronous at a certain moment, only to tick along at their own pace in the next instant. The man turns around and sees the crowd of townspeople in the street. It is all about the same, people ticking along at their own time and speed, struggling, strolling, loitering, or hurrying to and from – the community is made up of this swarm of individuals at their own pace, with their many destinies, from where, to where. Nonetheless, they are all within the same existence, a perpetual row of parallel lives, encounters, departures through time.[21]

The many temporalities of planet Earth are decisive in how it is experienced. Human senses are tuned in to a specific segment of temporality, but there are many more. A TV documentary I watched displayed starfish moving along the seabed in fast-forward – it was fascinating to watch them shooting back and forth like mice. Frequently, they happened to meet. Each time, before passing, they felt the other, and raised one of their arms like a greeting. However, such movements are too slow for the human eye. In fact, temporal differences may be the key to the modernist notions of the culture-nature and animate-inanimate dichotomies – of will-powered and highly visible human actions, as opposed to the repetitive and seemingly unchanging natural world. Nevertheless, we cannot doubt the slow changes in the Amazonas ecosystem, continental drift, or the growth of crystals in the molten masses of the planet. Tim Morton tells about listening to *air pressure fluctuations* above the Atlantic Ocean in Felix Hess's sound art project in New York, the sound recordings sped up 360 times.[22] In the 27-kilometre-long ring of superconducting magnets in the Large Hadron Collider (LHC) in Cern, scientists seek glimpses of things too small and too fast for the human eye.[23] These are merely a fraction of the myriads of temporal rhythms in the machines in the world – rhythms that are decisive in if and how they co-operate.[24]

Jeffry C. Hall, Michael Rosbash and Michael W. Young were awarded a Nobel Prize in 2017 for their ground-breaking research on how 'short time' is embedded in organisms. The suprachiasmic nucleus (SCN) in nerve cells in humans, plants and animals includes a gene that produces a protein that builds up in cells overnight, then breaks down during the day.[25] We learn of the eternal pulses of life, and how their multitudes are included in notions of 'circadian time' – the wheel or spiral of time. Circadian time is opposed to the 'arrow of time', the unidirectional, linear notion of time that characterises modernity – 'big time', that includes the *long-durée*, the Stone Age, dinosaurs, continental drift and the Big Bang, alike with the eternal and the distant future.

As far as I can see, most dictionary definitions of 'time' pertain to linear time, 'what clocks measure', 'a linear continuum of instants', 'a continuum that lacks spatial dimensions',[26] as is the case in the *Oxford Dictionary*:

> The indefinite continued progress of existence and events in the past, present, and future regarded as a whole.[27]

Perhaps the British philosopher J.M.E. McTaggart's famous 1908 paper 'The Unreality of Time'[28] messed up something straightforward that most people thought they already knew, in elaborating on 'tensed and tenseless theories of the passage of time'. Tenseless time entails an understanding similar to that of the Yanomamö Indian Rerebawä, a close proximity between past, present and future – before, now and after, as parts of a unity. There are ample thoughtful and elegant writings that expand on this theme of things and time, in philosophy and fiction as well as in archaeology, of which I unfortunately only know fragments and am by no means in position to surpass.[29]

The many-sided debates surrounding the physical phenomena of time are plenty interesting. However, the issue here is more in the line with how time is sensed, experienced and accumulated in human remembrance – and how this has changed over time. Presumably, there must be a difference in how notions of time, yesterdays, today and tomorrows are thought of in the present, in accelerating modernity, compared to the flow of seemingly identical everydays in deep pre-modernity. Quite commonly, time is referred to as running fast, or as dragging along too slowly. These contrasting adverbs have little to do with the accuracy in how time is measured – fast and slow are personal experiences that relate to individual circumstances. Are there reasons to suspect that people of the past did not also sense this variability in the passing of time? How was time experienced in the past?

Above all, 'circadian time' is accentuated in the highly distinguishable circles of life – night and day, tidal movements, lunar sequences and constellations of stars, years and seasons, the return of migratory birds and fish, the season of eggs and spawning – life and death. Similar asynchronous pulses are also noticeable within human bodies – heartbeats, the need to sleep, the female menstruation sequence, birth, learning to grab, walk and speak, the breaking of the male voice, ageing and death.

I believe that there might be some timeless commonplace ground in these orbits – independent of time itself, so to speak. My father and uncle, and myself, along with the readers of these lines, are all similarly involved in circadian time, the circles of life, the physical clocks embedded in the rotations of the earth and its circling around the sun, that also spill over into our repeated routines during the days. My father's life circulated according to coffee and news on radio, the chewing of his almonds 30-fold, the checking of the mailbox, the planning of dinner, the preparing and of eating it, the post-dinner nap, the routine of television (including a snack). These routines were the small circles within the bigger ones – the season for spouting snowdrops, the springtime when the willow bark would loosen to allow for the making of flutes, the busy time in mid-May when all too many wanted new garments for the national day, the forthcoming preparations to launch the boat, the coming of mackerels, the season for crabs, and the spectacular colouring of the autumn trees, which also marked the time to land the boat on its winter docking rack in the garden.

I suspect that my father could have had lengthy and meaningful conversations with Rerebawä about the spirals of time, and how it spills into our routines. The subject could also be common ground for myself and my imagined Stoneager friend, frequently bringing attention to phenomena we both know. Perhaps my father (and I) would have leaned more heavily on what we have learned from science about causal effects and the correlation of physical relations – as opposed to the considerably higher level of attentiveness to environmental detail from them. All of us, nonetheless, would have been similarly confident in how the world works, mixing myths, observations and science.

The perpetual pulses of circadian time are constants in the world – they belong to the planetary 'symbiotic real',[30] are facts of life that were perhaps even more important and tangible to past people than to members of modernity. The sensible aspect of unidirectional linear time is different. In our time, we are immersed in a swarm of arrows of time, in signs of accelerating changes – in technology, photography and written accounts, fashions and styles, professions, political regimes. The list of changes is hard to exhaust. We remember our own childhood as something that happened in a different world. The toys cherished, the plays played, the sweets, house rules and chances of summer jobs – they are all different, and most of our losses are compensated by new things and traditions. In Annie Ernaux's words, 'new things emerged with shorter and shorter intervals, and made the past move backwards'.[31] Inevitably, the accelerating changes in materiality signify the arrow of time. We are surrounded by reminders of linear time:

> ...time measurements that homogenise every moment of our life and then enable us to quantify it. As a result, people of today think of time as something that can be saved, consumed, lost, gained and sold, just as money is.[32]

The material remains from deep time display another, much slower pace – things seem to change little over centuries and even millennia. Partly, this could be explained by the coarse-grained archaeological record. Of course, people in deep time, Stoneagers, must have been able to sense elements of linear time, in happenings, fatal accidents or bygone scarcities, an abandoned encampment or a truce among clans that traditionally had been hostile. Nevertheless, *long-durée* remembrance is essential to understanding the ability of past peoples to sense and act upon the considerable environmental changes of past millennia. What they sensed and assessed in active life was normally local weather – what mechanisms could bring the much slower, unseen changes to attention?[33]

Deep time may easily have been included in a notion of perpetual past-present-future confinement, as Rerebawä expressed after seeing the Roman ruins. It would also have been possible to find places that were seemingly outside of the circles of life, in the darkness of caves, devoid of sounds, scents, movements, and time.[34] In spite of observing decay and layers of dust, there are reasons to believe that time was sensed differently back then, in the Stone Age – and it is reasonable to believe that notions of circadian time dominated.

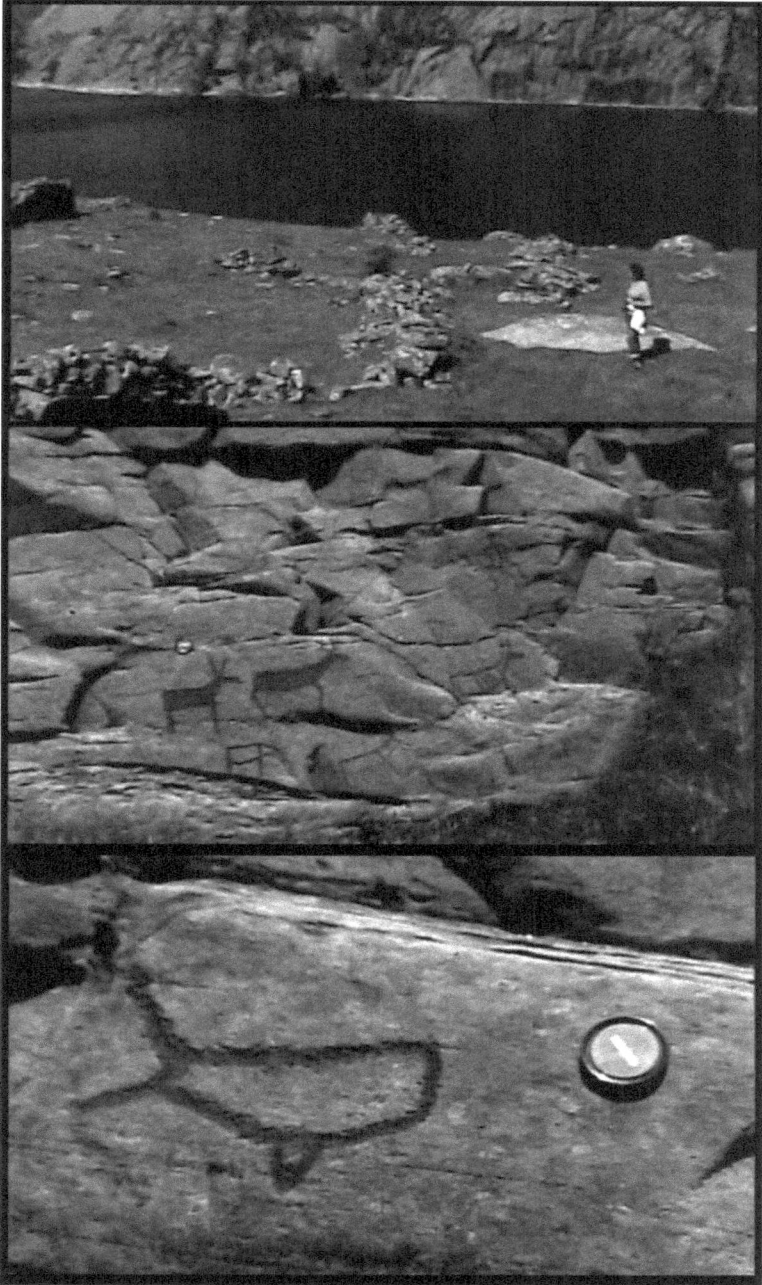

Figure 50. From my father's movie of a visit to the rock art site in Vingen, Western Norway.

Of course, how time is sensed is closely connected to environmental interplay, as Pelle Tejsner has shown in the responses to climate change among the fishermen in Qeqertarsuaq, Western Greenland.[35] The research-based supermodern climate-crisis narrative blends in nicely with a notion of a linear and unidirectional timescale – there is no going back, and to deviate ill-fated trends demands substantial effort on a global scale. Global environmental change needs to be halted, forced to stabilise, frozen to its 'natural state'. Naturally, one would suspect marginal societies like that in Qeqertarsuaq to be more exposed and vulnerable to the effects of the recorded changes, in parallel with amplified concerns for the future – in short, that the climate-crisis narrative would be the same, but with amplified consequences and anxieties.

However, what Tejsner encountered was a notion of the environment as being in 'a constant process of becoming'.[36] To adapt, humans have to 'move *with* the forces in their surroundings, not attempting to control, master or fundamentally alter them'.[37] Embedded in the fishermen's ontology is 'Sila', which includes both environmental 'moods' and how their engagements with local habitats must be handled with flexibility, patience and enduring openness. Subsequently, 'time' is envisioned differently – preconceived timetables, clock and calendars are useless in administering actions. A great many parallel examples of similar worldviews can probably be found in other 'untamed' societies around the world.

By all means, worries about climate change should not be cancelled, but the notion of 'Sila' is worth reflecting upon. There are quite a few problems that we ascribe to environmental change that could be redeemed by more spatial elasticity and timely patience – not to cross the mountain or fjord during the worst days, to avoid structural investments in terrains that are occasionally owned by unmanageable forces. The lack of patience and flexibility and enduring openness in modernity are perhaps as much to blame for our calamities as changes in the environment. Perhaps this seeking to combine linear and circular time is somewhat similar to the 'Generative Life Cycle Model' suggested by Yoko Yamada and Kato Yoshinobu.[38]

Mingled in these notes, willingly or not, are my own involvements in sensing the world and the passage of time. I keep wondering about how many of the things harvested from these individual, personal perceptions are relevant to the understanding of being a member of deep time. Perhaps it is worthwhile consulting the only human that I truly know (?) in life in this assessment: myself. Admittedly, this person is a white male in his late 60s, and so much more that clearly disqualifies him from general insights. Despite this, I will risk being more explicit about my lived experiences, about my encounters with life, things, time and remembrance, along with thoughts about people who lived other lives in the past.

Imploding megastructures

The gradual and hesitant acknowledgement of the fact that you have more past than future in life is perhaps a mellow moment. Fortunately, my own age is well beyond this, and yet nowhere near the point in life when my father reached his last day. Nevertheless, I hesitate to calculate and mark this date in my own calendar. It is a day of concern that the invention of the calendar involuntarily imposed on linear-timers. Göran Tunström measured out the 54 years, nine months and 23 days of his father's life in his own almanac.[39] I now know what Tunström probably never could work out – that he surpassed the age of his father by eight years, eight months and 21 days.

My friend Henning once told me that he had read that routinely jogging adds two more years to your life. Unfortunately, he added, this is also the approximate time you have spent jogging. His unspoken meaning was that calculators and statistics are perhaps not the best instruments to learn about 'being alive'.

They are certainly not to be counted in days, the two phases I can sense in my own life. Initially, when you are brought into the world, there is a phase of learning, adapting and adhering to the world. It is a pursuit to grasp ever-larger pieces of the world as it *is*, as some kind of *static planetary entity*. The second phase in life occurred to me as I realised that very few things in the world can be seen as stable – in fact, most things, even the precious things I want to keep, are fluctuant. The struggle for 'more' is redirected towards 'containing' things, to preserve the existentials that I have adhered to and based my life on.

Children are known to be very receptive, and the human ability to learn, to copy and cope, to communicate and so much more early in life is probably embedded in the depths of humanity. Subsequently, there is an unstoppable urge to consume more of the entities that make up the world – people, materiality, creatures, the laws of physics, the ever-expanding accumulation of skills, places you have been, things you have done, achievements and lavish corrective responses. You need more time, more initiative, more strength and effort to enlarge your share of planetary affluence. *Time is all too slow.*

This initial phase gradually evolves into an awareness of failing to keep it all contained – an amplified consciousness of change, loss, deprivation. In parallel, there is an increased sense of an ever-moving world. *Time is all too fast.*

As this decisive and mellow moment unfolded to me at the age of 50-something, I was not prepared.

I was killing time in my hotel room during a conference, in the white hotel bathrobe, 'steaming off' after a shower, awaiting the time when I could meet people in the bar before dinner. I turned on the TV – as usual, I could not figure out the remote control, and happened to see channels rarely visited. It was the National Geographic Channel, showing a programme in their series *Demolishing Megastructures* – cunning arrangements of explosives designed to detonate in a certain sequence that made the huge constructions collapse in a controlled manner without damage to nearby structures. Large sports arenas, multi-storey car parks, hotels that city development had left behind in unfavourable places – one after another, the huge structures fell down into a perfect pile of rubble within a giant plume of dust. I liked to watch the slow-motion footage that showed the sequence of meticulously placed and timed detonations. There was a certain beauty to it – it was as though the megastructures melted, became fluid and slowly settled on the ground. The shape of the dust cloud that emerged from all openings – for a brief moment, the dust formation retained the ghostly shape of the structure that had been there the millisecond before, before gradually losing its shape as the cloud expanded towards the camera, which in the next moment was immersed in turbulent debris. Then, the same sequence from a different angle. There was a perverted aesthetic to this controlled destruction of the giants – the scale, the power, the know-how. It reminded me of the brief satisfaction of smashing glass bottles and lightbulbs as a kid.

I was already looking forward to the next monster falling, to seeing the scenic devastation of a new megastructure. It was the Seattle Kingdome Sports Arena.[40] The *Kingdome*? I could hardly believe it. I had been there, in that very building, in 1980 – it had been among the many wonders of my first visit to the USA. I was newly married, and our firstborn son Kyrre was only months old – it was a time in life when our days were saturated with future prospects. At the time, the Kingdome was less than four years old, new, enormous, impressive, one of the many proofs that everything was bigger in the 'States', a token of better times to come. I attended an indoor leisure-boat exhibition with powerful speed boats and huge yachts on display – never had I ever seen such an enormous building. Not long after, I watched an indoor motor-cross rally with artificial hilltops, broadcast on the TV from the same arena – the Kingdome was high on the list of things I had tried to describe to my friends upon returning to Norway: '...yes, you heard me right... an in-door M-C rally.'

It was new to me then, as I still thought in the moment of its controlled demolition on the TV in my hotel room that afternoon. In the wake of seeing this, I felt a sudden surge of age and loss, that a thing that was 'new' and spectacular to me could be deliberately taken out of the world, annihilated. It did not help much to discover that the video was several years old – the implosion of the Kingdome had happened in 2000, when the building was only 24 years old.

The fallen wonder in Seattle and the subsequent gentle touch of nostalgia made it clear that my ever-expanding connections to the world also entailed a loss. Embedded in this expansion was a parallel, ever-growing void, a loss of basal things I had trusted would continue – a feeling of being deprived of things that were dear.

First and foremost, it is things that visualise and make us sense the accelerating changes of modernity – they make us remember things we used to do that we do not practice any longer. Materiality makes us sense changes that are too slow for the naked eye, as they happen – they are fossils that remind us of practices that gradual reorientations in habits and routines obscure.

The atlas displays the French colonies, Yugoslavia and Persia, Burma. An old newspaper contains news that in hindsight seems strange, ads for sweets you cherished that have fallen out of production, forgotten TV programmes you uncritically gobbled. Talking with friends, you remember forgotten mates – the first time you tasted paprika. Houses that were pivotal are sold, demolished, exterminated. Hard-earned skills in athletics or music erode as they are no longer practised – origami, drumming, volleyball. My father's Jui-Jitsu book suggests defence strategies that no longer sound sane.

A different time in life comes to mind, as I hook up to associative chains in my memoryscape, evoking mundane trivialities of how learning to be an Earthling was experienced during childhood.

Figure 51. A stone age encampment I envisioned as a child – with skin versions of our own white canvas tents. A drawing from school.

In our living room back then, there was a dirty yellow carpet. Although hard and heavy, it could be lifted and thrown back in a certain twist to make a seemingly unruly shape that was in fact the very intention of the act: the carpet had now changed to a desert-coloured miniature world with hills and valleys. There were even cliffs and caves, and lowlands that bordered to the outside, which was the sea. My brothers and I moved into this landscape with our Lego men and houses (the nicest were our homes), fences and barns, sheep and cattle. Tractors and ploughed fields were aligned in parallel with the woven structure of the carpet, roads and parking lots for our matchbox vehicles. Boats were placed along the straight margins of the carpet – which looked like dock-sides – and (along with air-planes, helicopters and the occasional spaceship) could connect to other places (factories and cabins we owned, or hostile territories that had to be defeated). There could be a bear or a lion in the caves, perhaps a dinosaur behind the mountain, like in 'The Valley Time Forgot', a particularly enticing episode in the Tarzan magazine. There was a cowboy riding a horse on a hill, a gun at his hip. A police station with a jail, a hospital, and a quarter for the fire squad were musts – as dramatic incidents happened frequently: People fell into the water or got lost in the hills close to the dinosaur valley, houses caught fire, the lion escaped from the cave, cars crashed – emergency squads of all kinds were kept busy. All actors were voiced with a particular, estranged dialect we had learned from TV and radio – as spoken in Oslo. We never managed to fully develop this miniature world, there were always more arrangements to be done. Different scales were never an obstacle. On the side, I arranged an office, a stool and the smallest of the nested tables, and wrote a business letter:

> BLERCKSFIRESHOPSTATION
> WE NEED A HOSE WE SHALL USE TO PUT OUT FIRE WITH ≈≈≈ ≈≈≈≈≈ ≈≈
> (alluding to vigorous handwriting) AND A PUMP ≈≈ ≈≈≈≈ [41]

Outside, similar realities were played out on a larger canvas. We needed horses to get around, and it did not matter much that they were sticks – they were led to grass and water and cared for as much as any horse. Stick-horses were individually owned. As they were mounted, we mimicked the horse-like rhythm, and places that were normally close could suddenly be distant. An afternoon could contain many days and nights. More than attacking, we were attacked by imaginary enemies, and most times we got badly hurt. Nevertheless, we always got by – I strangely recall that I nourished my wounded state, enjoying the simple, bitter-sweet sensation of being hurt, but still managing to get by, despite a severe limp. The horse could always bring me to water if I could manage to mount it. I always could.

There was an intense presence in being immersed in this mixture of imagination, playing out things with playthings, actions and happenings. When things got going they were more real than reality.

A rare male bird that could lay eggs...

A vital part of adapting was the frequent disentangling of misunderstandings. I can vaguely remember believing that the pulsating, threatening sound from the fire-alarm siren in Florø, which alerted the volunteer fire brigade, was the sound of the actual fire. The dramatic incident of fire and the disturbing sound were one. Grown-ups who normally walked were running in the streets, people were shouting, there was the smoke, and sometimes a faint stingy scent and distant flames – we could see and hear it all by looking from the roof hatch. My father was among the volunteers. The 'sound of fire' meant that he had to let go of whatever he was doing – even if a pork cutlet had just been put on his dinner plate, he had to throw his fork and knife to the table and rush for his bike. On one occasion – I can remember it well because it included a trailblazing disentanglement – my father returned unexpectedly quickly, his cutlet still retaining enough heat to be relished. The alarm had been false, he explained. But how could that be – as I had evidently *heard* the fire? Thanks to my father, I now know the difference between the two.

I have learned about similar mixed-up beliefs. Our parents imprinted us with healthy advice about how to be attentive to traffic. This included 'never crossing the street before the car has passed'. My brother Snorre once told me that sometimes, when he was about to cross the road, there were no cars in sight. He was an obedient child, and patiently waited for a car to arrive and pass before he ventured to cross. Similarly, a colleague once told me that he could remember believing that it was waving branches in trees that made the wind – he could see that the two coincided, and observed that the more vigorously the branches flapped, the stronger the breeze. 'A man and a woman may not share a bed if they are not married', Mommo told me one time. As I could not understand the problem, she explained that they could 'end up having a baby'. I sensed that this narrowed in on unspoken territories and did not ask more questions – but I remember speculating on the fact that my parents actually *were* married, and had still ended up with me and my brothers.

I could have been eight or nine at the time, with an above average interest in birds. I had my own bird book, and was eagerly accompanying one of Pappa's friends, Hans, on bird-watching expeditions. I had learned the names of most of the local fowl, their songs and eggs, males from females, and dreamed about seeing exotic cranes or falcons, or herons close up. During this phase of attentiveness towards birds, there was a family Sunday dinner in our home. Now, it was the usual after-dinner conversations, my grandfather Oluf (snr.) in the yellow good chair, uncle Oluf (jnr.) in the other, uncle Magne and my father on the sofa – all in their tailored 'better suits' from the shop. The women were busy arranging coffee and cakes while brothers, nieces and nephews were running around. As the oldest of the kids, I liked to listen to this and that of what was talked about. Frequently there was something funny said – well-meant teasing was cherished – about close relatives, workmates and friends. For some reason, the chat floated onto the topic of birds – a subject I could skilfully contribute to. I happened to claim that 'I had heard about a bird species where it was the *male*, and not the *female*, that produced the eggs'. In the same instant, without even a millisecond of thinking, they all burst wholeheartedly into laughter. I could not understand their immediate and confident reaction – this gang of bird-ignorant tailors, how could they be so sure that no male bird, not even a rare toucan in the depths of the unexplored Amazonas, could lay eggs? The fact that it was the other way around, that the very definition of male and female was the egg-laying, did not occur to me. Anyway, the embarrassment led me to sort this out on my own.

Figure 52. Learning about the world by observing, listening, and making mistakes that are corrected. How could they know for sure that there didn't exist a single, rare fowl, where the male produced the eggs? From the left: my father, grandfather Oluf (snr.), me, and my uncles Alf and Andreas (husbands of my father's sisters, Ida and Ruth).

There is parental guidance, schools, education, hints and divulgences from friends – but a major part of how things in the world operate is ill-explained or unspoken. You have to engage with your surroundings to find out – with other people, animals and plants, sticks and stones. Confused beliefs are perhaps particularly common in childhood. Nevertheless, I must admit companionship with misunderstandings in times when I should have known better – as in the case of the 'steel wool'.

I can no longer remember where I got the bright yellow package of 'Svint stålull' (Swift Steel) wool from, but it was included in the modest toolkit brought to my simple kitchen when I moved to study at university. It was quite marginal in my regular chores – only in rare cases was it actually used, in accidents, to remove crusts from burned food. On one of the rare occasions it *was* used, I noticed the handwritten price on the box: 41 crowns. Jeeezus. I had never realized that steel wool was so costly – 41 crowns could have bought me seven pints of beer at the student club 'Hulen' (The Cave) at the time – and a hot dog on returning home. Strangely, steel wool was never mentioned by my father among his many other warnings of costly things we needed to be aware of – confectionery, steaks, long-distance calls or strawberry jam. After seeing the price, the wads of 'Svint' were applied even more carefully. When absolutely necessary, I ripped a small part off of the bigger pad – each time this nano-fine white powder was produced that instantly evoked a seemingly poisonous sting to the nose and throat. Perhaps it was this presumably advanced chemical component that drove the price up. Besides, it was annoying that the used slivers were short lived – they turned rusty after merely days and could only rarely be reused. Hence, my supply of steel wool lasted and lasted. Eventually, I needed to prioritise purchasing more. However, this revealed that the price was not 41 crowns, but only four. It turned out that I had misread the handwritten 4/- (four, sharp), believing that the decimal signifier '/' meant '1'.

In any case, it was a minor thing. Maybe it was exactly that miniscule importance that made it possible for the misunderstanding to live on for so long. Still, I had acted upon this misreading for years. How could I have known otherwise? Steel wool was never a theme during the years living with my family in Florø. Steel wool is among the mundane things that are rarely discussed – it was never touched upon during the next to all-encompassing beer-drinking conversations with my friends, nor did I ever dream of bringing up the price of steel wool in the engaged discussions. Ironically, I carried this very simple misreading alongside my university studies of geological principles, structure-functionalism in anthropology, and intricate relative dating methods in archaeology. The steel-wool truth was locked into a sphere that I had to learn of through my own engagement with the world, as with so many other things.

Even today, decades after learning the correct price of steel wool, an unspoken sense of steel-wool-stinginess lingers. As I know Elin would dispose of them on sight, I tend to hide the used wads behind the dishwasher detergent bottle, in the hope that they may be useful a second time.

Still, after more than half a century of apprenticeship in the 'school of life', I am far from fully educated in insights that involve choices, strategies and actions – politics, dietary components and what they do to the body, the habits of consumption and their consequences for global climate. I strongly suspect that this 'learning by engaging' – in parallel with 'getting by' with a portion of ignorance and misreading – is as true for the past as it is for the present, and as it will be in the future. Life depends on attuning to the planet Earth, but not on getting it all right at once.

I guess that past people adapted to the planet in much the same way as now, through this mix of being told things, of learning skills by playing and acting out, of feeling distress in failing or the bliss of success, of being corrected or advised.

I sense that there is a decisive difference in how time is sensed between 'now' and the distant past. Stone Age members adhered closer to the repeating circles of life, which spilled over into how they saw time. Certainly, the arrows of unidirectional time could be vaguely sensed – in the decay of things, the layers of dust that settled on things that stood still (probably more a question of the maintenance and renewal of the same parts), and in the communication of past events – but the signs of a changing world and a sense of loss were not by any means as distinctive as they are at our end of the timescale.

Circadian time, and how the world is learned, have probably not changed much. Stoneagers never experienced their accustomed bait suddenly failing to attract fish as before, flint not responding to the familiar techniques, or a certain tool-type suddenly becoming useless, like my own stereo-rack, and the myriads of piggy-banks that no longer receive coins.

Up until the game-changing Kingdome demolition, I had perhaps envisioned my engagement with the world as an ever-increasing operation of learning about an unruly-shaped mass – that the world was an existential entity that it was possible to embrace.

Perhaps most humans experience these fundamental stages in life at a certain age, the notion of expansion at some point shadowed by loss. But perhaps this sense of loss is related to a stage within the circles of time, announcing that a new, similar loop is under way.

I am confident that my father and uncle could sense their individual lives similarly. But how about people from a distant time? The initial adhering, the bouncy merging with what you are born into – this first phase likely pertains to most humans. The second phase, however, is perhaps more associated with the accelerating trajectories of modernity.

Owning slivers of eternity

How could it be that the exciting theories of Eric von Dänicken regarding extra-terrestrial influence were not acknowledged by scholarly authorities? As far as I could see at the time, he already possessed the images to prove his statements. How could it be questioned? I was in the final phase of my father's school of archaeology – my mentor was always eager to push bygone mysteries onto his sons. They were happy times, with few limitations as to what could be spun around the past. Like the fantasy-hinting at a buried pyramid, as he light-heartedly showed me the pointed rock in the path outside his workshop. It was not put forward as a fact, but it nevertheless had its effect – the slightest of possibilities are often the most tantalising. Maybe this was the first time that I felt an urge to excavate, to find out.

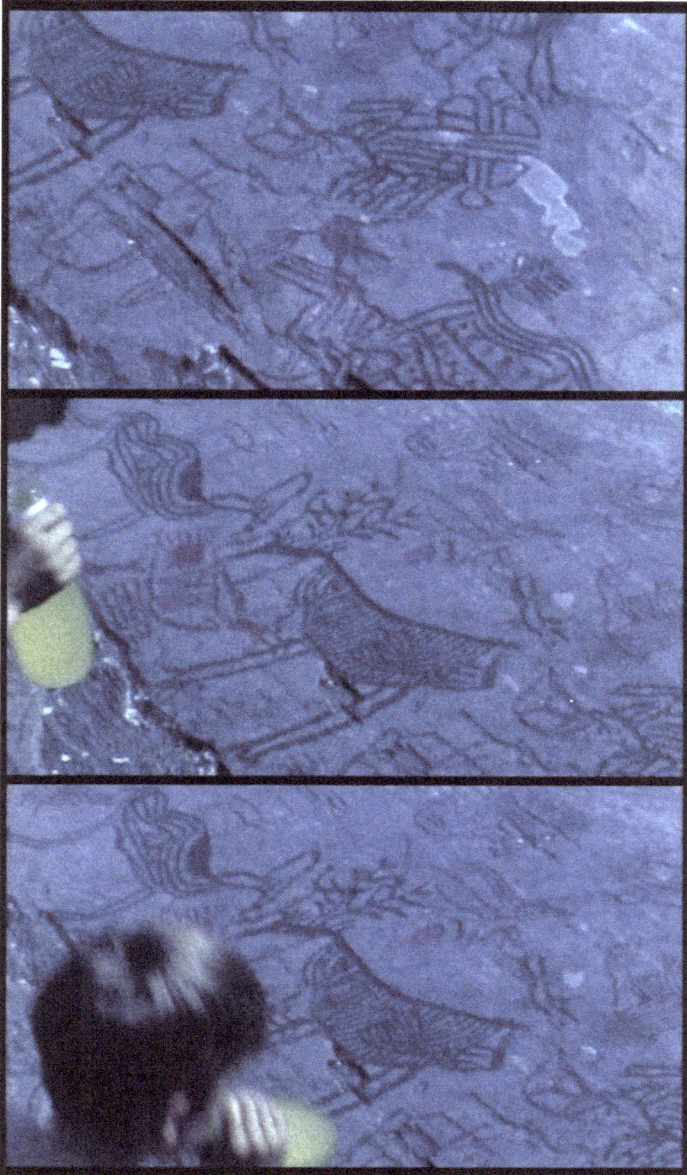

Figure 53. Stills from my father's 8 mm movie of Ausevik, a large rock art site only 15 kilometres by boat from Florø, which we heard about during our vacation in 1963. The visit to Ausevik was combined with a Sunday picnic. We sensed that we had arrived at a 'thin place', where the Stone Age was suddenly near to us. The eerie motifs qualified to be filmed. Suddenly, Børge appeared in the frame with a bottle of soft drink, accidentally bringing the moment back to our own time.

He brought us to thin places,[42] like the nearby 'Steindalen'. The exotic name, meaning 'The Stone Valley', resembled 'The Valley Time Forgot' from the Tarzan cartoon. To top it off, Steindalen contained a cave where ancient pottery had been reported. During the visit, Pappa's imaginings were so vivid that my brother Børge asked if a man passing in a nearby field could be a Stoneager.

> '...boys... think about all people who have sat here, at this very spot where are sitting now', he would say as he fed the fire with twigs. 'How did they manage? They had to hunt deer for food, with bow and arrows, they cooked the meat in the fireplaces – you know, as we do with blue mussels at the beach. No stores to get food and things. Think about how it was in the winter – steike (a mild swearing), those guys had to be really tough...'

We went for lengthy camping expeditions in the Ford Taunus with 'Bjerck's Garments Everywhere' on the rear door – they proved that the slogan was true. There was a decisive episode as we were slowly making our way along a gravel road in Østfold, near Oslo. We noticed a man lying on the ground, painting something in red. My father parked the Taunus at the road-side. 'Rock art', the man on the ground explained. We admired the shapes that the newly-painted lines enhanced, and could see the faint unpainted groves that showed the tremendous amount of time involved. The shapes had been made in the Bronze Age, 3000 years ago. My father filmed the man with his 8 mm camera – really, it was a thing to bring home from holiday. The rock-carving painter asked where we came from.

> '...from Florø?? Dear Lord... then you live close by Ausevik... and not too far from Vingen... they are the biggest rock art sites in the whole country!!'

To top it off, the man explained that these very images he was paint-ing now had in fact been discovered by a cow. The ancient lines were first seen in a spot where the cow's foot had slid and exposed the bedrock. This piece of trivia triggered something in me – if a cow could discover forgot-ten treasures, we certainly could. Immediately after coming home, we set off with the boat, it took only around an hour in-fjord to reach the mysterious messages in Ausevik. Most of the strange shapes we could see were evidently 'deer', but there were also shapes that looked like humans, spirals, and what a nearby sign labelled 'linjekrot' (line-entanglements). My father elaborated on what he learned from the sign as we fingered the faint grooves. As he filmed the ancient motifs, Børge accidentally appeared in the frame with a bottle of orange pop in his hand.

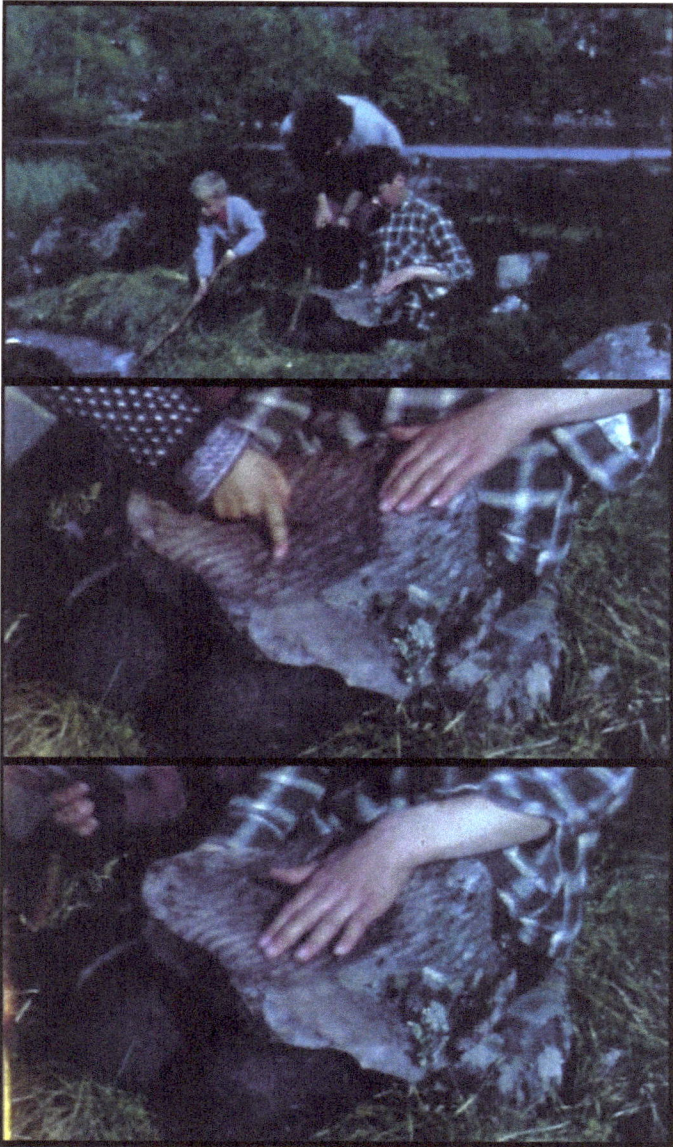

Figure 54. Still frames from my father's 8 mm movie, showing the discovery of the fossilised wave ripples in a slab of Devonian sandstone in Terdalen. This was one of the wonders of my childhood, perhaps a pivotal encounter with deep time – beyond everything we knew about, even outdating the 'beak-eroded mountain of eternity'. We all touched the ripples gently – our fingers were like gramophone pins playing the grooves of an ancient recording. The tune was familiar, singing the song of waves caressing a sandy shore.

Of course, I became deeply intrigued by all of the stories about the people who had lived in our homeland so many years ago. Their survival by simple means, and that you actually could discover things left by them, truth-bearing objects, evidence. The distant past, that was also close. Once, during a hike from the family cabin across the fjord, we discovered a sandstone slab that exhibited ripple marks. They were as sharp as on the beach we visited to swim – but my father knew (from his correspondence course in geology) that the waves that had inflicted these marks were 400 million years old, when this very sandstone massive was part of a large lake, at a time when Europe and America were joined.

We were amazed by this very tangible proof of a time before even the *dinosaurs*, which had hitherto been the most ancient time we could imagine. My father filmed as we touched the slab, feeling the familiar ripples turned to stone – we had to bring it home. The operation had to be prepared, and took place during a later, specifically-targeted expedition. The precious slab was suspended with ample rope from a sturdy wooden stake, carried in a similar way to how we imagined Stoneagers had brought a newly-killed deer to camp, escorted by Pappa's frequent reminders that we had be careful to find firm footing. We managed to lift it into the boat and transport it safely (and proudly) in the trolley to our home, where we displayed it in a prominent place in our living room. My uncles were invited to admire it.

At school, we had learned this:

> Imagine the biggest mountain. Once, every thousand years, a tiny bird lands at the mountain to sharpen its beak. When the mountain is worn down and gone, one single second of eternity has passed.

My father commented that eternity was even bigger, that eternity had neither beginning nor end. Like an orange. Still, I liked better the beak-sharpening metaphor. Anyway, with this 400-million-year-old memory in our home, it seemed as though we owned a sliver of eternity. This is what true souvenirs are about, owning slivers of something bigger.

A candy store in the basement

I was plenty old enough to be mortified when my father called the museum in Bergen and asked if his son could participate in an excavation that was going to happen in Brandsøy, close to Florø, but my interest overpowered the embarrassment. I had already decided to study archaeology, and the experience was a welcomed glance into the archaeological workshop – an opportunity to hold 6000-year-old things in my bare hands, and to learn the marks of stone-tool manufacture, the fossils of ancient handwork[43]. The excitement of learning all this was aroused to such a degree that I even wrote a piece for the local newspaper about 'percussion bulbs' – surely the first and only one on this subject in the *Firdaposten*. My father brought his new audio Super 8 camera to the excavation. He interviewed Asle, TV-style.

Figure 55. A still from my father's interview of Asle, recorded with the new Super 8 *audio* camera during the excavation in Brandsøy, the first Stone Age dig I attended. Asle, who conducted the operation, soon became my mentor and close friend. Shortly after this excavation, Svein Brandsøy, a local amateur archaeologist, discovered a huge stone quarry in a several-kilometres-long diabase dyke less than five kilometres further into the fjord. Asle wrote his academic thesis about this in the years to come (cf. Olsen and Alsaker 1984) – a major discovery in the Scandinavian Stone Age. It turned out that a considerable portion of the stone axes in the region came from the Stakaneset quarry, over more than 5000 years. Sitting up-front in Asle's ground-breaking research during my first years in archaeology was pivotal in my scholarly trajectory. It was all started by this excavation. What if my father had not called to the museum and asked for his son to participate?

Unfortunately, Asle passed away in 2018, long before his time. I believe, and take comfort in believing, that he now resides among the eternal hordes of people beyond time – and now knows most answers that his living colleagues still struggle to sort out.

Asle, in his dark green south-western, his back towards the camera, the tiny microphone in his hand, explained meticulously and solemnly (he later told me that he hated having do this), as my father eagerly zoomed in on details:

> 'What we see here is the excavation of a Stone Age settlement. (CUT.) The principle of such an excavation is that we excavate in square metres and wash out the masses with water in a sifting rack. (CUT.) Here, we have a situation where we have reached the lower part of the settlement layer. (Zooming in on the soil, CUT.) The cultural layer sits on a natural depression in the bedrock. Here, we have found a number of flakes of various raw material types, such as quartzite, flint, slate and greenstone, and some non-determined rock-art. (Asle, with the microphone on, calls to another crew member, 'Are you leaving now?', CUT.) Here, we can see the approximate location where we found the greenstone adze of Nøstvet-type. (Zooming in, as I point to the exact location in the muddy surface.) This can be dated to four to five thousand BC, and is presumably the most important implement we have found hitherto... (CUT.)

> Here we see Svein Brandsøy[44], who is excavating the south-western part of the locality. In this part of the settlement, we have found some slate artefacts, that are presumably younger than the greenstone adze that was found further to the north-east. We assume that this is a younger settlement that was used in the Younger Stone Age – to judge from the slate artefacts that were found here.'[45]

Even my uncle Magne arrived in his brown city shoes, struggling to find clean foothold in the soggy soils we were digging. It was amusing to watch his troubles – we had to laugh. Later he teased me back – he had seen the orderly paths of Danish excavations in books. Our excavation was a mess – could we not do better?

At the end of the excavation, I brought several artefacts to our home and displayed them on the red stool in our kitchen, along with a piece of broken ruler, for scale. My father organised artificial lighting for the camera, and filmed as I explained, pointing with a ballpoint pen:

> '...and here we have some fine microblades... well, this one is a blade, it is more than eight millimetres wide... the rest are microblades, and they bear witness to pretty good skills – it took quite elaborate craftsmanship to make these slivers of stone ... in fact... well... there are perhaps only two or three persons in the whole world today who are able to make them.'[46]

What was more, I had been handed a booklet about the legendary surveys of Per Fett, who had travelled around all of the counties of Western Norway to map monuments and locations of found prehistoric objects. I could hardly believe it. A stone adze had been found in the park just outside the school, a Bell-beaker arrowhead by the shores of lake Storevatnet in the middle of our town. The stone cairns along the channel Brandsøysund, which we frequently passed, were from pagan times, at least 1000 years old. It was deeply enthralling, and my home was expanded – it was like discovering a candy store in your own basement.

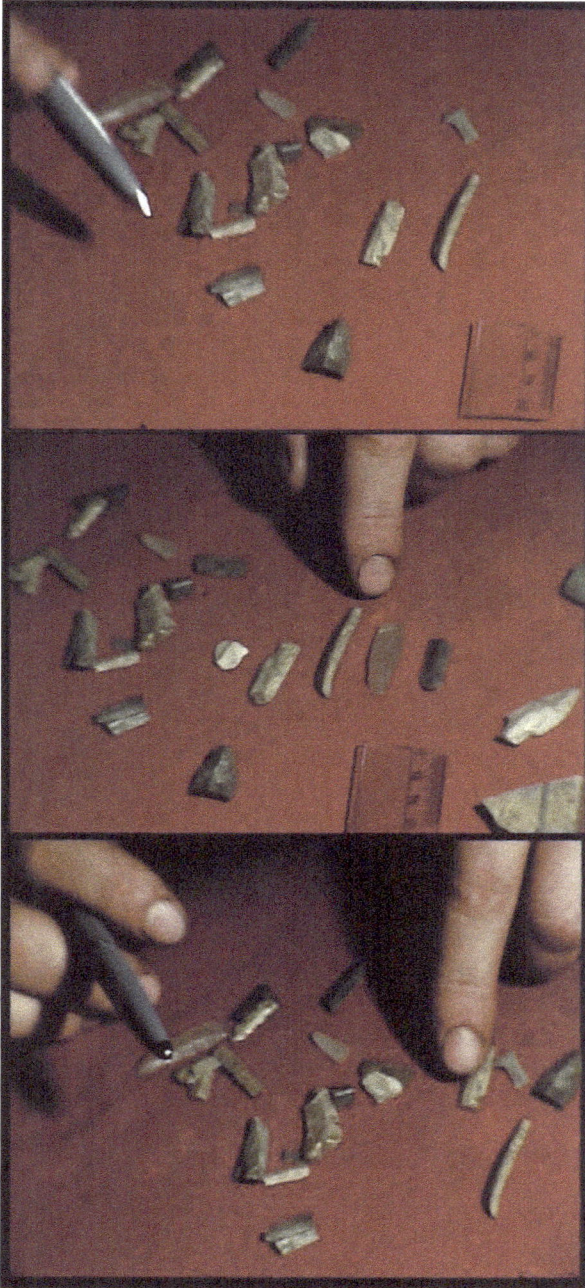

Figure 56. Explaining the lithic artefacts from the Sone Age site in Brandsøy, on the red stool in our kitchen.

My newfound knowledge, to be able to read ancient craftsmanship in stone, made it possible to discover things on my own, new places that would interest my mentor Asle in the museum in Bergen. The familiar world was estranged as the past unfolded itself so close to home. It was not exclusive to faraway places, as in the history classes at school.

Naturally, to study archaeology at university expanded this newfound realm of the past. In a lecture, amid the safe array of confident information, it was mentioned that a certain type of Iron Age glass bead had not been properly researched. To the lecturer, it was a most normal comment – to me it was remarkable to learn that there were things 'not being researched'. The astonishment brought forward an immediate readiness to engage in the shades of the unknown, which was greatly nourished during the course.

However, as I learned the formal archaeological discipline, something was also lost. What before had been a wild world of possible elucidations was narrowed down, in a way. The scientific truths were far more limited than the previous untamed visions of the past that my father had readily elaborated. I learned to refer to things as artefacts, the typology and terminology of the different shapes labelled according to the line-drawings in a reprint of 'Morphological Classification of Fractured Lithic Artefacts'.[47] More than openings to vibrant distant times, things became instruments for dating – to track down what was 'chronologically significant'. In a way, this was a necessary exercise to be able to communicate about lithic remains among members of the scholarly community. At the same time, the formal handling deprived them of the role they had acted among the Stoneagers. The scientific handling changed them to 'specimens', neutral objects that no longer retained what they had had as part of the deeds of past people.

Important hallmarks of the New Archaeology[48] of the 1970s were positivism and objectivity, meaning that lithic objects were labelled as neutral, their typology based on the intended shapes that could be directly observed. What (unintentionally) followed included an alienating of the things from their being a part of the lived Stone Age machinery. One of the most common functions of lithic tools – cutting – never appeared in the inventory lists from the Mesolithic settlements we excavated. The tool category 'knife' was non-existent, as we could not know for sure the function of the objects – at best, knives (...I still sense the urge to say 'possible cutting tool' as I now write 'knife') were referred to as lithic artefacts with lateral retouch, or artefacts with use-wear. It was as close as we could get on safe grounds. Still, today, the discipline has not sorted out the dilemma between formal types, technological morphologies and functional tools – the need for comparable precision in scientific communication vs. deciding what things actually did in past actions.

He never said, but surely my father must have struggled to keep up his vivid interest among all the formal measures that his now educated son eagerly communicated. I doubt that he could find much to nourish his enticing images of vital Stone Age hunters and how they had managed. His juicy embellishments of Stoneager hardships faded in parallel with my academic learning. Himself, he had collected flints during a former vacation in Denmark, and was very proud of their mounting on the wooden board he had made to display, label and date them. The arrangement was suspended from a decorative brass chain, a thing to show astonished friends. To the best of his ability, he had classified them as various tools according to the similar shapes he had found in books. To me, it was all wrong, I blew it apart – his efforts were turned to embarrassment. To him, the 'correct classifications' served to alienate things into cryptic evidence, no longer recognisable as things that were integrated into what he envisioned. Now, I regret that I failed to be more compassionate, to indulge and attune myself better to his sphere of interest. Now, I am happy to remember that he did not take the display down.

Once, during a new excavation in Brandsøy, I spent the weekend with my father at our cabin in Terdal, across the fjord. We paid a visit to Anna and Abraham on the farm nearby, and I mentioned the excavation. Anna asked about our findings.

> 'Well, we find things made out of stone, quartz and diabase, and abundant pieces of charcoal, in fact, a lot of burned hazelnut shells', I explained enthusiastically.
> 'Oh!', Anna exclaimed in a concluding tone, '...but you cannot use THAT for anything!'

I recall that my father laughed wholeheartedly at this, and even retold the conversation several times on later occasions. Now, I wonder if his amusement from the episode was nourished by my recent and insensitive critique of his display of the Danish flints...

Things' uncanny ability to be alive without moving

In the mid-1990s, I was offered a position as a cultural heritage officer at the office of the Governor of Svalbard. The position brought forward a different archaeology – an 'archaeology of the recent past'. In this remote Arctic island, there seem to be no prehistoric cultural remains. Nobody has been able to find vestiges older than the Dutch whaling ventures of the 1600s, and hence the written accounts of Willem Barentz in AD 1596 have granted him pioneer status. This, and the fact that most things were burned off as Svalbard was evacuated prior to the German invasion during WW2, has meant that cultural remains older than 1946 are lawfully protected – I had to look for things other than the Stone Age legacy to nourish my scholarly interest.

Shortly after moving to Svalbard, I witnessed a traumatic incident, an accident of the worst gravity, so dreadful that I have had serious doubts about including it here. Nevertheless, the incident was also a grim awakening of things left by their people. A Russian plane crashed into a mountain just outside Longyearbyen – 141 people were killed instantly.[49] It was terrible – a catastrophe that overwhelmed both capacities and competence in Longyearbyen. The Governor's staff was hastily reorganised. The non-operative part of the staff (myself among them) was included in task group P4 – with the responsibility for organising a number of auxiliary tasks in the operation that followed: food for the operative personnel at the crash-site, accommodation for specially-trained personnel from the mainland, making up temporary beds for the more than 100 Russian and Ukrainian employees who were supposed to return with the plane that had crashed, collecting and shipping all kinds of equipment that was needed in the mountain, and helping to unload the anonymous but heavy (in all senses) body bags from the helicopters as they returned.

During the next few days, even the P4 crew learned about how it was up there. The plane had hit the edge of the mountain mesa – the front half was still on the mesa, while the back part had slid down the steep slope. There were disturbing details, evoking even more troubling images. After almost a week in P4, I volunteered to take part in the operation at the crash site. I needed to calm down troubled fantasies with facts – and the reasons for my request were respected. I recall a numb anticipation as the helicopter landed some distance from the site – '...there is so much debris, things could be whirled up in the rotors'. It was a surprise that things could be worse than they already were in this mayhem.

The rear part of the plane had caused an avalanche several hundred metres long, a grim mix of snow, body parts and fragments from the plane – horrible in all senses of the word. Still, there was a strange eerie comfort in the gruesome scene. Of the big aircraft, only very few recognisable parts remained. The myriad sharp metal scraps demonstrated that the impact of the crash had been so abrupt and powerful that the 141 casualties would have experienced neither horror nor suffering. They had been taken out of life in the very millisecond of the collision. They had probably never realised what had hit them, not even that something *had* hit them. In all its horror, the scene calmed the worst of my wild imagination – in all the brutality, it was exactly this roughness embedded in the things that provided a sort of calming, not unlike the much later scene of my father's death.

What I had not expected were the amounts of passenger belongings that were also present and intermingled. I had not thought of the fact of all this mundane materiality. Winter coats and boots, woollen mittens and jackets, scarves and hats from the luggage compartments. Books and magazines that had perhaps been read in the very moment of the fatal accident. Sweets in wrappings. A half-knitted sweaters with the pins still resting in their stitches, still connected to its ball of yarn. Passports and wallets, lighters and cigarette packages, some with health warnings. Even a few bottles had miraculously survived, their contents intact – alike with a few jars with pickled cucumbers. A small plaque that read 'Life vest under your seat' – a touching remainder of a time when death was as distant to the passengers as it was to me in that moment. All of these all-too-normal things were included in this brutal context, all of the things that were 'alive' in their silenced and stagnant state, simultaneously both abject and deeply touching. Many of them could still be handled, could re-enter their traditional functions in the hands of humans. They would prove their ability to come back, but definitely to something else, all these things that the day before had been carefully picked to accompany their people on a prosperous two-year stay in Svalbard.

Now, I think that the repercussions from this gruesome scene re-emerged in seeing the derelict homes in Florø many years later – the masses of departed things and belongings, their uncanny ability to appear alive in still-stand, their unsentimental readiness to enter something new.

'Persistent Memories'

I doubt that my attentiveness to the things at the crash-site was related to lack of empathy with the unfortunate victims and the many others who were left behind. I would perhaps have seen it differently had I not known Bjørnar and his remarkable thing-indulgence. Archaeology brings on a special social 'glue', there being quite a number of joint arenas where you learn to know fellows quite well – the common enthusiasm for the discipline (most evenings are too short to exhaust interesting talks, and so nights must frequently be included), fieldwork (where you have to indulge in a collective, decide a menu, share the burden of mundane chores), and seminars and conferences (where you may display successful findings). All in all, they are abundant grounds for life-long friendships, as well as being pivotal in professional networks.

I had met Bjørnar at a Nordic seminar of archaeology students in Denmark in the early 1980s – he was student in Tromsø, me in Bergen. More than a joint interest in the entanglements of lithics, I was drawn to him by his willingness to spend late nights retelling hilarious episodes from his fieldwork, and also his more theoretical approaches to archaeology. We happened to graduate the same week in 1984. As opposed to most graduated students, who hastily seek whatever paid jobs that are available, Bjørnar chose to spend a year of further study in Cambridge, and returned to Tromsø with a number of new ideas and ample ingredients to make Indian curries. He willingly shared both. The mix of poppadums, chutney, cumin, talking and beer drinking during cooking – the food and alternative approaches to archaeology were both as spicy as they were tasty.

In 1995, it happened that Bjørnar asked me to join him in fieldwork in Disco Bay, Western Greenland – he had been asked to take part in a project, to survey and excavate ancient Inuit settlements, by Jens Fog Jensen, who was the director of the museum in the nearby village of Aasiaat. We enjoyed exciting days travelling along the shores by boat, occasionally going ashore to places where sites were expected, and finding a number of forgotten campsites. In our own base-camp, where the crew of Inuits, Danes, Canadians and Norwegians resided, Bjørnar and I constituted one of the kitchen teams. When it was our turn, I suggested making fish gratin – it is one of my favourite dishes, and I also believe that I am particularly good at preparing it, thanks to life-long experience and knowing my mother's well-proven recipe by heart.

As usual, we did most of the preparation the evening before, to save time for our hungry comrades when they returned from the field the next day. It was almost midnight before we started the operation in the separate kitchen tent, gathering the ingredients in parallel with having beer and joyful conversations, boiling the macaroni in milk, cutting pieces of fish fillets. I was getting ready to mix in the eggs when Bjørnar stopped me. He insisted that the dish should be made otherwise, by parting the eggs, mixing the yolk into the macaroni, whipping the egg whites to foam, and then 'folding' the stiff egg whites very gently into the mixture with the rubber spatula, taking care not to lose too much of the air in the foam – 'to make the dish fluffier and more tender.'

I objected, but Bjørnar insisted and continued to 'fluff' the gratin 'au-gratin-style'. My own gratin-skills were reduced to slicing up the bacon that was to go on top of the dish. We finished in silence, before going to the communal tent to have a last beer for the night. I could see that Bjørnar was not happy, that something was wrong. When asked what was the matter, he admitted that he thought my bacon slices were 'too thick'. He wanted them thinner. As this was my sole contribution to the dish, it was a sore point:

> 'Okay. Well. Then I think perhaps that you should go back to the kitchen tent', I said, annoyed, 'and slice the slices in two', knowing how hard it is to slice already-sliced bacon. 'Take the beer with you, and good luck!'

> 'Yes, that is exactly what I intend to do...', Bjørnar replied, and left.

I heard no more sounds from the kitchen tent, but I guessed his task was a rather silent operation – and saw no more of him until the morning. Somehow, he had actually managed what he had announced, and the gratin was to everybody's liking the next evening. I was a bit disappointed that nobody commented that the bacon was sliced too thin.

Now, I like to amuse Bjørnar by retelling our comic Disco Bay dispute – the 'Bacon Battle'. Anyway, the reason for mentioning the episode is not merely its funny aspect, but rather the subtle revealing of his (and perhaps my) character, our friendship, and Bjørnar's desire for perfection, for the best possible, and his willingness to take on missions impossible to get there. I guess this stubborn persistence has spilled into his archaeological crafts-manship and academic standing (and my tendency towards the safer, more traditional, more easily doable).

In a similar way, Bjørnar took an immediate interest in the ample recent remains in Svalbard. It happened that the Russian coal mining company 'Trust Arcticugol' had announced their plan to leave Pyramiden, one of the major settlements in Svalbard. Things had become different in the post-Soviet era – the willingness to prioritise investments to continue mining in Pyramiden was not as before. Subsequently, the company town that had recently hosted around 1000 inhabitants was (temporarily) abandoned. I had visited many times when the town had thrived and functioned – enjoy-ing the outstanding hospitality and traditions, lavish dinners with vodka, attending impressive dance and music performances in the 'Cultural Palace', where I once happened to present a Christmas greeting from the Governor of Svalbard. Then, Pyramiden had suddenly been deserted. On my first visit to the abandoned settlement, there was a distinct difference – without its people, the material remains suddenly acted differently. When populated, the human inhabitants had subdued things – the things were there and acted, seen, but obscured by their mundane familiarity. Now, as things had to speak for themselves, they brought on an accentuated attention. Bjørnar and I discussed this phenomenon eagerly, and planned a project to study the abandoned Pyramiden in detail.

During all of this, I met Elin. She was a newly educated artist who was allotted an artist-in-residence grant in Longyearbyen. I could not help but notice this woman. The town was accustomed to photographers who arrived to capture the famous 'blue light', the flaming Aurora Borealis, or the faint shapes of snow-covered peaks in the ever-darkness during winter. Well, not Elin. She took an interest in a stack of plastic bottle cases outside a storage building by the harbour, erecting her tripod in the snow for a lengthy, non-flash photo session. Then, photographing a shelf with toilet paper in the lady's room at 'Huset', the combined café and nightclub in town. Evidently, we shared an interest in things. However, her vision differed from mine – she saw, combined, contrasted, noticed, scrutinised and attuned herself to things that I barely noticed. My scholarly habit of the accurate documenta-tion of amounts and measurements was seriously challenged by her skills in sensing things that were not necessarily unambiguously delimited. Maybe the subtle meaning in the arrangement of things in a room was more impor-tant than positions and exact dimensions?

It was during one of the eternal nights of the Arctic winter, with ribbons of Aurora Borealis dancing its gentle ballet over Longyear City. It was 20 degrees below Celsius, although the full moon was as merry as in a summer night by the Mediterranean. I brought Elin to 'Kullkrana på Hotellneset', the crane for loading coal from the mines onto bulk ships – a huge piece of machinery that was now abandoned. I needed to bring a loaded gun in case we bumped into polar bears – we could observe their tracks in the snow. This was all to my benefit in this early phase of getting to know Elin – I believed that I could demonstrate my protective gene, my bravery and masculinity, as well as my attentiveness to the abandoned all at once. Elin later revealed that she thought I was a chicken to carry a loaded gun all the time, but she loved the mechanical monster.

It turned out later that the gun had been loaded with the wrong ammunition, proving to her that even the best man can make mistakes, in addition to being a chicken. Anyway, and luckily for me, Elin took an immediate interest in the abandoned thingly realm I planned to explore with Bjørnar, and we invited her on our Pyramiden expedition. More than her skills in photographing, we were interested in including her non-archaeological gaze in our appreciation of things – luckily, she was able to provide both.

We completed the Pyramiden study and co-authored a book,[50] combining Bjørnar's theoretical perspectives in defence of things, Elin's non-archaeological, artistic attentiveness to things, and my own close encounters with both the living and the abandoned Pyramiden.

In later years, we both were invited on Bjørnar's enticing projects, meeting many different fellows in this field of research – which pretty much led to the beginning of this book.

Figure 57. A photo from the 2006 fieldwork in the Soviet mining town of Pyramiden, in Svalbard, showing Elin, Bjørnar and myself. The roof of Hotel Tulip stood above the dust of the abandoned town and out of reach of polar bears – a place to relax. We later authored the book *Persistent Memories*, based on our findings.

'...the dark twin of every scientific paper...'

Looking back on beginnings and trajectories in academia, it is quite common to start with formative academic awakenings, mentors and scientific publications. The things referred to are all safe within some kind of disciplinary path, elaborating on the 'isms' that were passed along the way. These narratives are all valid and correct, and interesting to read. However, they tend to be thoroughly cleansed of all non-academic noise, like the things addressed by Merlin Sheldrake in his conversation with Robert Macfarlane – the non-mentioned 'dark twin of every scientific paper... this frothy, mad network that underlies and interconnects all scientific knowledge.'[51]

I think that all disciplinary engagement includes more than what may be defined as scholarly. After all, and as with most people, archaeologists happen to read novels that stick, have decisive conversations with friends, watch movies, perhaps have caring parents and happy childhoods and kids that happen to say unexpected things, or on occasion see someone dear putting on a bold face in shame.

At times, I wonder about how much my professional engagement exists in the things I never refer to. An episode recurrently comes to mind – it must have been more than 30 years ago, when my father was visiting us in Bodø one summer. We were on the path to the legendary Mjelle beach, Trygve and Kyrre already way ahead in their colourful shorts, eager to reach the destination. My father suddenly halted, staring up the steep slope above the path.

> 'Hein... look Hein, look... do you see that rock up there, the black boulder? Do you know what it could be? Perhaps we should check it out?'
> 'No... come on, Pappa, I will not bother with that now', I replied. It would have meant climbing up the hill (actually not that far), and letting the boys get even further ahead. He let go of the things he carried, and put on the fatherly tone I could instantly recognise:
> 'Hein. I will tell you this. You must never turn into somebody that doesn't bother... you know the type of guy that doesn't take the trouble to do this or that, not being curious, not bothering to check out things. You know the sort.'

We left the gear by the path, climbed up to the rock, and discussed if it could be gabbro.

Later, on the beach, he collected an eolith, a pointed sand-blown stone with a peculiar surface texture that he had never seen before. He brought it back to his home in Florø. It is one of the things I have kept from his home. Sometimes, I wonder how much of my performance in archaeology may be ascribed to my father... and how much of him I brought along into the discipline. How can this be measured?

Sometimes, in retrospect, I parallel my struggle to be a proper archaeologist with an alpinist during a slalom exercise, paying close attention to the prescribed flags I have to round along the way, knowing that if I should miss a single one, even if it should be the last, my great success – with the difficult hang at the start and all my other skilful efforts – would turn to nothing. And, to make it even worse, I have contributed even more flags to the slope, to be adhered to by others – in making reading lists, lectures, giving grades, editing publications. Perhaps the mandatory gates that must be passed in the race are now so many that they threaten speed and flow – the very essence of the exercise.

Only few have asked about what was actually seen and sensed along the way – the tree-tops, a rare bird, the view down the valley or the joy from the rush of the airflow, the pain from the lactic acid in coping with the centrifugal forces in the tricky curves, or the fierce vibrations in the ground on the last slope before 'Finish'. Likewise, I have perhaps failed to stimulate a wider awareness in what others can sense in archaeology.

As with alpinists, what matters is time and distance, and that all gates are passed as prescribed.

Now, I may not have the same speed as before (the skis have perhaps lost their wax), and there are flags that I do not bother to attune myself to as I once did. On the other hand, I am perhaps more attuned to the calmer freedom of a slower pace, am more attentive to the margins, to following a path that leads another way, to looking for a triviality that could explain Bryant's 'machines' to the students, to sensing a sudden memory from Florø in a whiff of air in a rainy morning, and to reflecting on the way Pirlo speaks with her face and tail as I come home – to speculating on how I can know who is cuddling who as I touch her soft neck.

Figure 58. My father did not much approve of the sailable canoe that Børge bought with his own money in his teens – 'It is unstable – what if it capsizes in open sea? How will you manage to return home up-wind?' Himself, he preferred more safety and control – we could sense his distress if we deviated from the accustomed sea route to and from our cabin in Terdalen. Florø is in the middle of the more than 100-kilometre-wide zone between open ocean to the west and the bottoms of the fjords to the east. My father preferred the fjords – less wind, fewer skerries, and shorter distances to shore if something should happen. This is where he brought us during numerous boat trips. However, fjords may be large or small, wide or narrow, but they all have ends, defining how far you can travel. I was in my teens before I saw the unbroken horizon of the ocean for the first time – this limitless body that had had no end, and the eerie freedom in sensing that it was up to you how far you would go. Would I have become a different archaeologist if my father had dared to show me this earlier – the prospects of the unsafe and limitless?

Notes

Acknowledgements

1 Meis 2021.

Chapter 1

1 This is elaborated on under the label 'Presentism', e.g., Olivier 2004; 2015.
2 'Mesolithic' denotes the oldest part of the Stone Age, in Norway the time period from 11,500 to 6000 years BP (Before Present), Bjerck 2010.
3 ...a person from past times, as per the imaginary time-travellers that miraculously appear from the water in the HBO series 'Beforeigners' (2019).
4 Chagnon 1968.
5 Hazelwood 2000.
6 'Stoneager' – a person from the Stone Age, similar to 'Beforeigner'.
7 Chagnon 1968: 144.
8 See also Shanks 1992; 2012.
9 For an interesting discussion on this, see Pillatt 2012.
10 Lowenthal 1985.
11 E.g., Olsen and Pétursdóttir 2021.
12 Macfarlane 2019: 108–109.
13 Morton 2017: 1.
14 Or 'object withdrawal' – 'so in your face that you can't see them', Morton 2017: 37.
15 Olsen 2003.
16 E.g., Olsen and Pétursdóttir 2021.
17 These are Bjørnar Olsen's productive research groups *Ruin Memories*, http://ruinmemories.org/ (Olsen and Pétursdóttir 2014), *After Discourse*, https://cas.oslo.no/research-groups/after-discourse-things-archaeology-and-heritage-in-the-21st-century-article1802-827.html (Olsen *et al.* 2021) and *Objects Matter*, http://objectmatters.ruinmemories.org/.
18 Harrison and Schofield 2010: 30.
19 Binford 1978; Bonnichsen 1973.
20 E.g., Buchli and Lucas 2001; Olsen 2010; Harrison and Schofield 2010.
21 A selection of readings: Bogost 2012; González-Ruibal 2006; 2019; Graves-Brown and Harrison 2013; Ingold 2011; 2015; Harman 2010; 2016; Harrison and Schofield 2010; Latour 2005; Lucas 2005; Morton 2017; Olivier 2011; Olsen 2010; Olsen *et al.* 2012.
22 Morton 2017: 1.
23 Gonzáles-Ruibal 2008: 262.
24 Harman 2016: 7.
25 Harrison and Schofield 2009, later elaborated on in Harrison and Schofield 2010.
26 E.g, Holtorf 2015, edited essays circling around the question 'Are we all archeologists now?'
27 E.g., a selection of Robert Macfarlane's books – 2012; 2015; 2019.
28 Harari 2015; 2017.
29 Macfarlane 2019.
30 Olsen 2011.

31 Witmore 2020.
32 Byrne 2017; 2021.
33 Byrne 2021: 116.
34 Pétursdóttir 2017.
35 González-Ruibal 2014.
36 Burström 2014.
37 Olivier 2015: 4.
38 Brate and Kiddey 2015.
39 Farstadvoll 2019; Introna 2021; Bailey 2021.
40 Haraway 1988.
41 E.g., Tilley 1994, and the critical debate in Bruck 2005.
42 Strathern 1987.
43 E.g., Goldschmidt 1977: 293–308; Richardson 2000, Adams *et al.* 2015.
44 Ellis *et al.* 2010.
45 Ellingson and Ellis 2008: 450.
46 (*ibid.*) See also Ellis 2004.
47 Wikipedia hosts a brief, but adequate account of 'Autoethnography', https://en.wikipedia.org/wiki/Autoethnography. A special issue of *Journal of Contemporary Ethnography* (35[4], August 2006) debates and seeks to define 'autoethnography'.
48 Richardson 2000: 254.
49 Adams *et al.* 2015.
50 Pillatt 2012.
51 Bryant 2014.
52 Bryant 2014: 6.
53 Bryant 2014: 38.
54 Olsen *et al.* 2012.
55 Bryant 2014: 93.
56 Morton 2013.

Chapter 2

1 Loe 2021.
2 *Firdaposten*, the local newspaper in Florø.
3 Melberg 1942.

Chapter 3

1 Hilmar Reksten – his daughter Bjørg Nora Reksten briefly mentions Alma and Nils in her chapter in Svendsen 1999: 28.
2 The last part of Mommo's typed draft for her 'Gentlemen's speech' reads like this: 'That is him who is the man XXXXXX in our thoughts, and it is for this boy, who takes a standing, I ask all my fellow sisters to XXXXXXX cheer for in this evening. May he live; Hipp, hipp hurray.' In the free space below, there is a hastily handwritten note on a diagonal; a sudden reminder that these past days were also connected to the bigger picture, in spite of their fragmentary state: 'The 22.11.1963. News reported at an irregular time: President Kennedy is shot in the chest with three shots.'
3 Uncle Faste produced a number of booklets of detailed memoirs that he handed out to family members.
4 Cf. 'habit memory', Olsen 2010: 116.

5 Glassie 1999: 58; quoted in Olsen 2010: 49.
6 Harman 2010: 93ff.

Chapter 4

1 The past in the present is elaborated on in a number of publications, e.g., Ingold 1993; Olsen 2010: 107ff; 2013; Olivier 2015.
2 ...from John Grant's song 'Disappointing' (*Grey Tickles, Black Pressure*, Bella Union, 2015).
3 Olsen 2013: 6.
4 1985–1988, see Acknowledgements.
5 Elaborated on in Bjerck 1989.
6 Foragers, a common term for hunter-fisher-gatherers.
7 See Acknowledgements.
8 See an inspiring elaboration in Macfarlane 2015.
9 To be exact, the sample was dated to 8330± 90 ^{14}C-years Before Present (T-7790) – calibrated to ca. 9400 calendar years old.
10 E.g., Andrefsky 2008.
11 E.g., Hayden 1979.
12 E.g., the marvellous finds from Ronæs Skov (Andersen 2009) and Tybrind Vig (Andersen 2013) in Denmark.
13 Bjerck 1990: fig. 26.
14 Bryant 2014.
15 In the final year of the three-year-long Vega Project (1985–1958), we arranged a similar survey along a much lower shoreline, at a 25-metre elevation, corresponding to the late part of the Stone Age, ca. 4000–5000 years BP. The idea was to see the arrangement of camps – to determine any stability or change in the pattern of settlement and lifestyle.

However, the settlement pattern had obviously changed prior to the Late Stone Age, as the camps along the 25-metre shoreline displayed other features: one to three houses were grouped at what appeared to be prosperous fishing locations. Most camps contained remains of a midden (refuse disposal) on the downside of the huts, towards what was the shore. The combination of locations, the houses and the build-up of middens suggested a certain stability, repeated and long-lasting occupations, perhaps of a few co-residing and co-working groups that relied on the stable fish resources nearby. Seascapes had changed along with the receding shoreline – a myriad of smaller islands, shallows and skerries surrounded Vega, which calmed the seas and resulted in a considerable increase in natural harbours. To what extent these people also spent time on other settlements with larger parts of their community, perhaps outside Vega, is, while likely, still unclear (Bjerck 1989).
16 More details in Bjerck 1989; 1990.
17 Harari 2017.
18 Bjerck *et al.* 2008: 285–294.
19 Per Morten Gullsvåg, former employee of the Vega municipality and Helgeland Museum.
20 The Vega Archipelago World Heritage, https://www.verdensarvvega.no/
21 My primary publications on the Vega Project are Bjerck 1989 and 1990. However, the Vega sites are included in several later publications, e.g., Bjerck 2007; 2010; 2013; 2014; Bjerck and Breivik 2012; Bjerck and Zangrando 2013.
22 E.g., Damlien *et al.* 2018; Sørensen *et al.* 2013.
23 Holen 2020.
24 Associate Professor Birgitte Skar, NTNU University Museum, Trondheim. See a similar study in Skar and Coulson 1986.

25 PhD candidate Jo Sindre Eidshaug and Associate Professor Ole Risbøl, NTNU University Museum, Trondheim.
26 Associate Professor Heidi M. Breivik, NTNU University Museum, Trondheim.

Chapter 5

1 Cf. a similar trauma elaborated on in Lollar 2010.
2 Bryant 2014.
3 Like one of Harman's 'sleeping giants', Harman 2016: 7.
4 MOO (Machine-Oriented-Ontology) was formulated by the philosopher Levi Bryant (2014). The theory is rooted in the 'Speculative Realism' foregrounded by Graham Harman in OOO (Object-Oriented Ontology; see Harman 2010; 2016). The theoretical basis is similar to Actor-Network Theory, which is also pivotal in 'Symmetrical Archaeology' (e.g. Olsen 2003; 2007; Witmore 2007; 2019). Recently, another contribution to similar thinking in archaeology has been presented in 'Assemblage Theory' (Jervis 2019).
5 Harman 2016: 2–3.
6 https://www.overstock.com/Home-Garden/Dimensional-D-cor/27962376/product.html
7 https://www.posterlounge.ie/p/696011.html#paid=19110
8 Allen 2000.
9 ...'the broken hammer', as in Heidegger's famous illustration of 'thing awareness' (Heidegger 1962). See elaboration in Olsen 2010: 68.
10 Karl Ove Knausgård 2020: 179 – my translation.
11 Olsen 2013: 8; see also Olsen 2010: 107ff.
12 Persson 2014: 44; see also Eriksen 1999; Kverndokk 2009.
13 Knausgård 2010: 14 (my translation); see also Burström 2009.
14 Olsen 2010: 66–67.
15 Jackson 1986.
16 Tunström 1986.
17 Allen 2000.
18 https://www.ebay.com/itm/Removable-the-Fondest-Memories-Wall-Decal-Kitchen-Stickers-Art-Vinyl-Decor-Ideas/254716265835?hash=item3b4e45c56b:g:9vUAAOSwtsNfXAxd
19 Ingold 2011.
20 Bird *et al.* 1988.
21 Tunström 1983.
22 Morton 2013: 56.
23 https://home.cern/science/accelerators/large-hadron-collider
24 Bryant 2014: 157ff.
25 https://www.nobelprize.org/prizes/medicine/2017/press-release/
26 http://www.exactlywhatistime.com/definition-of-time/
27 Oxford Dictionaries: Time. Oxford University Press, 2011.
28 McTaggart 1908.
29 There are numerous excellent scholarly writings on 'deep time' (e.g., Bailey 2007; Bryant 2014; Byrne 2021; González-Ruibal 2019; Harman 2016; Ingold 1993; 2011; 2015; Morton 2013; 2017; Olivier 2015; Olsen 2010). However, my understanding of the many aspects of time is just as much shaped by readings of Jackson's (2011) fabulous 'The Westward-Moving House', Yuval Harari's *Sapiens* (2015) and *Homo Deus* (2017), in addition to fiction, visual art and feature movies, e.g., Jean M. Auel's *The Clan of the Cave Bear* (1980), the works of Paul Auster (2006) and Annie Ernaux (1983; 1987; 2008), and

the six volumes of *My Struggle* by Karl Ove Knausgård (2009–2011), which demonstrate that even six volumes are not nearly enough to unfold a young man's life in full, Carl Frode Tiller's receding time perspective in *Begynnelser* (2017), Salvador Dali's melted clocks; Annaud's fabulous movie *Quest for Fire* (1981), Bill Murray's repetitive struggle in *Groundhog Day* (1993), the HBO series *Beforeigners* (2019), and a number of Stone Age novels for kids that I can no longer recall by name.

30 Morton 2017: 1.
31 Ernaux 2008: 85 – my translation.
32 Attali 1982, quoted in Yamada and Yoshinobu 2006.
33 Cf. Pillatt 2012, including debate.
34 Bjerck 2021.
35 Tejsner 2019.
36 Nuttall 2009: 299, referred to in Tejsner 2019: 260.
37 Nelson 1983: 240, referred to in Tejsner 2019: 262–263.
38 Yamada and Yoshinobu 2006.
39 Tunström 1993: 12.
40 Controlled Demolition, Inc. (CDI) of Phoenix, Maryland (acting as Implosion Subcontractor to Aman Environmental Construction, Inc. of Oakland, California), captures a GUINNESS WORLD RECORD for the 'Largest Structure (by volume) To Be Demolished Using Explosives' in their performance of the successful implosion of the 19.821 million cubic foot, reinforced concrete Kingdome Sports Arena in Seattle, Washington at 8:30 AM on Sunday, March 26, 2000. http://www.controlled-demolition. com; https://www.youtube.com/watch?v=oiftDBtCFt8
41 My mother kept the letter and dated it to September 1961. It still exists among my possessions, glued to the inside cover of 'My Very First Book'.
42 Macfarlane 2019: 270.
43 I am forever grateful to Asle Bruen Olsen, Kjersti Randers and Tore Bjørgo for introducing me to the mysteries of Stone Age craftsmanship.
44 Svein Brandsøy, the local amateur archaeologist who had found the site.
45 Asle's comments in my father's movie, transcribed and translated.
46 From my own comments in my father's movie, transcribed and translated.
47 Helskog *et al.* 1976.
48 Also labelled 'Processual Archaeology'.
49 https://en.wikipedia.org/wiki/Vnukovo_Airlines_Flight_2801
50 Andreassen *et al.* 2010.
51 The mentioned quote in Macfarlane 2019: 108–109.

Photo Credits

Photos and drawings are from private collections (albums, paper images and negatives) from Rolf Bjerck, Siv Liset (formerly Siv Bjartmann Bjerck), Ruth Liset, Erlend Book Bjerck, Børge Bjartmann Bjerck, alongside some of my own. Åge Hojem, NTNU Vitenskapsmuseet, has photographed/scanned old images. Elin Andreassen has assisted in the selection, adjustment and arrangement of photos and stills. Except for the following figures, the drawings and photos are by the author:

Figures 3, 8, 9: Photos by Siv Liset.

Figure 6: Drawing by Bjørn Faste Bjartmann.

Figures 10, 11, 12, 14, 17, 23, 28, 29, 32, 33, 34, 35, 38, 49, 52: Photographer Unknown.

Figures 15, 18, 50, 53, 54, 55, 56: Movie by Rolf Bjerck, stills selected and arranged by Elin Andreassen.

Figure 16 (Top): Photo by Rolf Bjerck.

Figures Cover photo, 16 (Bottom): Photos by Oluf Bjerck (jnr.).

Figures 26, 47: Photos by Erlend Book Bjerck.

Figures 30, 58: Photos by Børge Bjartmann Bjerck.

Figures 36, 57: Photos by Elin Andreassen.

Figure 37: Original photos by Ruth Liset.

Figure 40: Photo by Hilde Wika.

References

Adams, Tony E., Stacy Holman Jones and Carolyn Ellis (2015) *Autoethnography: Understanding Qualitative Research*. New York: Oxford University Press.

Allen, R. (consultant ed.) (2000) *The New Penguin English Dictionary*. London. Penguin Books.

Andersen, Søren. H. (2009) *Ronæs Skov. Marinarkæologiske undersøgelser af en kystboplads fra Ertebølletid*. Højbjerg: Jutland Archaeological Society.

Andersen, Søren H. (2013) *Tybrind Vig. Submerged Mesolithic Settlements in Denmark* Højbjerg: Jutland Archaeological Society.

Andreassen, Elin, Hein B. Bjerck and Bjørnar J. Olsen (2010) *Pyramiden – A Soviet Mining Town in the High Arctic*. Trondheim: Tapir Academic Press.

Andrefsky, William Jnr. (2008) *Lithic Technology: Measures of Production, Use and Curation*. New York: Cambridge University Press.
https://doi.org/10.1017/CBO9780511499661

Attali, Jaques (1982) *Histoires du temps*. Paris: Libraire Arthème Frayard.

Auster, Paul (2006) *The New York Trilogy*. London: Penguin Books.

Bailey, Doug (2021) Releasing the visual archive: On the ethics of destruction. In Bjørnar J. Olsen, Þóra Pétursdóttir, Mats Burström and Caitlin DeSilvey (eds.), *After Discourse: Things, Affects, Ethics*, 232–256. London: Routledge.
https://doi.org/10.4324/9780429200014-17

Bailey, Geoff (2007) Time perspectives, palimpsests and the archaeology of time. *Journal of Anthropological Archaeology* 26(2): 198–223.
https://doi.org/10.1016/j.jaa.2006.08.002

Binford, Lewis R. (1978) Dimensional analysis of behavior and site structure: Learning from an Eskimo hunting stand. *American Antiquity* 43: 330–361.
https://doi.org/10.2307/279390

Bird, Junius, John Hyslop, Margaret Bird and Gordon R Willey (1988) *Travels and Archaeology in South Chile*. Iowa City: University of Iowa Press.
https://doi.org/10.2307/j.ctt20h6v8q

Bjerck, Hein B. (1989) *Forskningsstyrt kulturminneforvaltning på Vega, Nordland. En studie av steinaldermenneskenes boplassmønstre og arkeologiske letemetoder*. Gunneria 61. Trondheim: University of Trondheim.

Bjerck, Hein B. (1990) Mesolithic site types and settlement patterns at Vega, Northern Norway. *Acta Archaeologica* 60(1989): 1–32.

Bjerck, Hein B. (2007) Mesolithic coastal settlements and shell middens (?) in Norway. In N. Milner, O. E. Craig and G. N. Bailey (eds.), *Shell Middens in Atlantic Europe*, 5–31. Oxford: Oxbow.

Bjerck, Hein B. (2010) Norwegian Mesolithic trends: a review. In Geoff Bailey and Penny Spikins (eds.), *Mesolithic Europe*, 60–106. Cambridge: Cambridge University Press.

Bjerck, Hein B. (2013) Looking with both eyes. Comments to Håkon Glørstad: 'Where are the missing boats?'. *Norwegian Archaeological Review* 46(1): 83–87.
https://doi.org/10.1080/00293652.2013.777101

Bjerck, Hein B. (2014) Kap 2. Kolonisering av den skandinaviske skjærgårdskysten og begynnelsen til sjøfangsten (10 000–9000 f.Kr.), Kap 3. Utvikling av sjøfangsten og steinalderens fangstsamfunn (9500–6500 f.Kr.), Kap 4. Fra steinalderens sjøfangst til metaltidens sjøfart (6500–500 f.Kr.). In Kolle, N. (ed.), *Norges fiskeri- og kysthistorie*. Bind 1. Trondheim: Fagbokforlaget.

Bjerck, Hein B. (2021) Out of the day, time and life: Phenomenology and cavescapes. In Bjørnar J. Olsen, Þóra Pétursdóttir, Mats Burström and Caitlin DeSilvey (eds.), *After Discourse: Things, Affects, Ethics*, 145–161. London: Routledge. https://doi.org/10.4324/9780429200014-11

Bjerck, Hein B. and Atilio F. Zangrando (2013) Marine Ventures: Comparative perspectives on the dynamics of early human approaches to the seascapes of Tierra del Fuego and Norway. *The Journal of Island and Coastal Archaeology* 8(1): 79–90. https://doi.org/10.1080/15564894.2012.756083

Bjerck, Hein B. and Heidi M. Breivik (2012) Off shore pioneers: Scandinavian and Patagonian lifestyles compared in the Marine Ventures project. *Antiquity* 86(333). http://antiquity.ac.uk/projgall/bjerck333/

Bjerck, Hein B., Leif Inge Åstveit, Trond Meling, Jostein Gundersen, Guro Jørgensen and Staale Normann (2008) *NTNU Vitenskapsmuseets arkeologiske undersøkelser Ormen Lange Nyhamna*. Trondheim: Tapir Akademisk Forlag.

Bogost, Ian (2012) *Alien Phenomenology or WHAT It's LIKE to Be a THING*. Minneapolis: University of Minnesota Press. https://doi.org/10.5749/minnesota/9780816678976.001.0001

Bonnichsen, Robson (1973) Millie's camp: an experiment in archaeology. *World Archaeology* 4(39): 276–291. https://doi.org/10.1080/00438243.1973.9979539

Brate, Mats and Rachel Kiddey (2015) Journeys in the city: Homeless archaeologists or archaeologies of homelessness. *Journal of Contemporary Archaeology* 2(2): 235–245. https://doi.org/10.1558/jca.v2i2.29592

Bruck, Joanna (2005) Experiencing the past? The development of a phenomenological archaeology in British prehistory. *Archaeological Dialogues* 12(1): 45–67. https://doi.org/10.1017/S1380203805001583

Bryant, Levi (2014) *Onto-Cartography: An Ontology of Machines and Media*. Edinburgh: Edinburgh University Press.

Buchli, Victor and Gavin Lucas (2001) *Archaeologies of the Contemporary Past*. London, New York: Routledge. https://doi.org/10.4324/9780203185100

Burström, Mats (2009) Selective remembrance: Memories from a Second World War refugee camp in Sweden. *Norwegian Archaeological Review* 42(2): 159–172. https://doi.org/10.1080/00293650903351045

Burström, Mats (2014) Treasured memories: An anecdotal mapping of wartime caches in Estonia. In Bjørnar J. Olsen and Þóra Pétursdóttir (eds.), *Ruin Memories: Materialities, Aesthetics and the Archaeology of the Recent Past*, 143–161. London: Routledge.

Byrne, Denis (2017) Remembering the Elizabath Bay reclamation and the Holocene sunset in Sydney Harbour. *Environmental Humanities* 9(1): 40–59. https://doi.org/10.1215/22011919-3829127

Byrne, Denis (2021) The view from somewhere: Liquid, geologic, and queer bodies. In Bjørnar J. Olsen, Þóra Pétursdóttir, Mats Burström and Caitlin DeSilvey (eds.), *After Discourse: Things, Affects, Ethics*, 113–128. London: Routledge. https://doi.org/10.4324/9780429200014-9

Chagnon, Napoleon A. (1968) *Yanomamö: The Fierce People*. New York: Holt, Rinehart and Winston.

Damlien, Hege, Mathilda Kjällquist and Kjel Knutsson (2018) The pioneer settlement of Scandinavia and its aftermath: New evidence from Western and Central Scandinavia. In Kjel Knutsson, Helena Knutsson, Jan Apel and Håkon Glørstad (eds.), *Technology of Early Settlement in Northern Europe – Transmission of Knowledge and Culture*, 99–137. Sheffield: Equinox Publishing.

Ellingson, Laura and Carolyn Ellis (2008) Autoethnography as constructionist project. In J. A. Holstein and J. F. Gubrium (eds), *Handbook of Constructionist Research*, 445–466. New York: Guilford Press.

Ellis, Carolyn (2004) *The Ethnographic I: A Methodological Novel about Autoethnograpy*. Walnut Creek: AltaMira Press.

Ellis, Carolyn, Tony E. Adams and Arthur P. Bochner (2010) Autoethnography: An overview. *Qualitative Social Research* 12(1): Art. 10.

Eriksen, Anne (1999) *Historie, Minner, Myter*. Oslo: Pax.

Ernaux, Annie (1983) *La place*. Paris: Éditions Gallimard.

Ernaux, Annie (1987) *Une femme*. Paris: Éditions Gallimard.

Ernaux, Annie (2008) *Les années*. Paris: Éditions Gallimard.

Farstadvoll, Stein (2019) Growing concerns: Plants and their roots in the past. *Journal of Contemporary Archaeology* 5(2): 174–193. https://doi.org/10.1558/jca.35117

Glassie, Henry (1999) *Material culture*. Bloomington: Indiana University Press.

Goldschmidt, Walter (1977) Anthropology and the coming crisis: An autoethnographic appraisal. *Anthropologist* 79(2): 293–308. https://doi.org/10.1525/aa.1977.79.2.02a00060

González-Ruibal, Alfredo (2006) The past is tomorrow: towards an archaeology of the vanishing present. *Norwegian Archaeological Review* 39(2): 110–126. https://doi.org/10.1080/00293650601030073

González-Ruibal, Alfredo (2008) Time to destroy. *Current Anthropology* 49(2): 247–279. https://doi.org/10.1086/526099

González-Ruibal, Alfredo (2014) Returning to where we have never been: Excavating the ruins of modernity. In Bjørnar J. Olsen and Þóra Pétursdóttir (eds.), *Ruin Memories: Materialities, Aesthetics and the Archaeology of the Recent Past*, 367–389. London: Routledge.

González-Ruibal, Alfredo (2019) *An Archaeology of the Contemporary Era*. London: Routledge. https://doi.org/10.4324/9780429441752

Graves-Brown, Paul and Rodney Harrison (eds.) (2013) *The Oxford Handbook of the Archaeology of the Recent Past*. New York: Oxford University Press. https://doi.org/10.1093/oxfordhb/9780199602001.001.0001

Harari, Yuval N. (2015) *Sapiens: A Brief History of Humankind*. London: Vintage.

Harari, Yuval N. (2017) *Homo Deus: A Brief History of Tomorrow*. London: Vintage. https://doi.org/10.17104/9783406704024

Haraway, Donna (1988) Situated knowledges: The science question in feminism and the privilege of partial perspective. *Feminist Studies* 14(3): 575–599. https://doi.org/10.2307/3178066

Harman, Graham (2010) *Towards Speculative Realism*. Winchester: Zero Books.

Harman, Graham (2016) *Immaterialism: Objects and Social Theory*. Cambridge: Polity Press.

Harrison, Rodney and John Schofield (2009) Archaeo-ethnography, auto-archaeology: Introducing archaeologies of the contemporary past. *Journal of the World Archaeological Congress* 5(2): 185–201. https://doi.org/10.1007/s11759-009-9100-5

Harrison, Rodney and John Schofield (2010) *After Modernity: Archaeological Approaches to the Contemporary Past.* Oxford, New York: Oxford University Press. https://doi.org/10.1093/oso/9780199548071.001.0001

Hayden, Brian (ed.) (1979) *Lithic Use-Wear Analysis.* New York: Academic Press.

Hazelwood, Nick (2000) *Savage: Survival, Revenge and the Theory of Evolution.* London: Sceptre.

Heidegger, Martin (1962) *Being and Time.* New York: Harper & Row.

Helskog, Knut, Svein Indrelid and Egil Mikkelsen (1976) Morfologisk klassifisering av slåtte steinartefakter. *Universitetets Oldsaksamling Årbok* 1972–74: 9–40.

Holen, Magnus N. (2020) Mellommesolittisk flekketeknologi i Trøndelag og Nordland. *Primitive tider* 22: 7–30. https://doi.org/10.5617/pt.8411

Holtorf, Cornelius (2015) Are we all archaeologists now? *Journal of Contemporary Archaeology* 2(2): 217–259. https://doi.org/10.1558/jca.v2i2.28463

Ingold, Tim (1993) The temporality of the landscape. *World Archaeology* 25(2): 152–174. https://doi.org/10.1080/00438243.1993.9980235

Ingold, Tim (2011) *Being Alive: Essays on Movement, Knowledge and Description.* London: Routledge.

Ingold, Tim (2015) *The Life of Lines.* London: Routledge. https://doi.org/10.4324/9781315727240

Introna, Lucas (2021) Touching tactfully: The impossible community. In Bjørnar J. Olsen, Þóra Pétursdóttir, Mats Burström and Caitlin DeSilvey (eds.), *After Discourse: Things, Affects, Ethics*, 207–218. London: Routledge. https://doi.org/10.4324/9780429200014-15

Jackson, John B. (2011) The westward-moving house. *Places Journal*, July 2011. https://placesjournal.org/article/the-westward-moving-house

Jackson, F. (1986) What Mary didn't know. *The Journal of Philosophy* 83(5): 291–295. https://doi.org/10.2307/2026143

Jervis, Ben (2019) *Assemblage Thought and Archaeology: Themes in Archaeology.* London: Routledge. https://doi.org/10.4324/9781315158594

Knausgård, Karl Ove (2020) Navnet og tallet. In Anne Gjelsvik (ed.), *Bearbeidelser. 22 Juli i ord og bilder*, 178–185. Oslo: Oslo Universitetsforlaget.

Knausgård, Karl Ove (2010) *Min kamp, Tredje bok*, 14. Oslo: Forlaget Oktober.

Kverndokk, Kyrre (2009) Resan til ondskan: Skoleelever på bussreise til Auschwitz. In Aronsson, P. (ed.), *Platser för en bättre värld: Auschwitz, Ruhr och röda stugor*, 45–89. Lund: Nordic Academic Press.

Latour, Bruno (2005) *Reassembling the Social: An Introduction to Actor-Network-Theory.* Oxford: Oxford University Press.

Liset, Ruth (n.d.) *Ruth's Bok,* I–III. Unpublished memoirs.

Loe, Erlend (2021) Denne teksten er ærlig, rederlig og generøs: Anmeldelse av Annie Ernaux, Far/Enkvinne. *Aftenposten* March 6, 2021: 94.

Lollar, Karen (2010) The liminal experience: Loss of extended self after the fire. *Qualitative Inquiry* 16(4): 262–270. https://doi.org/10.1177/1077800409354066

Lowenthal, David (1985) *The Past is a Foreign Country.* Cambridge: Cambridge University Press.

Lucas, Gavin (2005) *The Archaeology of Time.* London: Routledge. https://doi.org/10.4324/9780203004920

Macfarlane, Robert (2012) *The Old Ways: A Journey on Foot*. London: Penguin.

Macfarlane, Robert (2015) *Landmarks*. London: Penguin.

Macfarlane, Robert (2019) *Underland: A Deep Time Journey*. London: Penguin

McTaggart, J.M. Ellis (1908) The unreality of time. *Mind*, New Series 17(2): 457–474. https://doi.org/10.1093/mind/XVII.4.457

Meis, Morgan (2021) Timothy Morton's hyper-pandemic. *The New Yorker* June 8, 2021. https://www.newyorker.com/culture/persons-of-interest/ timothy-mortons-hyper-pandemic

Melberg, Sam (1942) *Jiu-Jitsu: Knep og parader til selvforsvar*. Oslo: Forlagshuset.

Morton, Timothy (2013) *Hyperobjects*. Minneapolis: University of Minnesota Press.

Morton, Timothy (2017) *Humankind: Solidarity with Nonhuman People*. London, New York: Verso.

Nelson, Richard K. (1983) *Make Prayers to the Raven: A Koyukon View of the Northern Forest*. Chicago: University of Chicago Press.

Nuttall, Mark (2009) Living in a world of movement: Human resilience to environmental instability in Greenland. In Susan Crate and Mark Nuttall (eds.), *Anthropology and Climate Change: From Encounter to Action*, 292–310. Walnut Creek: Left Coast Press.

Olivier, Laurent (2004) The past of the present: Archaeological memory and time. *Archaeological Dialogues* 10(2): 204–213. https://doi.org/10.1017/S1380203804001254

Olivier, Laurent (2015) *The Dark Abyss of Time: Archaeology and Memory*. London: Rowman & Littlefield.

Olsen, Asle Bruen and Sigmund Alsaker (1984) Greenstone and diabase utilization in the Stone Age of Western Norway. *Norwegian Archaeological Review* 17(2): 71–103. https://doi.org/10.1080/00293652.1984.9965401

Olsen, Bjørnar J. (2003) Material culture after text: Re-membering things. *Norwegian Archaeological Review* 36(2): 87–104. https://doi.org/10.1080/00293650310000650

Olsen, Bjørnar J. (2007) Keeping things at arm's length: A genealogy of asymmetry. *World Archaeology* 39(4): 579–588. https://doi.org/10.1080/00438240701679643

Olsen, Bjørnar J. (2010) *In Defense of Things: Archaeology and the Ontology of Objects*. Lanham: AltaMira Press.

Olsen, Bjørnar J. (2011) Halldors lastebil og jakten på tingenes mening. *Kunst og kultur* 94(4): 180–189. https://doi.org/10.18261/ISSN1504-3029-2011-04-02

Olsen, Bjørnar J. (2013) Memory. In Paul Graves-Brown, Rodney Harrison and Angela Piccini (eds.), *The Oxford Handbook of the Archaeology of the Contemporary World*. Oxford: Oxford University Press. https://doi.org/10.1093/oxfordhb/9780199602001.013.026

Olsen, Bjørnar J. and Þóra Pétursdóttir (2021) Writing things after discourse. In Bjørnar J. Olsen, Þóra Pétursdóttir, Mats Burström and Caitlin DeSilvey (eds.), *After Discourse: Things, Affects, Ethics*, 23–41. London: Routledge. https://doi.org/10.4324/9780429200014-3

Olsen, Bjørnar J. and Þóra Pétursdóttir (eds.) (2014) *Ruin Memories: Materialities, Aesthetics and the Archaeology of the Recent Past*. London: Routledge.

Olsen, Bjørnar J., Michael Shanks, Timothy Webmoor and Christopher Witmore (2012) *Archaeology: The Discipline of Things*. Berkeley: University of California Press. https://doi.org/10.1525/9780520954007

Olsen, Bjørnar J., Þóra Pétursdóttir, Mats Burström and Caitlin DeSilvey (eds.) (2021) *After Discourse: Things, Affects, Ethics*. London: Routledge. https://doi.org/10.4324/9780429200014

Persson, Maria (2014) *Minnen från vår samtid: Arkeologi, materialitet och samtidshistoria*. PhD dissertation. Gotark Serie B Gothenburg Archaeological Thesis 62. Gothenburg: Gothenburg University.

Pétursdóttir, Þóra (2017) Climate change? Archaeology and Anthropocene. *Archaeological Dialogues* 24(2): 175–205. https://doi.org/10.1017/S1380203817000216

Pillatt, Toby (2012) From climate and social memory to weather and landscape (Comments from M. Bell, J. Cooper, A. Davies, D. Groenborn and T. J. Wilkinson). *Archaeological Dialogues* 19(1): 29–74. https://doi.org/10.1017/S1380203812000049

Richardson, Laurel (2000) Evaluating ethnography. *Qualitative Inquiry* 6(2): 253–255. https://doi.org/10.1177/107780040000600207

Shanks, Michael (1992) *Experiencing the Past: On the Character of Archaeology*. London: Routledge.

Shanks, Michael (2012) *The Archaeological Imagination*. Walnut Creek: Left Coast Press.

Skar, Birgitte and Sheila Coulson (1986) Evidence of behavior from refitting – a case study. *Norwegian Archaeological Review* 19(2): 90–102. https://doi.org/10.1080/00293652.1986.9965434

Sørensen, Mikkel, Tuja Rankama, Jarmo Kankaanpaa, Kjel Knutsson, Helena Knutsson, Stine Melvold, Berit V. Eriksen and Håkon Glørstad (2013) The first eastern migrations of people and knowledge into Scandinavia: Evidence from studies of Mesolithic technology, 9th–8th millennium BC. *Norwegian Archaeological Review* 46(1): 19–56. https://doi.org/10.1080/00293652.2013.770416

Strathern, Marilyn (1987) The limits of auto-anthropology. In Jackson, A. (ed.), *Anthropology at Home*, 56–67. London: Travistock.

Svendsen, Arnljot S. (1999) *Hilmar Reksten. Stridbar, raus, elsket*. Bergen: Hilmar Rekstens Almennyttige Fond.

Tejsner, Pelle (2019) 'It is windier nowadays': Coastal livelihood and seascape-making in Qeqertarsuaq, West Greenland. In Tanya J. King and Gary Robinson (eds), *At Home on the Waves: Human Habitation of the Sea from the Mesolithic to Today*, 250–267. New York: Berghahn Books. https://doi.org/10.2307/j.ctv12pns49.18

Tiller, Carl Frode (2017) *Begynnelser*. Oslo: Aschehoug.

Tilley, Christopher (1994) *A Phenomenology of Landscape: Places, Paths, and Monuments*. Oxford: Berg.

Tunström, Göran (1983) *Juleoratoriet*. Stockholm: Albert Bonniers Förlag.

Tunström, Göran (1986) *Tjuven*. Stockholm: Albert Bonniers Förlag.

Tunström, Göran (1993) *Under tiden*. Stockholm: Albert Bonniers Förlag.

Witmore, Christopher (2007) Symmetrical archaeology: excerpts of a manifesto. *World Archaeology* 39(4): 546–562. https://doi.org/10.1080/00438240701679411

Witmore, Christopher (2019) Symmetrical archaeology. In S.L. López Varela (ed.), *The SAS Encyclopedia of Archaeological Sciences*. Wiley Blackwell. https://doi.org/10.1002/9781119188230.saseas0563

Witmore, Christopher (2020) *Old Lands: A Chorography of the Eastern Peloponnese*. London: Routledge. https://doi.org/10.4324/9781351109437

Yamada, Yoko and Yoshinobu Kato (2006) Images of circular time and spiral repetition: The generative life cycle model. *Culture and Psychology* 12(2): 143–160. https://doi.org/10.1177/1354067X06064575

About the Author

Hein Bjartmann Bjerck (born in Florø, 1954) is a professor in archaeology at the NTNU University Museum (Norwegian University of Science and Technology in Trondheim), where he conducts teaching and research. His research interests have developed from Stone Age studies to contemporary archaeology, which he tries to combine in the present book. He has been a fellow in several of Bjørnar J. Olsen's research projects, focusing on things, heritage and the archaeology of the recent past (*Ruin Memories* (Routledge 2014), *After Discourse* (Routledge 2021), *Objects Matters* (yet to be published)).

Bjerck has conducted/joined archaeological field studies in various Norwegian regions, as well as in Maine (USA), Svalbard, Disco Bay (Greenland), British Columbia (Canada), Chile and Argentina – Tierra del Fuego in particular. A pivotal point in his research is the roots and further developments of marine foraging. He directed *Marine Ventures*, a comparative study in this research field in Norway and Argentinian Tierra del Fuego. The project included an international symposium on the subject, published in the volume *Marine Ventures – Archaeological Perspectives on Human-Sea Relations* (Equinox, 2016).

Praise for Archaeology at Home

A majestic work, full of experiment and sensuous detail. Equally haunting, melancholic, and amusing: a narrative *tour-de-force*. Hein Bjerck writes with a unique voice, evoking place, people, and emotion with affect seldom, if ever, found in archaeological or historic text. Part love-letter to his father, uncle, and his own past, part meditation on objects, things, memory, humanity, relationships, and the passage of time, *Archaeology at Home* exceeds the boundaries of any one discipline. An instant classic.

Professor Doug Bailey, Department of Anthropology, San Francisco State University

We are being convinced that the future of archaeology lies in technology, but the future of archaeology lies in imagination: our capacity to recreate other pasts, other futures and other ways of telling them. In this fascinating book, Hein Bjerck tells us about 9,500-year old houses and his own family's homes, and explores in an original way memory, materiality and experiences of domesticity that are at the same time intimate and remote. In so doing, he shows us the path to a new kind of archaeology: one that is tremendously creative and full of emotion, an archaeology that mixes past and present, the social and the personal, self and others, science and narrative. This book will be essential reading for anybody interested in the archaeology of the contemporary past, the archaeology of domestic space and new forms of storytelling in the humanities and the social sciences.

Alfredo González-Ruibal, Institute of Heritage Sciences (Spanish National Research Council)

It is a deep and moving book, that seems to begin as a funny challenge: may an archaeologist do an archaeology of his/her own home? Far beyond family chronicles, Bjerck has written a remarkable and sensitive essay on things, life and time, seen from inside.

Professor Laurent Olivier, Curator in chief, Musée d'Archéologie nationale, Saint-Germain-en-Laye, France

Archaeology at Home is a book that causes us to stop and think, to re-evaluate our practice and approach both collectively and individually; a book that challenges archaeologists to do what we do better. In a masterful blend of contemporary archaeology and early prehistory, Bjerck breathes life into the past and its fragments of humankind. This book asks us to re-position ourselves in archaeological interpretation and narrative, to 'write from somewhere', and to consider how the lives we live can inform the lives lived in the recent and distant pasts. It is a book about relationships: between the past and present; between humans and non-humans; between worlds; between memory and the tangible; between lost and found. *Archaeology at Home* is inspiring, thought provoking and evocative. It also contains an ingredient rarely found in archaeological writing and research – humour.

Dr. Marion Dowd, Lecturer in Prehistoric Archaeology, Institute of Technology Sligo

In 1790, a young writer locked himself at home to study the wonders of what lay closest by. The resulting account, *A Journey Around My Room*, now holds renewed significance following two years of a Pandemic confining many of us to our homes. During my confinement, I started to wonder what an excavation of my own life might reveal – what I might learn about myself that I hadn't otherwise realised. But my entangled domestic mess remains untouched, for now. I am therefore both envious and admiring of *Archaeology at Home*, an eloquent and close encounter which stands as a modern day *Journey*, not around a room but of a life, or lives to be precise. The work is unashamedly and unmistakably an archaeology book, reflecting on people's stories told through the itineraries of material objects, places and landscape. In a unique and highly readable account, the author reveals what all archaeologists know but others may not – that archaeologists make the best story-tellers, and that our stories will be contemporary and can be deeply intimate. And aren't those stories always the best?!

Professor John Schofield, Archaeology, University of York

This is a book that addresses one of the deepest paradoxes of archaeology: its desire, on the one hand, to understand and re-connect with past human lives and on the other, the realization 'that most of what relates to being a human in the past are outside the fragments of our archaeological record'. What do you do when faced with such a paradox? Pretend it doesn't exist and carry on as before, trying to overcome the limitations of the archaeological record? Or accept that archaeology has the potential to be something else? In this book, Bjerck bravely chooses the second option. Drawing on the wide field of new materialisms, symmetrical archaeology and a machine-oriented ontology, he explores three 'homes' as case studies: his late father's; an uncle's house consumed by flames; and a Mesolithic camp. For Bjerck, these homes are best seen as thing-regimes, special human-thing collectives. But what makes his approach unique is his personal connection to all three sites. This is an object-oriented ontology with a human face. Ultimately, what makes Bjerck's solution to the paradox so compelling is that even if past lives will always elude our grasp, the situated nature of our own engagement with these remains ensures that the human dimension in this object-oriented world is never lost. It is what frames everything; these homes take on the contours they have, precisely because Hein Bjerck is part of them, he is writing from a position fully immersed within these thing-regimes. As he himself describes it, this is a kind of auto-archaeology; but it is also more. This is also an exercise in archaeology as memory, and as we read it, we realize we are not just visiting three homes, but also, in a way, returning home.

Professor Gavin Lucas, Archaeology, University of Iceland

www.ingramcontent.com/pod-product-compliance
Lightning Source LLC
Chambersburg PA
CBHW040140270326
41928CB00022B/3272